REVOLUTION
AT THE MARGINS

REVOLUTION AT THE MARGINS

*The Impact of Competition
on Urban School Systems*

FREDERICK M. HESS

BROOKINGS INSTITUTION PRESS
Washington, D.C.

Copyright © 2002
THE BROOKINGS INSTITUTION
1775 Massachusetts Avenue, N.W., Washington, D.C. 20036
www.brookings.edu

Library of Congress Cataloging-in-Publication data

Hess, Frederick M.
  Revolution at the margins : the impact of competition on urban school systems / Frederick M. Hess.
    p. cm.
  Includes bibliographical references (p.) and index.
    ISBN 0-8157-0208-6 (cloth : alk. paper)—
    ISBN 0-8157-0209-4 (pbk. : alk. paper)
    1. School choice—United States. 2. Educational change—United States. 3. Urban schools—United States. I. Title.
    LB1027.9.H49 2002   2001007901
    379.1'11'0973—dc21   CIP

9 8 7 6 5 4 3 2 1

The paper used in this publication meets minimum requirements of the American National Standard for Information Sciences—Permanence of Paper for Printed Library Materials: ANSI Z39.48-1992.

Typeset in Sabon

Composition by Stephen McDougal
Mechanicsville, Maryland

Printed by R. R. Donnelly and Sons
Harrisonburg, Virginia

To my grandparents,
Fred and Bernice Hess
and
Stanley and Edythe Rosenzwog,
for all their sacrifices,
love, and support.

Contents

Preface

THIS IS A BOOK about how urban school systems respond to the competition posed by school vouchers or charter schooling. My goal is not to provide a definitive work on the topic. Rather, I hope to encourage scholars and policymakers to reevaluate some of the facile presumptions regarding market-based education reform.

Given the likelihood that conventional public systems will educate a substantial majority of students for the foreseeable future, the way that choice-induced competition affects public schooling is likely to prove more significant for American education than are individual schools of choice. I focus on urban schooling because these systems particularly concern educators and policymakers. These systems are the most frequent targets for choice-based reform, the ones in which hopes for such reform are highest, and lie in the dense urban communities most likely to provide fruitful education marketplaces.

I have been interested in urban school systems for roughly ten years, which is about the same period of time that school voucher and charter school programs have existed in the United States. When I first became interested in urban schooling, while teaching high school social studies at Scotlandville Magnet High in East Baton Rouge Parish, Louisiana, school choice was not yet prominent in the national dialogue about urban schooling. Instead, attention centered on reform efforts that relied more heavily on new curricula, site-based management, professional development, and similar measures. These efforts failed to deliver the hoped-for results, in large part due to political dynamics (which I explore in an earlier work,

Spinning Wheels: The Politics of Urban School Reform). The resultant frustration fed the hunger for more radical reform and helped choice-based reform gain new visibility among those considering ways to reform urban schooling.

I conducted the research that led to *Spinning Wheels* at Harvard University under the mentoring of Paul E. Peterson and Richard F. Elmore. At the time, both of those eminent scholars were becoming increasingly active in the nation's school choice discourse, helping to make Harvard a hotbed of research and commentary on the topic. Pursuing research on urban school politics and reform in that environment highlighted for me just how divorced conversation regarding school choice was from the broader consideration of efforts to improve schooling. I was in the unusual position of conducting doctoral work in the Department of Government while teaching in the Graduate School of Education, a vantage point that afforded an unobstructed view of the bifurcation that characterized scholarship on educational policy in the 1990s. Choice-based reform became increasingly the province of economists, political scientists, and neoconservative policy advocates, while the community of education scholars tended to concentrate on questions of more immediate applicability to teaching, learning, assessment, and leadership in the public schools.

Although in the 1970s and 1980s the discussion of both types of reform had been primarily the province of the education community, now there was less overlap in the discourse. One consequence was a growing methodological, disciplinary, and normative chasm between the two communities. Today, the two topics tend to be addressed at different conferences and in different journals, in different ways, by different sets of scholars and policy advocates. I believe this state of affairs has had pernicious effects on both discourses.

I have three broad hopes for this work. First, I hope that a more nuanced consideration of the way education competition works in practice may help us approach questions of choice-based reform in a more measured and less polemical fashion. It strikes me that there is widespread confusion on both sides of the normative fence about how competition is likely to affect urban education. This confusion is rooted in a failure to fully comprehend the dynamics of market competition, the organizational nature of urban schooling, or how these will shape responses to competition. Thus one goal of the work is to clarify how competition is likely to play out in urban education and what this suggests for policymakers. Attention to these considerations promises to significantly increase the so-phistication and usefulness of debates over school choice.

Such discussion may help to shift the parameters of the national discourse regarding choice-based school reform. In the past decade that discussion has tended to focus on how attending choice schools affects student performance and on concerns regarding the possible segregative consequences of choice-based reform. While these questions are certainly significant, the debate has tended to harden into two hostile camps, one in favor of school vouchers and the other opposed to them. More significantly, permitting the choice discourse to become increasingly detached from broader discussions regarding school improvement and school change has been a mistake. In fact, as I argue here, the competitive effects of school choice will be contingent on the kinds of change that are made or are not made in the larger educational system. In the absence of broader organizational and institutional changes, choice-driven competition is unlikely to deliver the results that its proponents desire.

Second, I seek to shed light on the ways in which urban system structure and practice hamper efforts to improve urban schooling. Examining how public school systems respond to market incentives provides a fruitful opportunity to more fully understand the implications of their organization and culture. Because so much consideration of urban schooling takes for granted the traditional milieu and public monopoly of school systems, it is possible to miss institutional and organizational characteristics that set urban school systems apart from many other organizations. The response of urban systems to competition may illuminate the constraints and patterns of behavior that are distinctive to school systems. I hope that bridging the gap between the conversation about choice-based reform and conversations over accountability, teacher training, and so on will enrich both sets of discussions.

Finally, I hope this work might contribute more broadly to understanding the promise that market-driven reform holds for the provision of public services. I hope that it might be particularly useful in illustrating the way that context will influence the effects of such reforms and what kinds of organizational change are necessary to realize the promise of market-driven reform.

This book is based on case studies conducted in three school districts that were at the center of the school choice debate during the 1990s. Milwaukee and Cleveland are the only two school districts to have been the site of single-city public voucher programs; Edgewood, Texas, was deliberately targeted for the most ambitious private voucher effort launched to date. The case studies examine each of these three districts from the inception of their school choice program up through the conclusion of the 1998–99 school year or, in the case of the nascent Edgewood program, through the 1999–2000 school year. Why do the studies end at these points? First, quite simply, fieldwork inevitably has to come to an end. Second, the time frames were sufficient to permit analysis of the three quite different programs through varying stages of development. Third, by these dates I had accumulated so much material that I felt I had reached a point of diminishing returns.

Scholars of urban education tend to discuss urban school systems as part of a self-enclosed bubble. We look at them on their own terms and regard them as unique. In fact, urban school systems are not unique; they are organizations that tackle a difficult task (educating large numbers of disadvantaged children) under the heavy hand of often dysfunctional managerial, accountability, and regulatory systems. By examining how they respond to competitive forces, by seeing how they handle the kinds of threat that are routinely managed by other kinds of organizations, we can better understand the nature of these systems.

In that sense, this volume can be viewed as a companion and extension of my earlier book, *Spinning Wheels*. However, whereas that work explores the reasons that urban school systems routinely launch ambitious reforms, with often perverse consequences, here I focus more narrowly on whether the "cleansing" force of competition is alone sufficient to replace that churning with a more focused and effective model of governance.

Before proceeding, the reader is cautioned that this book is not a conventional work about choice-based school reform. I do not seek to weigh the merits of choice-based reform in any broad sense and do not attempt to make the case for or against choice-based school reform. Instead, I explicitly focus on one facet of the school choice debate, examining the impact of choice-based competition on urban school systems, seeking what light it may shed on the nature of urban schooling more generally. If the reader is interested in scholarship that examines school choice from a broader and more prescriptive perspective, I recommend concise and tightly argued works such as Jeffrey Henig's *Rethinking School Choice*; Joseph Viteritti's *Choosing Equality*; John Witte's *The Market Approach to Education*; Mark Schneider, Paul Teske, and Melissa Marschall's *Choosing Schools*; and Bryan Hassel's *The Charter School Challenge*. The interested reader might also want to consider the collections edited by Paul E. Peterson and Bryan Hassel or Peterson and David Campbell; Stephen Sugarman and Frank Kemerer; Bruce Fuller and Richard Elmore; Hank Levin; and Robert Maranto, Scott Milliman, April Gresham, and myself.

I am deeply appreciative of a number of people and organizations for their assistance with this project. I am especially grateful to the educators, officials, activists, scholars, and other respondents in the three school districts who so generously shared with me their thoughts and often their personal files or records.

I owe a lasting debt to Dick Elmore, Gary King, and Paul E. Peterson for training me to be a scholar and for the long years of guidance, mentoring, and friendship they have provided. I would like to thank the Spencer Foundation, the National Academy of Education, the Olin Foundation, the Bradley Foundation, the WKBJ Foundation, the Harvard Program in Educational Policy and Governance, and the University of Virginia for providing the support that made this research possible. I owe particular thanks to Bruno Manno, whose comments one day in 1999 helped give rise to the analysis that structures this volume. I also thank David Baker, Glenn Beamer, Bill Boyd, John Brandl, Eric Bredo, Dave Breneman, Amy Bunger, Hal Burbach, Ted Fiske, John Gardner, Jay Greene, Jim Guthrie, Bryan Hassel, Jeffrey Henig, Paul Hill, Jennifer Hochschild, Caroline Hoxby, Tom Kane, Sunny Ladd, David Leal, Hank Levin, Tom Loveless, Robert Maranto, Ken Meier, Scott Milliman, George Mitchell, Terry Moe, Alex Molnar, Alan Parker, David Plank, Eric Rofes, Clarence Stone, Paul Teske, Sarah Turner, Sandra Vergari, Joseph Viteritti, Sammis White, Amber Winkler, John Witte, Pat Wolf, and Ken Wong for sharing thoughts and providing crucial assistance at various stages of this project. I am also grateful to Erika Austin, John Bertsch, Dana Brower, Christine Countryman, Deb DeMania, Michele Davis, Amy Dowis, Lee Hark, Nick Jabbour, Jim Lawson, Joleen Okun, Andy Oldham, Michelle Tolbert, and Rhonda Tooley for their assistance with researching, editing, and preparing the manuscript. Finally, Patrick McGuinn deserves special thanks for his role in conducting the Cleveland research and in helping to draft chapter 6.

Various portions of this work have been presented at annual meetings of the American Political Science Association, the American Educational Research Association, and the Association for Policy Analysis and Management; at conferences held at the Harvard University Kennedy School of Government and the Chicago Federal Reserve; and in talks delivered to indulgent university and policy audiences. I would like to thank the colleagues and advocates who participated in these various forums for their many useful comments and suggestions.

As with all scholarship, this work is the accomplishment of many hands, including my own teachers, my colleagues, my students, and my sources in the locales studied. Of course, the fact that other individuals are largely responsible for whatever contribution this volume may make in no way implies that they bear any commensurate responsibility for my errors of fact, judgment, or interpretation. Any such errors are entirely mine.

REVOLUTION AT THE MARGINS

ONE   *Introduction*

In the fall of 1998 I pulled into the parking lot outside the Milwaukee Public Schools administration building on West Vliet Street. I was visiting the site of the nation's leading experiment in school choice. Entering the administration building, I passed a rally of the Milwaukee Teachers Education Association (MTEA); its members were there to press for ratification of the new, long-delayed union contract. About 250 MTEA members were already inside the board meeting room as the nine school board members trickled in. Behind the board's seats hung a massive orange and black sunburst banner proclaiming "High Standards Start Here." At-large board member John Gardner spoke frequently on topics ranging from board members' health insurance to the structure of the union contract. Each comment was met with hissing by the predominantly union audience.

Although the scene was in many ways typical of an urban school system meeting, the debates and politics seemed remarkably energized and coherent. The unusual dynamic seemed somehow related to Milwaukee's school choice experiment, but it was not clear how or why. Puzzled, I decided to retrace events in Milwaukee and in two other urban school systems with large-scale choice programs, hoping that such a course would make clear what had happened and how school vouchers and charter schooling factored into it. This volume represents my efforts to explore and understand how such competition affects urban school systems.

The way in which such systems respond to choice-driven competition may reveal as much about urban schooling as about the effects of market

1

competition. Studies of schools and schooling generally treat education as a unique good, fostering the mistaken impression that education reformers can learn little from a broader understanding of the ways in which governance, administration, and culture affect organizations. By changing the milieu in which a school system operates, choice-based reform can illuminate behaviors and arrangements that normally remain unremarked and unexamined.

Competition and School Performance

For more than a decade, school choice has been a flash point in debates over education. The 1990s saw the launching of charter schools in more than thirty states, public voucher programs in two cities and the state of Florida, and private voucher programs in dozens of cities across the nation. At the most elemental level, choice-based reforms seek to reshape education by transforming parents and students from clients of a public service agency into consumers of a marketed product. Advocates hope that markets will prove especially effective in urban areas, where there is intense dissatisfaction with current options. The presence of a large number of schools and a population able to support a wide variety of schools render these systems especially well suited to choice arrangements. Traditionally, educators control most decisions in public schools, with the community's major recourse being the electoral process or appeals to elected officials. Under school choice, however, families express their preferences by selecting their school. Before schools can be places of education, they must first be able to attract and retain a clientele. Advocates hope and expect that markets will force educators to focus on meeting the demands of their prospective clients.

Perhaps the most commonly advanced argument for school choice is that the market will force public school systems to improve.[1] Market ad-

---

1. An important, though generally ignored, qualification is that, even under perfect competition, existing school choice plans will force schools to compete primarily on services rather than on price. See Besanko, Dranove, and Shanley (2000, p. 317) for an economic analysis of the implications of nonprice competition. The reason for this is that voucher, charter, and open enrollment plans all involve the government (or other voucher provider) sending a set amount of money to the chosen school in the name of the child. Families do not reap any savings if they use a provider. Since families will not be cost conscious, there is little incentive for producers to compete on cost. Instead, given that voucher or charter students come with a fixed amount of attached revenue, the incentive is to provide families with the most attractive education. Consequently, competition-inspired

vocates assume that forcing these school systems to compete for students will prompt public schools to improve in order to ensure their survival and success.[2] Schools that lose students will presumably try either to lure them back or to attract new students, while successful schools will expand and attract imitators.

In a 1977 discussion of voucher proposals, David Cohen and Eleanor Farr observed that "everyone agreed that vouchers would promote 'competition,' which would loosen up public school systems grown rigid with age, size, and professional power. The fear of losing students and revenues would move schools to improve curricula and increase responsiveness."[3] The influential charter school advocate Ted Kolderie writes that for many advocates, "from the beginning, 'charter schools' has been about system-reform . . . a way for the state to cause the district system to improve."[4] David Osborne, a leader of the push to reinvent government, asserts that "those who invented charter schools . . . wanted to improve all 88,000 public schools in the country by creating enough competition for money and students to force school systems to improve" and goes on to claim that "empirical studies have demonstrated that, indeed, competition works just as the reformers predicted."[5] In fact the research provides little to support Osborne's strong claims.

---

benefits will take the form of higher-quality schools rather than lower-cost schools. If families were permitted to keep that part of a voucher that they did not use, then schools would be pressured to compete on price. The problem with introducing price competition, of course, is that some children—especially those from families in which money is tightest—would receive a cut-rate education. See Steuerle (2000) for a discussion of this issue and related concerns.

2. See Bradford and Shaviro (2000) for a straightforward explanation of the economic theory underlying the provision of public services through voucher programs. For an analysis of efficient provision of public goods, see Rosen (1999, pp. 61–254).

3. Cohen and Farrar (1977, pp. 72–73).

4. Kolderie (1995, p. 8).

5. David Osborne, "Healthy Competition," *New Republic*, October 4, 1999, pp. 31–33. Similar versions of this assertion are common. Milwaukee's mayor, John Norquist, a leading voucher advocate, argues that "most of us see each day how competition spurs achievement . . . choice challenges the complacency and stagnation of the public-school monopoly" (1998, p. 94). Jeanne Allen, president of the Center for Education Reform, predicts that under the ambitious Florida voucher program, "rather than see a mass exodus of children [from the public schools], we're going to see a dramatic improvement of the public schools in Florida." See Kenneth J. Cooper and Sue Anne Pressley, "Florida House Approves School Vouchers; Senate Votes Today," *Washington Post*, April 29, 1999, p. A2. In 1999 the Heritage Foundation educational policy expert Nina Shokraii Rees declared, "Though still in their infancy, school choice programs have improved overall student academic achievement in public schools. Evidently, competition is good for learning"

The market assumption is that competition rewards firms that efficiently deliver the goods and services that consumers desire. This dynamic encourages producers to continually improve their product and reduce costs. At the same time, it is understood that many factors can impede the smooth operation of the market. Consideration of these factors lies at the heart of most economic research.

Given the attention that economists devote to market imperfections, the question of how public schools respond to the market has received surprisingly little rigorous consideration. Education researchers have instead tended to focus on who uses choice options and how children fare in charter or voucher schools. Such inquiries invite the question of what happens to those who stay in traditional public schools. Since for the foreseeable future school choice programs are likely to serve only a small percentage of students, the question of those who remain in traditional public schools is crucial. Even if students in schools of choice benefit, the effects of choice-based reform could be negative if their public school peers are adversely affected. Conversely, even if students in choice programs do not benefit relative to their peers, such programs may constitute good policy if they compel public systems to become more effective.

Refining a Theory of Education Competition

The larger school choice debate has often paid little attention to schools as organizations.[6] Researchers frequently ask whether school choice will improve student performance, better satisfy families, or produce pernicious side effects. They pay much less attention to how or why educational competition will actually operate or how it may be affected by the

---

(1999, p. 16). Ladner and Brouillette (2000, p. 9) note that choice proponents believe "that just as businesses respond to heightened levels of competition by making better products, [so] schools will respond to competition by delivering higher-quality education." Proponents generally echo the economist Milton Friedman, who first suggested that educational competition would stimulate "the development and improvement of all schools" (Friedman 1982, p. 93). However, sounding a more cautious tone, Finn, Manno, and Vanourek (2000, p. 202) note that "not everyone in the charter movement believes that these schools are meant to change the system. For some, their school . . . is a haven . . . intended only to serve a particular population of children for whom conventional schools are not working."

6. A large body of literature addresses the complexities of applying standard economic principles to the operations of industrial organizations. When the simple "theory of the firm" becomes more nuanced, stylized conceptions of competition become poor guides as to how real-world actors will compete. See Besanko, Dranove, and Shanley (2000); North (1990).

nature of schools and schooling. If choice-based reforms are to be promoted as a tool for widespread school improvement, a more sophisticated understanding of education markets is essential.[7] The unqualified market claim that choice-based reforms, by unleashing competition, will radically and rapidly improve urban school systems is inaccurate, given the context and structure of these systems. However, framing the claim in this manner is disingenuous. What proponents of competition really suggest is that the discipline of the market will gradually lead to positive changes in monopolistic, rigid, public school bureaucracies.

Voucher proponents point, for instance, to increases in public school advertising and to the proliferation of innovative schools as evidence that competition compels school systems to operate like private sector firms. The changes that such proponents point to are real and often appear to be positive. However, advocates of education competition are likely mistaken when they interpret the distribution of videos and T-shirts and the launching of innovative programs as harbingers of a "businesslike" transformation that will enhance systemwide productivity and efficiency. In effect, they conflate a *publicity-oriented* competitive response with a *performance-oriented* competitive response, overlooking the deeper significance of this distinction.

School choice proponents may see this distinction as irrelevant or as a veiled attack on education competition. In fact the point is relevant and nonpartisan—and has important implications for the nature and consequences of education competition. To understand why this is so, it is necessary to consider the nature of urban public school systems, the market in which they compete, and the constraints under which they labor. This chapter briefly sketches the broader argument. The nature of the education marketplace and of urban school systems as competitors is discussed more fully in chapters 2 and 3.

Some proponents of choice may suggest that competitive systems have not had sufficient time to compel urban school bureaucracies to respond. In particular, such readers may point to the evidence of a growing response in Milwaukee over time. However, both theory and field research

---

7. The assumption is that school systems will begin to behave like businesses if sufficiently motivated. As a pamphlet written under the Workforce Investment Act to help organizations cope with vouchers explains, "An organization's success in responding to [a voucher-based market] will depend largely on how well it can adapt to thinking and operations as a business." See Maguire (2000, p. 19). That school systems may be unwilling or unable to behave in such a manner has received little systematic consideration.

provide little reason to believe that, absent changes in the structural or institutional constraints, future responses will be qualitatively different from the kinds of responses reported here. The muted effects to date are due not solely to the small scale and relatively recent inception of choice programs but also to structural and cultural factors that may continue to confound competition.

The programs examined in this volume are relatively small in an absolute sense, but the three represent perhaps the nation's most ambitious efforts at choice-based reform and confronted the local school systems with a radical and symbolically powerful threat. Given these parameters, there is much to be learned from these cases.

Unlooked-For Effects

Competition does bring change, but that change is likely be different from that anticipated by either proponents or critics. Rather than the simple school improvement anticipated by market enthusiasts, choice-induced changes are likely to be subtler and potentially more profound.[8] The response of these urban systems has not been to emphasize productivity or efficiency but has proven far more complex. It has been shaped by the public governance of these systems, the market context in which they operate, and their own structural and organizational limitations.

School choice advocates frequently suggest that the failure of existing programs to spur significant change in public school systems is a consequence of the small size of choice programs; they argue that competition would inspire systemic improvement if programs were expanded. While the effects of choice will increase if programs are expanded, the size and scope of the resulting school system response is likely to surprise and to disappoint market proponents. Why this is, what the implications are, and what can be done about it are the questions at the heart of this book.

Because market competition is normally observed in the context of a private sector dominated by for-profit firms, it is natural to assume that markets always operate in this fashion. However, such an assumption

---

8. Monk (1992) points out that the concept of "productivity" (or straightforward improvement) is a slippery one in the case of public goods like education, in which there are competing definitions of a satisfactory outcome. However, Odden and Picus (2000, p. 288) usefully suggest that "educational productivity" can be understood as "the improvement of student outcomes with little or no additional financial resources, or a consistent level of student performance at a lower level of spending."

may be mistaken. If consumers are limited in their ability to assess product quality, if the self-interest of producers does not compel them to satisfy consumer desires, or if producers lack the tools to respond to competitors, then markets may lead to results different from those predicted by abstract models.[9]

Urban school systems pose a number of challenges for market theory. They are highly visible public agencies charged with the delicate task of educating particularly disadvantaged children. The sensitive political demands on urban school leaders complicate their efforts to respond to market imperatives. The changes that choice produces in local school politics and the behavior of school officials will shape public schooling in important ways. Attempting to narrowly assess market impacts in isolation from such effects risks missing much of the unfolding story of school choice.

Markets can be immensely powerful engines of social change, but they do not always produce the hoped-for outcomes. What happens when school choice is introduced in urban communities? What shapes the impact of competition? What does their response to choice-based reform reveal about urban school systems? Finally, what actions should policymakers consider if they are dissatisfied with the results of choice-induced competition?

The Urban Public School Crisis

For decades there has been widespread agreement that America's urban school systems are in crisis.[10] Critics have described the manner in which bureaucracy, politics, organizational structure, teachers' unions, racial conflict, civic support and leadership, and the urban political economy have hindered urban schooling.[11]

In many urban areas two-thirds or more of students entering high school do not graduate. Urban schools are widely deemed unsafe; outdated and

---

9. Schumpeter famously explained how self-interested parties and entrepreneurs are essential to the free market: "The function of entrepreneurs is to reform or revolutionize the pattern of production by exploiting an invention or, more generally, an untried technological possibility for producing a new commodity or producing an old one in a new way, by opening up a new source of supply of materials or a new outlet for products, by reorganizing an industry and so on" (1942, p. 83).

10. Hill and Celio (1998).

11. Anyon (1997); Hess (1999); Hill and Celio (1998); Hill, Campbell, and Harvey (2000); Lieberman (1997); McDermott (2000); Ravitch and Viteritti (1997); Rich (1996); Sanders (1999); Henig and others (1999); Orr (1999); Portz, Stein, and Jones (1999); Stone (1998); Peltzman (1993).

overcrowded facilities are common. Gallup data throughout the 1990s showed that more than 80 percent of Americans believed it "very important" to improve inner-city schools.[12] Continued efforts to improve urban schooling through reforms targeted at pedagogy, curriculum, testing, and school governance failed to produce the desired results.[13] During the 1990s frustration with such efforts led to the consideration of increasingly radical remedies, including choice-based reform.[14]

Choice-based reform has been received most warmly in urban areas, and most choice-based activity has been centered in urban school systems, both because the status quo in these systems is seen as untenable and because these systems provide a dense enough network of schools and students for an education market to be feasible. In other words, advocates believe that it is in urban areas that choice-based markets are most likely to work and where their potential contribution will be greatest.

An Analytical Model

Markets are impersonal mechanisms that work by harnessing desire and fear. Market failure can upend lives, consume careers, and destroy fortunes. Market success can bring wealth, power, and material and creative opportunities. The power of the market lurks in the knowledge that even dominant firms may be only one innovation away from being overthrown and that garage inventors may be only one breakthrough away from success. In this environment, the handful of entrepreneurs who embrace risk and take chances drive innovation and growth.

Most individuals, however, are risk-averse; most people fear loss much more than they value potential gains.[15] The consequence is that markets cause most employees, especially those with the greatest professional and financial investments in the status quo, to live in a constant state of anxi-

---

12. Rose and Gallup (1998).

13. See Hess (1999, pp. 89–102) for discussion on the extent of attempted reform activity.

14. Of course, while public support for choice-based reform grew during the 1990s, it is still mixed and marked by a wealth of concerns. For a careful and nuanced discussion of public attitudes toward school choice, see Public Agenda (1999); Moe (2001).

15. For discussions of the dynamics of risk avoidance in a variety of contexts, see Weaver (1986); Kahneman and Tversky (1982); Shubik (1982, 1984); Acemoglu and Shimer (1999); Bjorgan, Liu, and Lawarree (1999); Carlson (1998); Landsberger and Meilijson (1996); Scott and Uhlig (1999).

ety. Workers are driven by the fear of losing their jobs and by the desire for promotions and raises. Investors and executives fear for their investment or their position. There is nothing relaxed or voluntary about responding to market imperatives. Market forces are not dependent on individual loyalty or commitment. After all, employees of large firms know that their individual efforts are unlikely to significantly affect the corporation's bottom line. These employees are not motivated by a vague hope that the benefits of one's contribution will trickle down. Instead, they are driven by concern with how their performance will be evaluated and the concrete effects these evaluations will have on their personal security, salary, and future. If employees are effective, producers will compete for their services. If they are ineffective, producers will no longer desire their services. Employees who do not respect this harsh truth are leapfrogged or displaced by those who do. Similarly, firms that do not police the quality or efficiency of their employees risk being overtaken by more disciplined competitors.

Such destruction of careers and firms is essential to the healthy operation of the market. By terminating unproductive employees, firms become more efficient and push their remaining employees to work harder. Likewise, by eliminating or punishing ineffective firms, the market clears room and frees up resources for new and more productive producers. This cycle of growth and destruction fosters continuing improvement in the quality and cost-effectiveness of goods and services, enhancing the quality of life for the community as a whole.[16] Over time, employees displaced or buffeted by destruction are absorbed back into a larger and more productive economy. However, recognizing macroeconomic market efficiency ought not obscure the reality that there are significant losses and disruptions at a personal level.

Naturally, people prefer not to live in fear of this wrathful market. They seek to erect barriers that offer protection from the relentless threat of competition. Investors and executives seek the security afforded by favorable government statute or by monopoly status, situations in which firms can make handsome returns without worrying about competitors stealing customers or threatening their prospects.[17] Unions try to protect their members from the market by restricting layoffs, curtailing the rights

16. Schumpeter (1942) calls the force of the free market "creative destruction."
17. For a classic discussion of monopoly and monopoly power, see Fisher (1991).

of employers to terminate workers, providing wage security, and limiting the monitoring and evaluation of workers.

In the private sector, when competition is threatening enough—such as when American automakers or electronic manufacturers confronted the onslaught of Japanese competitors in the 1980s—it can bring these protective edifices crashing down. Firms either uproot inefficient rules and procedures as they retool or they are reduced to rubble and replaced by more productive competitors.[18]

The public sector is an entirely different matter. Public agencies are unable to respond in a similarly direct manner. First, the market threat can be neutralized by political fiat. Public agencies are not threatened by bankruptcy in the same way that private firms are.[19] The legislature may require a public agency to compete against other providers, but it can also readily ensure that the agency's revenues remain stable regardless of how it fares. As long as the state opts to maintain funding for public agencies, private hospitals (for example) do not directly threaten public hospitals, and security guards in gated communities do not threaten the jobs of the community police force. Of course, since public agencies depend on public revenue and since such funding is linked to the way voters and legislators view these agencies, agencies are not unconcerned with loss of clients. However, public agencies are threatened less by the revenue lost due to consumer flight than by the possibility that a shrinking clientele may erode their political support and lead legislators to cut funding levels.[20] This observation has crucial implications for leadership and organizational behavior.

Another public-private distinction is less subtle. The incentives for officials steering public agencies are fundamentally different from those for executives directing private firms. Private firms are driven by investors,

18. All markets are not equally threatening and do not place equal demands. This point is discussed in chapter 2. The threat is much greater in markets where the danger of failure is higher, where more competitors exist, and where market actors are in peril of suffering personal losses and are aware of those dangers.

19. Stiglitz (2000, pp. 200–01).

20. For instance, a school system or a hospital with a shrinking clientele is likely to lose funding due to formulas that base allocation in significant part on the number of students or patients served. Unlike in the private sector, however, such losses are not etched in stone. If the school system or hospital has sufficient political support, it can win emergency allocations from the public purse or modifications in the funding formula. In other words, although public organizations are sensitive to the loss of clients, they have recourses that make the erosion of market share less dire than it is for private sector firms.

who keep a watch on profitability and who can, if disappointed, withdraw their investments (or by owner-managers who have their own wealth riding on the future of the firm). When confronted by competitors, the need to improve profitability propels executives of private firms to be alert to new market opportunities, to root out organizational inefficiencies, and to pursue increased profitability. If they do not take these steps, they risk being displaced by those who will.[21]

Public agencies are governed by public officials. Whereas private sector officials are judged by investors primarily on the basis of corporate profitability and growth, public officials are judged by more ambiguous criteria.[22] Because they do not have a direct personal stake in agency performance, unlike private sector investors, members of the voting public have little incentive to care whether public agencies are maximizing revenues or attracting new clients. Consequently, public officials are typically not rewarded for, say, attracting new patients to a public hospital or new recipients to a welfare office.[23] Moreover, although voters naturally wish government to operate efficiently, they rarely have clear measures with which to assess efficiency. Voters tend to evaluate public officials and public services on the basis of personal experiences and such readily available proxies as media depictions, visible activity, and the incidence of scandals.

Both because of the kinds of service that public agencies provide and because public employment rarely offers the material inducements available in the private sector, public employees frequently choose such work out of a sense of calling. This may incline them to reject market pressure when they deem the market-dictated response to be morally objectionable. A private sector firm that adopted such an approach would soon be razed by competitors. However, as long as a public agency retains politi-

---

21. This is of course a simplification of the way markets work. However, my point is to contrast productive responses to competition with political responses to competition and to explain how the nature of the product produced and the means of production structure the way public organizations respond to market forces. Because political organizations are generally in the business of responding to political forces, political scientists have had relatively little reason to pay much attention to how political organizations respond to market-induced pressure. For a general discussion of the economics of the public sector, see Rosen (1999).

22. Moore (1995).

23. Policymakers could choose to reward public agency officials for attracting clients, but such incentives are generally seen as being at odds with the larger mission of public agencies. See DiIulio (1994).

cal support, its leaders need not make productivity or efficiency their first concern.[24]

Whether a producer is public or private, the push to answer market imperatives is driven by those executives or investors with the greatest personal or professional stake in the organization. In private firms, anxious investors demand results from the firms' executives, motivating them to tackle institutionalized protections, to change inefficient procedures, and to fire ineffective employees. In public organizations, it is the top elected officials or high-level administrators who reap the political or professional benefits from organizational outcomes, giving them strong incentives to address inefficient procedures and ineffective employees. However, public officials also have reasons not to undertake such efforts.

Counting Votes, Not Profits

Public officials depend on public support; they must marshal votes and win elections. Their present effectiveness and future prospects turn on their public backing and on their ability to cultivate—or at least to avoid provoking—influential, organized, and attentive constituencies. There is rarely an influential constituency attentive to quiet improvement in the productivity or efficiency of a public agency. Public agencies also lack a bottom-line measure, like profitability, to which officials can point in defending their performance.[25] The consequence is that "objective" measures of organizational performance tend to have little effect on the voting public. Meanwhile organized interests—especially public employee unions and civil rights organizations seeking government protection—are invested in the rules that protect employees and that ensure equitable service provision.[26]

24. In his classic work on bureaucratic behavior, Wilson (1989, p. 349) offers three reasons that public organizations are less efficient than private ones: government officials are less able to define an efficient course of action, have weaker incentives to identify such a course of action, and have less authority to impose such a course of action. This study seeks to place these insights into a broader context and examine how conditions may change when public bodies are subjected to market discipline.

25. See Wilson (1994) for discussion. Of course, publicly held private firms engage in some symbolic activity when the management believes it advantageous. However, these firms engage in much less of this than public agencies because such efforts have little effect if investors are unconvinced by bottom-line results.

26. In the case of education, efforts to modify work force protection like tenure and undifferentiated pay scales are staunchly opposed and generally blocked by teachers' unions. Even those measures that get enacted tend to only modestly curtail these protections. See Ballou and Podgursky (1997, pp. 123–24).

Many public agencies also have a reservoir of community goodwill or sentimental attachment on which to draw. While the level of support varies, service providers that enjoy strong psychic attachments or emotive support—like local fire departments and public schools—are able to draw upon this goodwill when seeking to convince the public that they deserve to be protected from the vagaries of the market.[27]

Generally, individuals have less directly at stake as voters than as investors. Voters experience gains and losses that are more diffuse, less immediate, and less visible, giving them less reason to carefully attend to organizational performance. As a result, public officials have less incentive to focus on internal organizational efficiency or productivity than on ensuring that their organization's public face is positive and reassuring. This is particularly true for officials of public organizations that are highly visible, that have an exceptionally ambiguous output, or whose service provision it is difficult to noticeably improve in the short term.[28]

Suggesting that public officials will not tackle inefficiencies is not to say that they will ignore the challenge posed by competition. The enhanced scrutiny brought by competition does pressure officials to respond in some fashion. If competition threatens to embarrass the organization or the community or if it makes public officials look ineffective, the ensuing air of crisis will ratchet up the incentive to react. Typically, public officials are risk-averse and inclined to caution.[29] However, when confronted with a crisis—or a perceived crisis—inaction becomes costly.[30] To do nothing in a crisis is to appear ineffectual, while activity can calm public concerns and position leaders to claim credit for any perceived improvement.[31]

Managing large public bureaucracies is a daunting task. Officials tend to cope by relying upon rules and procedure, largely out of a concern that organizational actions be consistent with legislative direction and not anger the elected officials who control policy and funding. Officials desire to reassure the public and to satisfy critics without offending powerful, watch-

---

27. One possible response is simply to allow these public systems to be replaced by private producers. In the case of school choice, however, thus far almost all advocates of choice-based reform have explicitly rejected proposals to eliminate traditional public schools. One exception is Coulson (1999), who calls for the abolition of publicly governed schools.

28. Hess (1999, pp. 30–40).

29. Arnold (1990, p. 51).

30. As I have argued previously, "Inaction is the worst possible sin for a public official facing a crisis" (Hess 1999, p. 12). Also see Edelman (1972, p. 78); Stone (1997, pp. 188–209).

31. Wilson (1989); Kingdon (1995); Stone (1997).

ful constituencies. Such constituencies use their resources and influence with legislators to help craft policies and rules to their liking. Officials who seek to alter these rules or strictures risk offending these constituencies or their legislative allies in the name of an amorphous, fragmented, and inattentive public.

Public employees face extensive procedural requirements, which elected officials have instituted for the express purpose of ensuring that public servants conform to the wishes of the lawmakers.[32] Given substantial penalties for violating statutes or offending lawmakers, and the lack of commensurate rewards for productivity, public servants have incentives to hew to legal and procedural requirements, even when they deem such measures problematic.[33] Public employees who respect rules and procedures tend to prosper, while those who violate norms or offend powerful constituencies do not. It is not that bureaucracies are devoid of entrepreneurial personalities, only that these individuals tend to be discouraged and to have their professional progress hampered.

When compelled to publicly respond to market competition, officials of public bureaucracies are restricted by organizational procedures and cultures. These restrictions often leave these officials with only a few potential responses. One is to enhance the bureaucracy's advertising, public outreach, and public relations. Such measures offend no one, upset no routines, build public support, and can be easily tacked onto existing practices. Moreover, because such measures are visible and easily replicated, they enable organization subunits (such as individual schools) to imitate impressive efforts with a minimal investment of resources or energy. This response, which I label the *pickax*, will prove to be of particular interest.

Two Models of Market Response

It is useful to imagine two very different kinds of market competition, which I label *bulldozer* and *pickax* competition. Bulldozer competition demands wrenching change, while the pickax encourages incremental change. The bulldozer harnesses the desire for self-preservation and uses it to compel improvements in efficiency or productivity. The pickax rests on intrinsic motivation: change is produced when individuals choose to take advantage of new opportunities. The bulldozer uses systematic and

---

32. Chubb and Moe (1990, pp. 26–28).
33. Barzelay and Armajani (1992, p. 4).

impersonal incentives to drive systemic change throughout an organization; the pickax permits leaders to engage in the easier task of creating an impression of organizational improvement. Pickax change does not necessarily lead to bulldozer change, although school choice proponents often treat evidence of pickax change as proof that the effects of the bulldozer will soon follow.

In most productive activity, the bulldozer works by coupling the extrinsic and intrinsic impulses, using extrinsic motivation to bolster the intrinsic. This introduction of extrinsic incentives is why market competition tends to commodify all products, from rebellious music to handmade crafts. Efforts to introduce extrinsic incentives into human service fields—like education and medicine—create a fundamental conflict. In those fields, extrinsic incentives often clash with the impulses that impel many of the best and most committed workers.

The Pickax

Imposing significant organizational change is arduous and unpleasant work; it requires that comfortable routines and secure arrangements be overturned. Private sector executives and managers undertake such efforts only when they have to, and they are able to make them work only because they can make employees cooperate by monitoring performance, sanctioning the uncooperative, and rewarding the cooperative.

Public managers lack many of these essential tools. Consequently, rather than forcing change upon their subordinates, public managers—especially those atop resistant organizations or forced to negotiate political constraints—prefer reforms that allow entrepreneurial employees to step forward.[34] Rather than compelling systemwide changes that yield bottom-line results, these managers relax organizational strictures enough to allow self-selected reformers to step forward.[35] This solution avoids the conflicts provoked by coercion, while producing clear evidence that organizational improvement is under way.

Opportunities to provide new services or programs appeal to the less conventional members of public organizations. The entrepreneurial per-

34. Wilson (1989, pp. 218–32) explains at length why bureaucratic organizations tend to reform by supplementing existing practices rather than by trying to change them.

35. Of course the impact of these measures will depend on the number of potential entrepreneurs and on their energy and managerial skill. See Gustafson (1999, pp. 108–33) for an eye-opening discussion of this issue in the context of 1990s Russian capitalism.

sonalities with the energy to seize such opportunities are the individuals who tend to be marginalized in public sector agencies. In fields like education and social work, these entrepreneurs are rarely motivated by self-interest as it is conventionally understood in economic discourse. "Public interest entrepreneurs" have forgone the more lucrative opportunities of the private sector and generally stand to reap few rewards for their extra exertions. These entrepreneurs are motivated by a sense of calling and intrinsic desire.

New initiatives designed to meet public demands for visible evidence of improvement frequently relax the strictures that protect and insulate organization members. Public pressure encourages influential constituencies, such as unions, to accept changes in organizational procedures in order to avoid being labeled obstructionist. Such relaxation is easier for these groups to accept when market competition features new providers unencumbered by such strictures.

Under pickax competition new programs and initiatives spring up beside existing practices. Inefficient practices are not rooted out, but rules that protect employees or constituencies are relaxed. The result is a series of holes punched in the protective barriers that have been erected over time. Pressed to provide some response, administrators begin to chip holes in the rules, regulations, and procedures that pervade public agencies. Entrepreneurs emerge through these holes, creating new models of activity and bypassing traditional avenues of advancement. This process may eventually overwhelm the status quo, changing the organizational culture and pulling down the old edifice, or it may result in a few desultory weeds growing limply through small cracks in an otherwise unchanged organization.

The Argument in Brief

A number of scholars, including Richard Elmore, Jeffrey Henig, Hank Levin, Richard Murnane, and Frank Levy, elucidate the challenges that arise when education is conceptualized as a market good.[36] They make it clear that the effect of markets, in education as elsewhere, depends on how these markets are structured, how producers respond to market pressure, and how consumers consider and make choices. Although these analy-

36. Elmore (1986, 1990); Henig (1994); Levin (1987, 1993, 1998); Murnane and Levy (1995).

ses do not focus on the question of education competition, their warnings regarding the importance of institutions and political constraints are highly salient.

The irony is that education competition—a market-based approach intended to decrease the political tensions that infuse urban schooling—operates largely by provoking *political* reactions. Although some of these reactions are likely to foster more effective and productive schooling, they are not systematic in their execution and are unlikely to match the size or immediacy of changes conventionally observed in private sector firms confronted with competition.

The market bulldozer is not in evidence in urban school systems, although there are hints of the pickax, as competition leads officials to chip away at regulations and bureaucracy. In determining the substantive effects of the pickax, context appears crucial. It matters whether schools are led and staffed by entrepreneurial educators, whether education leaders have reason to fear competition, and whether those leaders have the means to respond to competition. For instance, in some suburban systems and in select schools in which jobs are more desirable and harder to come by, educators displaced due to competition may find it hard to find new working conditions as pleasant or rewarding. In such cases, the response to competition is likely to be quicker and more visceral than elsewhere.

The limited and political response to competition in urban school systems is due to three sets of constraints. First, these systems are heavily burdened by balky structures, executives lacking effective tools, and a culture that insulates educators. Many of these constraints, however, can be relaxed by policymakers or may evolve with time.

Second, if urban school systems do respond to competition, they will not necessarily do so by providing a better or more cost-effective product. Even if menacing competition were to emerge, the nature of the current education marketplace is such that school systems have incentives to respond with symbolic gestures rather than with substantive improvement. However, policymakers can take steps to clarify the outcomes on which schools will be judged and to simplify education consumption, altering the marketplace so as to compel educators to compete in ways more likely to yield concrete benefits.

Third, even if urban school systems and the market context are made more amenable to competition, public systems will continue to be driven by political, rather than market, logic. School officials will continue to be guided by public opinion and the pressures of concentrated constituencies. Such officials have little incentive to force wrenching changes that may upset constituencies or resistant subordinates. Policymakers can address these constraints by altering governance structures and by giving school officials a more direct stake in organizational performance.

The changes necessary to produce significant market effects will fundamentally alter the culture of schooling. Whereas extrinsic and intrinsic incentives tend to be mutually reinforcing in private sector endeavors, selective incentives are at odds with the ethos that characterizes most public agencies—especially in the case of education. Voters and policymakers will have to decide whether to trade the comforts of the status quo for the benefits of a more rugged and less accepting system of schooling. Market-driven schools will be more focused on outcome and productivity, will have teachers who feel more pressure to demonstrate productivity, will place more emphasis on measurable outcomes, and will have leaders more concerned with consumer preferences. Although these changes may be desirable, they are a far cry from a simple "improvement" in public schooling. They are potentially revolutionary and ought to be regarded as such.

The Study

My aim is to enhance the understanding of education markets and urban school systems by focusing on how communities, education constituencies, school system officials, school-level personnel, and private educators respond to competition. Although such responses are not the ultimate concern of parents or policymakers, they are pivotal in determining how competition alters public schooling. Systemic changes will emerge only when urban school system leaders adopt them and channel them down through the schools and into the classrooms.

In this volume I examine how choice-based programs have affected schooling in three urban systems. Public voucher programs operate in two of the nation's school systems.[37] The larger, longer-running, and more

---

37. Three very small statewide public voucher programs exist in Florida, Vermont, and Maine. Operating with small numbers, they lack the concentrated impact that could drive a competitive response. Moreover, the Vermont and Maine programs have long been a stable part of the educational system in those states, making them unlikely to provoke a sudden competitive response. The Florida program, initiated in 1999, offers vouchers to only those students in the schools judged to be the state's very worst and included just fifty-two students at the beginning of the 2000–01 school year. Of the 3,500 schools in Florida only two were labeled chronic failures in that year.

instructive program is in Milwaukee, Wisconsin. The smaller program was launched in Cleveland, Ohio, in 1995. Additionally, during the 1990s philanthropists also funded private voucher programs in dozens of cities. The most ambitious was launched in Edgewood Independent School District in San Antonio, Texas. Here, I examine the experiences of Milwaukee, Cleveland, and Edgewood. The three school systems, while all urban and all poor, vary in size, ethnic makeup, governance, the nature and role of the teachers' union, political milieu, and historical context. Taken together, the experiences of the three systems can teach a great deal about the effects of competition and the impact of program design and local context.

The research involved more than 230 interviews with education participants and observers in the three systems; repeated visits to the districts, school offices, and public and private schools; archival searches of daily newspapers and other local weeklies and publications; and reviews of school system records and documents, board minutes, private papers, and other secondary documents.[38] Research was conducted between September 1998 and November 2000.[39]

This work posed several challenges. In particular, it is difficult to gauge which competitive effects may be idiosyncratic to particular systems or to separate choice-induced effects from the churning and noise present in any urban school system. Further, as it turns out, much of my story is one of nonresponse. In the end, I found myself largely studying why the dog did not bark. To address these challenges I studied systems with distinct choice programs and pursued all available sources to tease out cause and effect. However, in the end, my efforts to assess the scope of response and to determine the reasons for the observed behavior are more suggestive than conclusive. It is difficult to demonstrate that something did not hap-

38. The school districts studied provided varying degrees of access for the conduct of this research. Milwaukee Public Schools employees provided significant access, while efforts to gain access to the Cleveland and Edgewood school systems were much less fruitful. In particular, until the fall of 2000, the Edgewood Independent School District officially refused any formal access. Such conditions are not unusual in the world of urban schooling.

39. As in my previous work on urban schooling, I do not directly attribute respondent quotes except where unavoidable. Instead, observers are identified by position descriptions, which offer relevant information on the perspective of the observer. This anonymity is afforded to respondents although the vast majority were willing to speak for attribution. The reader will notice that some quotations are attributed; these are taken from other published sources, generally newspapers.

pen, to document the extent of its "not happening," or to conclusively explain why it did not happen.[40] Characterizations of observed effects and of noneffects are inevitably subjective.

In the case studies, I focus on the effects of voucher programs. Other choice-based reforms (such as charter schooling) generally play a more marginal role in this work.[41] This is because the sample systems were selected for their voucher programs and happened to host limited other sources of competition during the period under study. The sample was selected on the basis of voucher programs because meaningful school voucher proposals have more potential to create a marketplace, redirect money from public to private providers, and threaten public educators than more regulated reforms like charter schooling and open enrollment. Of course, as is discussed later in the volume, the reality of large-scale charter schooling in cities like Washington, D.C., and Philadelphia could very well prove more threatening than more limited voucher programs.

The Wisconsin legislature created a tiny Milwaukee voucher program in 1990. In 1995 the legislature dramatically expanded the program and included sectarian schools. These measures were almost immediately halted by a union-backed lawsuit, which produced a court injunction. In the fall of 1997 a period of increasingly aggressive competition started with the launch of the first city charter schools and gained steam when the Wisconsin Supreme Court upheld the voucher program expansion in June 1998.

The Cleveland voucher program was launched in 1996. It was slightly larger in both absolute and relative size than the initial Milwaukee program. Beset by court challenges, plagued by visible logistical problems, and overshadowed by Ohio's takeover of the city's school board, the program never had the impact eventually achieved by the Milwaukee program.

40. On studying nonevents, see Crenson (1971).

41. Voucher programs—in which families are offered a tuition grant to pay for their child's education and the child is free to attend a public school or to use the grant to attend a private school—can provide a particularly useful opportunity to examine the competition hypothesis. The programs make competitive use of existing private school capacity, threaten the loss of public education dollars, explicitly draw upon market logic, and make it relatively easy for new firms to enter the market. The three districts studied all faced notable voucher programs in the 1990s. For an overview of education vouchers, see Sawhill and Smith (2000); Bishop (2000). Charter schools, which are independently run schools that receive a charter from some state-determined agency and receive state funding on a per pupil basis, provide another kind of competition. The competitive effect of charter schooling depends on the nature of the laws scripted by the state. See Finn, Manno, and Vanourek (2000); Hassel (1998).

The Horizon scholarship program was launched in the Edgewood Independent School District in April 1998. A privately funded experiment that offered scholarships to more than 90 percent of the students in this impoverished district, the Edgewood program provides a useful comparison to the public efforts in Milwaukee and Cleveland.

Each case also offers insights into specific dimensions of the urban education marketplace. Milwaukee produced the clearest hints of the pickax response, while Cleveland shows how program design and contextual constraints can muffle competition. Edgewood illustrates that school districts may respond in ways that have little to do with educational quality and can teach some useful lessons about how the supply of private schooling may evolve in a market setting.

I do not attempt to assess the effects of competition by analyzing outcome data. Other scholars have taken this approach, and this is entirely proper, as multiple lines of research can advance our understanding in various ways. However, my goal is to develop a broader understanding of how education competition affects schools and schooling. Since choice-induced competition is not hypothesized to impact public classrooms directly but to initiate a chain reaction in which market pressure will induce system officials to change practices that affect school and classrooms, it may be foolhardy in this case to rely too heavily on short-term outcome data.[42]

A particular complication in determining whether competition improves schooling is a lack of agreement about what constitutes a good education. Instead of taking a position as to the educational desirability of certain changes, I focus on simply understanding what these changes are and why they emerged. I leave it to the reader to gauge the desirability of specific responses. Another complication is that extant school voucher and charter school programs tend to be highly restrictive, reducing the incidence of competitive response. However, even these limited experiments can yield useful insights. Moreover, the program constraints themselves are worthy of examination.

Previous Research

To date the body of research on competitive effects is still relatively undeveloped. As Patrick McEwan concludes in the most recent review of exist-

42. Bryk, Kerbow, and Rollow (1997, p. 174); Hess (1999, pp. 32–35).

ing research, "Evidence on the effects of competition on public school efficiency is sparse."[43]

The research into how choice-induced competition affects school systems tends to explore the question in two ways. One approach focuses on how competition affects the quality of the educational product, using data on student test performance or graduation rates, future student earnings, the cost of education services, or similar measures. The second approach tends to rely upon surveys, case studies, and field research to examine how schools or school systems respond to competition.

The two bodies of research focus on somewhat different debates. The first centers on whether education competition produces measurable improvements in performance or efficiency, the second on understanding how schools and school systems actually react to competition. The larger problem for both approaches is the absence of a conceptual model that explains how and why public schools are likely to respond to competition, given their context and their institutional structure.[44] Absent an understanding of the motives and incentives impelling educators and the constraints under which they operate, empirical findings are of limited value. In this work, I seek to advance such an understanding, providing an opportunity to synthesize the existing research.

Effects on Outcomes

The lack of choice-based schooling in the United States forces scholars examining the impact of competition on outcomes to tease out such findings from existing arrangements. In particular, researchers seek to use the incidence of local private schooling or the number of other nearby public systems as proxies for competition.

The most systematic efforts to assess the effect of natural competition on public schooling are those of the economist Caroline Hoxby.[45] Using national data to examine the effects of competing with a large number of neighboring public school systems or with a large local private school community, Hoxby finds that competition leads to higher student test

---

43. McEwan (2001, p. 136).

44. Epple and Romano (1998) make one such effort, discussing how the importance of peer effects and the nature of education may influence competition. However, their goal is not to explore how the broad structural or organizational context may influence the nature of competitive effects.

45. Hoxby (1994, 1998, 2000).

scores and lower per pupil district costs. Less ambitious studies also find evidence that private schools tend to boost the performance of local public school students.[46] Other, less far-reaching studies do not find a systematic link between competition and measures of school system performance.[47] The challenge for this body of work is that, even if one accepts the cross-sectional link between competition and system performance and sets aside concern about possible sources of bias, it is not clear how the association came to exist, how rapidly the effects emerged, or whether choice-based reform will necessarily produce similar effects.[48]

An approach that has the potential to shed more light on how public schools actually respond to choice programs is one that considers how choice experiments have affected public school student performance. Unfortunately, the newness of most choice-based reform limits research along these lines. Moreover, because choice-based reform tends to be adopted in concert with other kinds of reform or by systems that are changing in other ways, such analyses are inevitably plagued by problems of endogeneity and omitted variable bias.

Hoxby goes furthest in considering these problems by adopting a new research approach.[49] She analyzes test score data from Milwaukee public schools subjected to voucher and charter competition, comparing the test score performance of these schools to similar schools elsewhere in Wisconsin that did not face this type of competition, finding that student test scores in the schools subject to the voucher program increased more rapidly than test scores of students in the other Wisconsin schools.[50] Hoxby also reports significant improvement in the Arizona and Michigan public schools that faced charter school competition.

Another effort that seeks to link choice-based reforms to changes in performance finds that low-performing Florida schools significantly improved their test score performance when the state threatened to issue vouchers to students at schools performing at the lowest level of the Florida

46. Dee (1998); Borland and Howsen (1992).
47. Sander (1999); Jepsen (1999); Smith and Meier (1995); Wrinkle, Stewart, and Polinard (1999).
48. See McEwan (2001, pp. 125–30) for discussion of possible sources of bias in these analyses.
49. Hoxby (2001).
50. Hoxby's findings contrast with the more muted Milwaukee effects reported in this volume. Hoxby focuses on test scores, while this study focuses on evidence of broader system change. Further, most of Hoxby's reported results occurred in 1998–2000, a period of growing choice competition.

Comprehensive Assessment Test (FCAT).[51] It is unclear whether the gains are due to improved teaching, a shift in instructional focus from nontested to tested material, or some other cause.[52] Significantly, these findings are consistent with those from other states that introduced high-stakes performance tests. Schools subjected to such concerted pressure tend to improve their test scores as employees seek to avert sanctions, whether those sanctions are vouchers, a state takeover, or more intrusive monitoring.

Mark Schneider, Paul Teske, and Melissa Marschall also address the question of how choice experiments have affected student test scores.[53] Examining three public choice experiments, they find some evidence that competition may have contributed to marginally improved test scores in two of the school systems, though their effort illustrates just how difficult it is to identify effects produced by competition.[54]

The central problem for this line of research is that, regardless of substantive findings, it cannot offer explicit direction to policymakers. If the research suggests that competition does produce desirable results, it cannot say very much about how or why it does. The causal explanations are generally limited to restating the premises of classic (bulldozer-style) competition. Statistical relationships simply do not illuminate the processes

51. Greene (2001). This study illustrates just how program design can matter. Individual schools were given clear direction and subjected to significant pressure. Principals had professional incentives to boost test scores, while jobs at specific schools could be lost if students were to depart via vouchers. The explicit outcomes and school-level focus made it possible to evaluate teacher performance and monitor teacher cooperation. Results similar to Greene's emerge when schools are subjected to high-stakes testing whether or not school choice is involved. When educational organizations are pressed to produce a discrete outcome, they will do so. Such pressure works most effectively at the school level, where the connection among educators, outcomes, and sanctions or rewards is clearest.

52. Amelia Newcomb, "In Florida, Lessons on Vouchers," *Christian Science Monitor*, February 16, 2001.

53. Schneider, Teske, and Marschall (2000).

54. The authors report test score improvement in the public schools of Montclair, N.J., and District 4 in New York City that coincided with the existence of public school choice. However, it is difficult to determine whether such improvement is due to the effects of competition or to the many other reforms adopted along with public choice. In the case of Montclair, the authors acknowledge that "there are many possible explanations" for the observed improvement in test scores and that they cannot necessarily attribute it to competition (p. 200). In the case of District 4, the authors seek to account for "the effects of improved leadership, more school flexibility, access to greater resources, and retention of better students" so as to isolate the effect of competition (p. 198). However, the adoption of public choice is linked to other leadership and reform activity that helped to make District 4 a magnet for talented teachers and principals. As a consequence, it is hard to know what actually produced the tiny improvements that the authors attribute to competition.

producing the reported effects. Because the research cannot tell us what caused the observed effects, it cannot foretell whether the results of choice-based reform will be consistent with those produced by naturally occurring competition or how variations in program design or context will change outcomes.[55] On the other hand, studies finding that "natural" competition has no effects are not necessarily persuasive, partly because the analyses offer no theoretical reason to believe that markets will not work in education and partly because the outcome measures they use are inevitably imperfect.

School System Behavior

A second body of work seeks to understand how public schools or school systems respond to market competition. The presumption is that findings can be extrapolated to illuminate how a more developed system of school choice would work. Of course, just as there is difficulty extrapolating from findings on "natural" competition, so are there dangers with using small-scale experiments to anticipate the effects of a large-scale system of school choice.

The research examining how public schools and school systems respond to competition produces three findings, all of them more consistent with the pickax, rather than the bulldozer, conception of competitive response. Schools and school systems sometimes answer competitive pressure by taking apparently positive steps, such as adding programs or increasing publicity; they sometimes adopt measures that offer cause for concern, such as cutting popular programs in order to marshal community support; and they sometimes become defensive or disheartened.

Because most of the research on system behavior is anecdotal or based upon case studies, it is difficult for researchers to gauge how frequently or forcefully school systems actually do respond to competition. However, a few scholars have studied this question in a systematic fashion, finding that something between a third and a half of school systems respond to charter school competition in some fashion.[56] In an effort to assess the impact of charter school competition on nearly a hundred Arizona public

---

55. A problem with measuring the effects of "traditional" choice situations, rather than school choice policies, is that the findings may not necessarily depict what would happen under new institutional arrangements. See Armor and Peiser (1998, p. 159).

56. Rofes (1998); Armor and Peiser (1997, 1998); Aud (1999).

schools (rather than on school systems), two colleagues and I surveyed classroom teachers and found that competition had relatively limited effects on school outreach efforts and leadership.[57]

By way of explaining the rate at which systems did not respond to competition, Amy Stuart Wells notes in a study of several California schools that public school principals sometimes did not respond to charter school competition because they saw the charter schools as holding unfair advantages; rather than engage in what seemed to them a pointless effort, they circled the wagons and resisted change.[58]

The previous research effort most similar to the current study is that of Paul Teske and colleagues.[59] They examine the impact of charter school competition on five urban districts and find that response varied across districts, with superintendents in two of the five districts using the threat of competition as a tool for advocating change. They find that the link between charter competition and local school response was "tenuous at best," with school systems insulated by legislative design and hampered by organizational constraints. Meanwhile, they served consumers unable to accurately assess efficiency or demonstrated performance. The researchers do observe some response to competition, as school personnel sought in some instances to add new programs, launch innovative efforts, or increase their efforts to communicate with and respond to parents.

The competitive effects reported throughout this body of research tend to be relatively consistent: the opening of new schools organized around a specific philosophy or theme, the addition of programs such as all-day kindergarten, an increase in curricular resources, the introduction of new programs consistent with parent preferences, new concern with publicity efforts, and replacement of the superintendent with a "reformer."[60] School systems also respond to competition in less positive ways: using the courts or legislation to derail or restrict charter schools, refusing to provide student records, cutting popular programs—such as art or advanced placement courses—and then blaming the cuts on charter schooling and seeking to galvanize parental opposition to school choice.[61]

---

57. Hess, Maranto, and Milliman (2001, forthcoming a).

58. Wells (1998).

59. Teske and others (2001).

60. Rofes (1998); Hess, Maranto, and Milliman (forthcoming b); Ladner and Brouillette (2000).

61. Hassel (1998, 1999); Hess, Maranto, and Milliman (forthcoming b); Loveless and Jasin (1998); Millott and Lake (1996).

Evidence from Abroad

While the role of context makes it difficult to generalize too casually from the effects of school choice in other nations, such research is clearly relevant. The evidence from abroad, in particular research based on the British experience with school choice, shows that schools frequently respond to competition by devoting more energy to public relations.

A high-profile study of sixteen schools in South Wales finds no evidence that competition improved educational performance but that, on the contrary, it encouraged schools to divert resources to marketing. Another oft-cited study finds that schools in three British towns devoted substantial attention to advertising, public relations, and improving the physical appearance of the school but that lack of consumer information on the various schools limited the ability of competition to drive improvement. Earlier studies also report that competition encouraged schools to emphasize public relations, marketing, and visible, quick-fix reforms.[62]

A study of New Zealand's decade-long experience with charterlike schooling suggests that the simplest way for schools to compete effectively may be by attracting more socioeconomically privileged and higher-performing students.[63] Unlike most firms, schools can readily influence the quality of the "raw material" they receive—and the quality of that "material" has a massive and direct effect on outcomes. The New Zealand scholarship raises an important caution, pointing out that competitive schools may have incentives to abandon the moral imperative that they serve all students and to instead focus on recruiting the most able or profitable students.

Other Concerns in the Choice Debate

Before pressing forward, it is useful—if only to place this volume in context—to briefly mention the three debates that generally dominate scholarship on school choice. The first of these is the question of whether enrollment in schools of choice materially benefits the participating students. This question has been the most widely researched of the choice-related disputes. Choice advocates argue that empowering parents and students to select schools allows these children to benefit educationally

62. Gorard (1997); Woods, Bagley, and Glatter (1998); Walford (1994).
63. Fiske and Ladd (2000); Ladd and Fiske (2001).

and socially. It is presumed that new, quality schools will blossom in a choice environment, presenting families with a range of desirable schools to accommodate a variety of students. Research into this issue has dominated the choice debate, with much of the work seeking to compare the performance of students in choice schools or private schools to those enrolled in traditional public schools.[64]

Second, some critics fear that choice-based reforms may be inequitable. They suggest that students attending schools of choice will come disproportionately from those families most concerned with education, thus draining public schools of their most concerned parents and most capable students.[65] Researchers examine whether choice programs may increase segregation or stratification by "skimming" disproportionate numbers of white students, advantaged students, and students from families in which the parents are most concerned with schooling.[66] Such flight is of particular concern both because racial and social heterogeneity are seen as desirable goods and because there is evidence that the presence of high achievers improves the performance of all students in a school. Researchers disagree, however, about whether markets increase or reduce stratification. Choice advocates argue that such fears are unfounded, pointing to evidence suggesting that satisfied and advantaged families are the least likely to avail themselves of new alternatives and that school

64. There are a number of studies on this question. For studies suggesting that students in voucher schools outperform their public school counterparts, see Greene, Peterson, and Du (1999); Greene, Howell, and Peterson (1998); Howell and others (2001); Rouse (1998). For work finding more mixed results on the effect of vouchers on student performance, see McEwan and Carnoy (2000); Metcalf (1999); Witte (1998, 2000). Evaluations of charter schooling have thus far not established any significant difference in performance, either positive or negative, between charter school students and their public school peers.

65. Albert O. Hirschman (1970) pointed out thirty years ago that allowing those who demand a high level of service to flee may result in a lack of pressure on organizations to improve.

66. For some recent work that addresses this issue, see Carnegie Foundation (1992); Ladd and Fiske (2001); Lee, Croninger, and Smith (1996); Martinez, Godwin, and Kemerer (1996); Plank and others (1993); Wells (1998); Whitty, Power, and Halpin (1998); Willms and Echols (1993). This work features disagreements about the extent to which segregation is likely to occur, the processes that may drive it, and just how problematic any effects will be. Market advocates argue that these fears are exaggerated. For instance, Vanourek and others (1997) present national data on charter schooling that suggest little evidence of segregation or skimming. Schneider and others (1998) argue that a small number of actively informed families are attracted by particular qualities of schooling and that choice permits these families to satisfy their preferences.

selection helps curb the segregation produced by residential housing patterns.[67]

Third, choice critics worry that introducing market mechanisms into schooling threatens the public purposes of education.[68] Those who view public education as central to enriching the democratic discourse, teaching democratic values, and serving as a melting pot fear that market arrangements may drive these values from schooling. Choice advocates counter by arguing that parents have the right to educate their children as they wish.[69] Moreover, choice proponents suggest that private schools may actually be more effective at fostering democratic virtues than are public schools.[70]

Layout of the Book

The first three chapters map out a framework to help the reader understand the constraints on market-driven reform in the public sector, particularly in the case of education. Chapter 2 addresses the context of the urban education market, examining the problematic nature of education as a market good and how the K–12 marketplace currently operates before considering how competitive capacity influences competitive threat. Chapter 3 discusses the constraints that may impede the response of urban school systems to market competition.

Chapters 4 through 7 provide case studies that illustrate and develop the issues posed by urban education markets. The larger implications of the case studies are culled and synthesized in chapter 8, which closes with an extended discussion of intrinsic motivation and its importance for efforts to introduce market-driven reform. Chapter 9 discusses the lessons learned and the implications for the long-term impact of urban education markets, providing some thoughts regarding what it will take to produce significant education competition and the costs that such competition will entail.

67. Milton Friedman made this argument when initially proposing school vouchers in 1962. Moe (2001) provides substantial support for the notion that poor and minority parents are the most likely to express interest in new educational alternatives. Schneider, Teske, and Marschall (2000, pp. 204–22) and Witte (2000, pp. 52–82) suggest that choice-based reforms will not necessarily result in "creaming" or increased stratification but that the results will depend heavily on the way choice programs are structured.

68. Barber (1992); Gutmann (1987); Henig (1994); Macedo (2000).

69. Gilles (1998).

70. Campbell (2001); Greene (1998); Wolf and others (2001); Greene and Mellow (1998).

TWO   *The Market and
the Urban Public
School System*

Markets work most efficiently when many producers compete to sell straightforward products to a large population of potential consumers. A market featuring a small number of sellers or buyers, or an ambiguous product, or a product with significant effects for nonconsumers tends to work imperfectly.[1] Nonetheless, discussion of education competition often proceeds as if markets operate without regard to the context of the market or the product. The reality is that the character of K–12 education and the manner in which it is produced by urban public school systems conspire to create a market that looks little like the textbook ideal.

Both the nature of schooling and the collective way in which urban public school systems provide it make for a product that fits poorly into the classic market model. In particular, the disputed nature of education and the ambiguity of educational outcomes have the potential to create a market in which symbolic gestures, rather than substantive performance, may influence consumer decisions. In such a market, producers have incentives to focus more on political and metaphorical appeals than on product quality or value. Markets are also shaped by both existing competitors and the prospect of emerging competitors.

This chapter discusses how the good produced, the manner in which it is consumed, and the extent of market threat shape producer responses to

1. See Schneider, Teske, and Mintrom (1995).

competition. Political scientists have written widely about the differences between activity in the economic and the political spheres, or what Deborah Stone terms the *market* and the *polis*. Stone, James Q. Wilson, Albert O. Hirschmann, Hugh Heclo, John Mueller, and others have illuminated the different worlds inhabited by members of public and private organizations.[2] While valuable, this work is limited for our purposes because it has generally discussed public organizations operating in the public sector and private organizations operating in the private sector. This volume explores what happens when public organizations are thrust into a competitive context. Meanwhile, a second body of economic scholarship examines how public sector firms or protected private sector monopolies react to deregulation.[3] Because such cases generally involve removing strictures from private firms or converting previously publicly managed organizations into private firms, it is unclear whether such research can illuminate how public organizations react to a competitive market context. Such questions have broad relevance in light of prominent government efforts to "reinvent government" and to improve publicly provided services through competition and private contracting.

Education as an Opaque Good

Education is an unwieldy market good, both because of the nature of the task and because of the way it is understood and provided in the American context.[4] This is the ultimate issue underlying the concerns of school choice critics when they voice fears that parents may not accurately assess school quality or that they may make decisions that are shortsighted or undesirable from the community's perspective. Most significant here is the obvious point that producers have less incentive to enhance the quality of a product if consumers find it difficult to evaluate quality.[5] Three

2. Stone (1997); Wilson (1989); Hirschmann (1970); Heclo (1977); Mueller (1999).

3. In particular, scholars have written widely about these issues as they have arisen in the areas of transportation, telecommunications, and cable television. See Chung and Szenberg (1996); Crandall and Furchtgott-Ross (1996); Duesterberg and Gordon (1997); Hazlett and Spitzer (1997); Levine (1987); McAvoy (1996); Morrison and Winston (1990, 1995); Robyn (1987); Schlesinger and others (1987); Teske, Best, and Mintrom (1995); Vogelsang and Mitchell (1997); Wiley (1984).

4. Henig (1994); Schneider (1999).

5. As Heclo (1977, p. 202) observes, "Knowing when a business has increased its market penetration from 40 percent to 42 percent is not like knowing when people have decent housing or proper health care." He might well add, "or when they have quality schools."

issues loom large in discussions about consumer evaluation of educational quality: disagreement about what constitutes educational quality, uncertainty about how to measure educational quality, and the realization that the ultimate consumers of education are not in fact the parents.

Defining Educational Quality

Consumers do not agree on what constitutes a quality education.[6] In the case of schooling, there is fundamental disagreement regarding the purpose of the good provided. While individual consumers are clear regarding their expectations of goods like a pair of shoes, a steak dinner, or an SAT preparation course and although the public is fairly clear about what it expects from services like municipal waste collection and the fire department, expectations about services like public education are immensely heterogeneous.[7]

As Liane Brouillette notes, "Most people agree, at least in a general way, about what constitutes good health. Agreement on what constitutes a 'good' education is harder to come by."[8] Some educators urge schools to foster self-expression, while others call for more discipline and structure. Some advocates believe schools should ensure that students master academic content, while others think it essential to increase instruction in art and music. If school districts attempt a multitude of tasks and succeed at some with some of their students, it is difficult to generate holistic assessments of district quality.[9]

6. A 1994 Public Agenda study, "What Americans Expect from the Public Schools," illustrates the mixed demands that Americans place upon educators. For instance, more than 80 percent of respondents thought it important for schools to emphasize self-esteem even as 37 percent said that too many teachers emphasize self-esteem at the expense of student learning. Strong disagreements about school-related issues include those over whether and how students should be disciplined, how teachers should dress and interact with students, how schools should approach controversial issues like racism and sexual activity, and whether reading or mathematics instruction ought to focus on acquiring basic proficiency or on fostering creativity.

7. Douglas (1987); Brouillette (1996); Lipsky (1980); McNeil (2000); Sizer (1996); Wagner (1994); Hirsch (1987); Shanker (1993); Ravitch (2000); Bierlein (1993); Lezotte (1992); Stout and others (1995); Tyack, Kirst, and Hansot (1983); Wirt and Kirst (1989).

8. Brouillette (1996, p. 2).

9. In practice, this problem is alleviated in part because people with certain tastes tend to sort themselves into communities. Schooling is likely to be very different, for instance, in Berkeley, California, and in small-town Alabama. See Tiebout (1956). Even within a school district there is variation across schools. Moreover, within schools, districts provide nonstandard services, such as gifted education and vocational education, to cater to different demands. See Powell, Farrar, and Cohen (1985).

In one sense, this heterogeneity poses no difficulty for choice advocates, who point out that markets permit an array of preferences to be satisfied. To the extent that school systems are disbanded or freed from the expectations that districtwide schooling be largely standardized, such an argument has much force. However, heterogeneous demands mean that public school systems charged with providing an education to all local children receive mixed messages as to what the public desires. While fragmented preferences may offer a promising opportunity for individual schools to cultivate a market niche, they may swamp public systems charged with providing standard services to a diverse community.

Market competition will enhance the efficiency and quality of schooling to the extent that consumers reward those qualities. If parents are concerned with school safety, school location, or electives offered, then school leaders will respond to those concerns.[10] Given that academic performance is not the only issue of concern to urban parents, it is not clear how strongly parental pressure will push school leaders to emphasize academic performance. The challenge for educational leaders is that they must negotiate the question of what they *should* be doing before they can focus on how to do it more effectively. When they are compelled to respond to competition, it is not clear to *which* demands they will respond.

This kind of confusion is not unique to education. Consumers also disagree about whether an elite sushi restaurant is delightful or disgusting, or whether a neighborhood "greasy spoon" is a good value or a health hazard. Such disagreements encourage vendors to target market niches, producing competition within and among the niche markets. Consequently, in the case of education, charter schools and private schools can readily arise to address the demands of particular families. The challenge for public school *systems* is that, because they are required to serve all local students and to provide a relatively standardized common education, they have limited freedom to cultivate niche markets.[11]

10. For a sampling of the recent evidence on this point, see Greene, Peterson, and Du (1998); Lee, Croninger, and Smith (1996); Martinez, Godwin, and Kemerer (1996); Meissner, Browne, and Van Dunk (1997); Weinschrott and Kilgore (1998). Researchers consistently find that many other concerns, such as safety, academic program, location, and the moral tone of the school, may rank above academic performance when families select a school. This is not necessarily a bad thing—such reasoning is perfectly understandable and may serve the child's best interests—but it means that responsive school leaders will be concerned with many issues in addition to academic outcomes.

11. This pressure has helped give rise to the "shopping mall" high school phenomenon. See Powell, Farrar, and Cohen (1985).

Measuring School Quality

Even when there is agreement regarding quality education, there is concern that testing instruments and technology do not accurately measure or provide reliable data on a school's delivery of that education.[12] Murky outcome measures and wide variation in student ability and needs make the assessment of educational quality difficult, especially in urban school systems, where troubled home environments mean that academic results may only dimly reflect school performance.

Concerns about the value of testing instruments complicate matters and foster doubts about the wisdom of using test scores to assess school quality.[13] Test results are highly reflective of students' socioeconomic circumstances, are influenced by the number of test-taking students, and can be manipulated or inflated by school officials.[14] It is possible to construct tests that are less susceptible to these problems, but such efforts have proceeded unevenly and are often subject to problems of their own.[15]

Private sector executives are able to examine and to demonstrate the profitability or input-output performance of discrete corporate units. Educational leaders lack a similar capability.[16] The lack of a clear metric to assess educational quality has two implications for urban school administrators. First, it is difficult for them to know what changes will improve quality or whether the changes they do make are working. Second, even if they are able to determine the success of the changes they have made, it may be difficult to publicly demonstrate this success.

None of the preceding addresses the fact that education is ultimately a developmental endeavor focused on long-term effects. Advocates of, say,

12. Kennedy (1999); Linn (2000).

13. Some argue that standardized assessments do not measure the things children should be learning, than an emphasis on test performance is pernicious, and that test scores may therefore be misleading. Such disagreement makes it difficult to generate agreed-upon assessments of school quality. See Kohn (2000); McNeil (2000); Ohanian (1999).

14. Cannell (1987); Clotfelter and Ladd (1996); Finn (1991); Lieberman (1993); Orfield and Ashkinaze (1991); Powell and Steelman (1996).

15. For a useful collection describing the design, promise, and problems of four such approaches, see Millman (1997b); also see Kane and Staiger (2001). States and districts are increasingly seeking tests that more accurately measure classroom learning rather than general student competence. Such approaches are likely to eventually make school quality much more transparent, but they are still works in progress.

16. For a seminal discussion of the difficulties in monitoring public agencies in which neither the process nor results of employees' work are readily observed, see Niskanen (1971).

school prayer or whole language often argue that the benefits of such measures may not be immediately apparent but will show up in behavior years or even decades in the future. For this reason, economists often evaluate educational effects using future educational attainment or earnings, outcomes that cannot be measured until years after a student has left school. In practice, of course, parents do negotiate these complexities and choose individual schools, often by relying on such proxies as word of mouth or their personal reaction to the school principal. However, it is unclear whether parental proxies accurately reflect a school's productivity or added value. More significantly, parents will find it much easier to gauge the performance of an individual school in this fashion than that of an entire school system.

Purchasing a Third-Party Service

Assessing the quality of a service one purchases for a third party is always difficult. This is especially true for parents in large urban school systems that include dozens of constituent schools. The parents choosing and monitoring schools do not actually use the good. Education is selected for someone else, making the quality of that education difficult for the buyer to judge. Parents have little more to base their evaluations on than their child's homework assignments, communications from the child's teacher, PTA newsletters, and parent-teacher conferences. Nonparent voters who try to assess the local system have even less to go on.

The large number of schools in an urban school district makes evaluation of the district even more difficult. In a small rural or suburban district, parents might reasonably judge the system's performance based on their view of their children's school and the opinions expressed by friends and neighbors. However, in a system of perhaps fifty or a hundred schools, parents are less likely to feel prepared to evaluate the system's overall performance. Popular perceptions therefore rest heavily upon elite perceptions and media coverage. Reliance on local leaders and the media for cues reduces school administrators' ability to directly shape perceptions of system quality through quiet educational improvement. Because of this dynamic, system leaders' public support is heavily dependent upon their ability to cultivate favorable relations with cue givers.[17] This situation

---

17. Roch (2000).

encourages these leaders to emphasize visible and dramatic initiatives that are likely to find favor with local leaders, the local media, and the general public.

Education as a Market Good

The formative nature of education also raises questions about the ability of consumers and producers to respond to market imperatives in accord with classic market theory. The importance that society attaches to the social development of children and to equality of educational opportunity may pose particular problems.

Switching Schools

Consumers are more likely to switch goods when it is simple to switch from one product to another. Two kinds of cost are involved in the calculus of such decisions: the transaction cost and the switching cost. The transaction cost is the cost of procuring the necessary information and arranging for service provision. Switching costs are the life-style changes and related disruptions associated with the switch.[18]

In K–12 schooling, switching products requires taking a child out of one school and placing her or him in another. While not prohibitive, the costs of this transaction may reduce the number of families desiring to switch schools and can therefore damp down the degree of competitive threat. Switching schools may separate children from their friends and social circles, interfere with extracurricular activities, create logistical or scheduling difficulties, and require students to adapt to new teachers or a new program of instruction. Particularly for parents who find it difficult to obtain good information or to assess school quality, such concerns may make them less likely to consider switching schools. None of this suggests that discontented families will not change schools, but these considerations will temper the potential threat posed by consumer flight.[19]

---

18. Pindyck and Rubinfeld (1998); Stiglitz (2000, pp. 82–83).

19. See, for instance, McGroaty (2000) for an impassioned argument that discontented parents will go to great lengths to utilize school vouchers or charter schools.

Handpicking the Student Body

The fact that education is a service "done to" the client rather than "provided to" him has important implications for competition. Unlike most producers, educational organizations can alter the apparent quality of their product by adjusting the mix of their clientele. Most firms sell a product or service to a consumer; in the case of educational organizations, the product is the development of the consumer's own skills and capacities. Because it is difficult to assess the quality of this "product," schools are generally judged on the basis of final outcomes, such as test scores or graduation rates, even if these outcomes are heavily influenced by factors beyond the school's control. Moreover, parents believe and researchers have long recognized that students benefit from attending school with high-achieving and well-behaved peers.

Given these realities, schools can make themselves more attractive by accepting successful students and by screening out those with difficulties.[20] In a competitive marketplace, individual schools have incentives to pursue promising or high-performing students.[21] This does not mean that schools necessarily handpick students—educators may reject such an approach on the basis of moral or philosophical qualms—but the market is likely to penalize schools that do not. This phenomenon is not unique to education but emerges any time an individual's experience is affected by the nature or identity of fellow consumers. For instance, many restaurants and resorts strive to attract a certain clientele in order to create an alluring atmosphere. This behavior is typically not perceived as problematic, because society is unconcerned with the fact that certain clients may be made more welcome than others in these establishments. However, because society decries such behavior in schools, policymakers seek to limit it. The result is a market featuring unusually broad constraints on the ability of producers to shape their product, to target customers, or to cater to their clientele's preferences.

Crucially, although individual schools can discriminate among students, school *systems* find it much more difficult to do so. Attempts by school

20. Epple and Romano (1998).
21. Universities and elite private schools do this as a matter of course, and elite public schools (such as magnet or governor's schools) rely upon rigorous screening processes. Significantly, most private schools and public universities do not adopt this strategy. That is a conscious decision they make to forgo market advantages out of a sense of mission or due to an insufficiently large applicant pool. On the use of selective practices by K–12 schools under New Zealand's choice-based system, see Fiske and Ladd (2000).

systems to lure high-achieving students through special programs or special schools tend to enjoy limited success, especially when such measures are attempted by urban systems viewed by residents of neighboring suburbs as unsafe and educationally poor. Frequently, such efforts merely shuffle students already enrolled in the system's schools. Moreover, school systems are required to educate all children who reside in the district, creating an incentive to either encourage troubled students to drop out or to use alternative local services. Urban systems currently use both approaches to some degree, though they may hesitate to increase the use of such frowned-upon measures to respond to a visible and public challenge.

Finally, it is important to note that education is widely regarded as a public good.[22] Public goods, like national defense and public highways, benefit the entire community and can be provided to an additional person without reducing the amount enjoyed by current consumers. Believing that education has significant spillover effects on other members of the local and national community, the broader society desires to have a say in how any individual child is educated. Because the larger community believes it will share in the costs and benefits of a child's education, there is some confusion about what part of schooling might be appropriately considered a consumer good and what part might be viewed as a community endeavor.

These concerns are true of all education to some extent, but American society has historically elevated them to a primary place in the case of K–12 education.[23] There is no need to dwell upon this issue; it should simply be noted that the mixture of private and public purposes raises concerns about whether parents making private decisions will respect public purposes.[24] The possibility that parents will not do so, or that their preferences may be at odds with the "public" purposes of schooling, raises questions about the appropriateness of viewing education as a consumer good.

22. For thorough discussions, see Buchanan (1968); Stiglitz (2000, pp. 127–55).

23. For useful discussions, see Gutmann (1987); Macedo (2000).

24. There is disagreement about the degree to which specific services, especially education, are public goods. For instance, many critics suggest that retirement programs, national parks, and federal aid for the arts have little or no public good component and that provision of these ought to therefore be left to the market. See Friedman (1982). Uncertainty about the scope of the public good component in education is a major concern, particularly in terms of choice-based reform. See Henig (1994, pp. 57–61); Levin (1987, 1993).

Given disagreement about the ultimate goal of education and about just what schools should be teaching, it is exceptionally challenging for school system officials to assess employee effectiveness in a straightforward fashion. When they set out to respond to public discontent, education officials face an array of conflicting marching orders.

Products, Producers, and Competition

Whereas most conventional (private) market goods are purchased by individuals and are relatively amenable to an individual's evaluation, district-based public schooling is a public good that is difficult to evaluate. Two dimensions of this market transaction prove essential in understanding how producers are likely to compete. The first is whether the product is being provided to individuals or to communities; the second is how consumers assess quality. While it is possible to conceive of each dimension as an either-or dichotomy, it is most useful to instead think of each as a continuum.

Divisible and Collective Goods

Most consideration of public goods emphasizes the tendency for markets to produce too little of these goods and the need for government to therefore provide or subsidize the provision of public goods. In this volume, on the other hand, the point of interest is how collective provision affects the behavior of consumers.[25]

Collective provision requires the government to use tax revenues to make services like education or environmental protection broadly available. Community members share the parks and schools that government then provides. Contrast this with the purchase of most goods or services, whether a car or a dental checkup; consumers operate as individuals interacting with particular firms. In the first case, where consumers are operating as part of a collective, while in the second they are operating as individuals.

Public services can be provided in a more or less collective fashion.[26] For instance, public parks that charge user fees are less collective than those

25. For a fuller discussion, see Hansmann's (1987) review of economic theories of nonprofit organization.
26. Douglas (1987, pp. 44–46).

that charge no fees. Similarly, divisible goods, such as a garden hose or a lawn mower, might be bought collectively and shared by several neighbors.

The difference between providing a collective good to a broad public and selling a specific product to a particular buyer is significant. First, individuals have more incentive to gather information on goods and services they purchase than on those that are publicly provided.[27] When individuals purchase a divisible product, they pay 100 percent of the cost and enjoy 100 percent of the benefits. When individuals use public services, they contribute only a tiny fraction of the actual cost, share the good with many others, and can adjust the size of their purchase only by agitating for systemwide change. If consumers are disappointed by the performance of a mechanic, they can simply visit another garage. However, if disappointed by the performance of the community police, they have no such recourse. They must either convince the police force to willingly change, mobilize political pressure to compel change, or move to a new community. Moreover, voters who do not use public parks or do not collect Social Security have even less incentive to obtain information on how effectively that service is provided.

When competition is introduced into a realm dominated by collective provision, only those who use the good have much incentive to gather information or compare producer performance. Those consumers unable or unwilling to take advantage of the divisible alternatives (such as families not provided with school vouchers or without a local charter school) have little incentive to increase efforts to acquaint themselves with the performance of their public provider or to agitate for its improvement.

Persistent families and individuals often obtain preferential treatment from public agencies if they complain with enough vigor. Such provisions result in a divisible product being delivered to individual consumers. The families are not agitating to improve service for all children but to win more resources for their child. Most incentives to observe and influence service provision focus on this relatively manageable and fruitful task of gaining divisible benefits rather than on the more frustrating task of advocating for systemwide improvement. For instance, parents often know a great deal about which teachers are better or worse at their child's school

---

27. Scholars have long recognized that citizens have much more information about private than about public goods. See Lupia (1992, 1994); Zaller (1992). However, some scholars suggest that the impact of the public-private provision on consumer awareness may be smaller than traditionally imagined. See Schneider, Teske, and Marschall (2000, pp. 46–58).

and may take pains to compare the quality of different local schools be-fore deciding where to purchase a house. However, they will invest far less time and energy assessing school board members or the superinten-dent. The difference is that, in the first case, parents are behaving as con-sumers of a divisible good. They care which teacher their child gets or which school their child attends, and they will take steps to obtain the desired good. In the second case, the judgment will have little impact, reducing the incentive to invest much time or energy in gathering infor-mation. In short, under both competitive and noncompetitive conditions, community members have little incentive to demand or recognize systemwide improvement in the provision of a public good.

Second, consumers purchasing divisible goods can procure whatever product they desire without regard to the preferences of others. Each pro-vider is equally free to serve only those consumers who desire its product. If a consumer wants to purchase a pack of cigarettes or the services of a chiropractor, it does not matter that other consumers may find the pur-chase offensive or foolish. On the other hand, unlike private firms that sell only to self-selected consumers, public organizations must provide their good to the entire community. This forces public providers to negotiate heterogeneous sensibilities and inclines public executives to steer clear of controversial products or production techniques even if product quality is compromised. When conflicts cannot be avoided—for instance, when some parents want the school to teach sex education and other parents do not—the indivisible nature of the good means that officials must either convert the product into a divisible good (that is, provide an opt-out provision) or offend some clients.

For providers of collective goods, the homogeneity or heterogeneity of consumer expectations matters greatly. If the public holds relatively clear expectations—in cases such as trash pickup—the ability of observers to evaluate performance and to disseminate these evaluations means that competition may encourage an emphasis on these key tasks. However, where public expectations are more heterogeneous, the effects of compe-tition will be less straightforward. One strategy that producers sometimes adopt is to convert a public good into a divisible good. For instance, mag-net schooling permits a single school system to provide parents with a variety of choices.[28] If unable or unwilling to take that route, producers

---

28. One much publicized example of choice-induced competition showed precisely how divisible consumption can spark a response. In 1997 an Albany, New York, philanthropist

must try to satisfy consumers who hold conflicting conceptions of " quality"; in this case, providing a "better" product is not necessarily an effective strategy, since what one consumer considers "better" another may not.

The Clarity of Quality

Producer behavior is also shaped by the ease with which consumers— be they communities or individuals—can assess product quality. Such evaluation is influenced by three factors: the immediacy of the product, the clarity of consumer expectations, and the clarity of outcomes. Producers have more incentive to attend to consumer preferences when consumers can readily evaluate goods or services. When consumers cannot—or when their evaluations turn on widely varying criteria, fluctuate dramatically, or are susceptible to manipulation—providing quality products becomes less critical.[29]

It is relatively simple for consumers to gauge their satisfaction with concrete goods and simple services like clothing and restaurants. It is also relatively easy to gauge satisfaction with the cost and quality of such public goods as a community park or a high school gym. These goods are visible, easily assessed, and characterized by relatively homogeneous consumer expectations.

It is harder to judge more complicated services, like dentistry and accounting, because consumers lack relevant expertise and because negative

---

offered to pay 90 percent of private school tuition (up to $2,000 per year) for families whose children attended Giffen Memorial Elementary School. Giffen's exceedingly poor student body had produced the worst test performance results of any school in the region. That fall, 20 percent of students departed for private schools. By offering a simple and divisible consumptive option (to stay at Giffen or to leave), the voucher made it a simple matter for parents to reach decisions about school quality and to make a change based on that decision. The result of the decision of large numbers of parents to exit the school created intensely negative publicity for the system and directly threatened the personnel at the specific producer (in this case, Giffen Elementary). Officials transferred the Giffen principal, added an assistant principal charged with boosting academic performance, found cause to remove 20 percent of the school's teachers, and replaced its language arts program with the Success for All model developed by researchers at Johns Hopkins University. For more detail, see Rees (1999, pp. 17–18).

29. The problem of "performance ambiguity" in public goods has long been recognized. See Ouchi (1980). In a related challenge, it has been observed that for-profit providers have the incentive and opportunity to take advantage of consumers when the quality of a service is ambiguous. See Hansmann (1980).

results may not show up for a while. Nonetheless, there are cues (ranging from office décor to published rankings) that make evaluating service providers a more manageable task. Similarly, some public services, like waste management and vehicle registration, can be assessed in a straightforward fashion. While not all the results of these services are immediate, consumers are reasonably clear about the purpose of the service and about what constitutes a desirable outcome.

It is particularly difficult to judge complex services or those that can be observed only from a distance. For instance, researchers have long noted that services like day care can be difficult to judge.[30] The same is true of health maintenance organizations, as these organizations are charged with sometimes conflicting tasks, such as keeping down costs and ensuring that patients receive quality care. This problem is particularly common in organizations that provide a collective good, like a public hospital or a public school.

In truth, service clarity is often a function of how consumers *think* about quality. It is, to a certain extent, a social construct. The case of parents shopping for an undergraduate institution for their child provides an excellent illustration. Most sophisticated observers of higher education argue that the relative quality of universities and colleges is difficult to judge and depends on the needs of the individual student. Such advice, however, offers little guidance to parents. Therefore a cottage industry has emerged publishing guides that rank universities and colleges in a straightforward manner. While derided by experts as misleading, these guides are widely used. And because consumers respond to these rankings, whatever their validity, university and colleges take pains to change in ways that will boost their rankings.[31]

The response of organizations to competition depends in a large part on what consumers reward. When there is disagreement about the ultimate purpose of a service, or when results are long term and amorphous, consumers will be relatively slow to react to changes in product quality.[32]

30. Nelson and Krashinsky (1973; Nelson (1977).

31. For a discussion of this general phenomenon in a variety of cases, see D. Stone (1997, chaps. 7, 13).

32. For the classic discussion of how consumers and voters respond to declines in quality, see Hirschman (1970). However, Hirschman does not attempt to raise the point addressed here, that both market and political transactions will be shaped in large part by the nature of the good itself.

Symbolic and Substantive Market Responses

Producers that provide readily assessed divisible products to individual consumers generally respond to competition by improving product quality in a straightforward fashion. In such markets, producers either provide a high-quality product or are pushed aside by firms that do. In such a market, the buying public will tend to be relatively well informed about the products, can readily assess product quality, and has reason to be concerned with value and cost. Because consumers have incentives to gather information and can assess the value and quality of the product, producers are pressed to focus on delivering quality and value. Producers will advertise in an effort to tout their product and to influence the tastes of consumers, but it will be relatively difficult to convince consumers to swallow an inferior or overpriced good. If a new producer emerges with a better or cheaper product, competitors in the market must respond in kind or risk consumer defection.[33]

When subjected to market forces, producers of collective goods that are easy to assess or divisible goods that are difficult to assess are subject to somewhat less pressure to improve product quality. Publicly provided goods and services that are easily observed or measured would include many public construction projects, efforts to control air and water pollution, or trash collection. Divisible services that are difficult for consumers to evaluate might include day care or accounting. In such markets—finding it challenging to assess the quality of the service provided with any precision but personally concerned with quality and willing to make an effort to collect information—consumers often rely upon proxies and rules of thumb. Meanwhile, providers have incentives to demonstrate to the consuming public the quality of their product, though the incentive to focus on demonstrating quality is weaker than for producers whose product is both divisible and easily evaluated.

Producers of collective goods that are difficult to assess have the weakest market incentives to compete by focusing on product quality, since individuals have little incentive or ability to assess product quality. The result, from the provider's perspective, is an exceptionally malleable mar-

---

33. Schumpeter (1942, p. 82) describes the forces of "creative destruction" inherent in the free market: "Capitalism, then, is by nature a form or method of economic change and not only never is but never can be stationary." Under the forces of unfettered competition, no producer or supplier of goods or services can rest safely on her laurels.

ketplace, in which consumers are relatively susceptible to advertising, symbolism, and similar appeals.

Unsurprisingly, discussions of quality in the case of hard-to-measure or publicly provided goods and services often turn on thematic appeals and anecdotal persuasion as much as on outcomes and costs.[34] Market competition does not abolish this dynamic; producers of a hard-to-assess collective good, even—and especially—in the face of competition, have incentives to focus on readily grasped symbolic appeals. In fact, if organizational officials feel threatened, they are likely to increase the extent of such efforts.[35] Popular discussion often distinguishes between these "political" appeals and the "market"-oriented response of firms producing divisible, easily evaluated goods. Such a distinction fails to recognize that the political activity can be a market response.

A public that cannot assess the quality of a good may instead assess the producer of the good. For such producers, reputation and perception of legitimacy take on an exaggerated importance.[36] In the case of an urban public school system, for instance, with its difficult-to-assess product, the system may signal its competence by hiring only certified teachers, by making sure its buildings fit the expectations of the public, and by following accepted practice in such areas as grading and school activities. When confronted by competition, the system may launch professionally endorsed changes that promise improvement and show that the system is tending to its responsibilities.[37]

Critically, although it may not be immediately apparent, marketplace context is subject to human manipulation. Both the "divisibility" of many collective products and the manner in which they are evaluated can be shaped by formal (political) and informal (social) arrangements. For instance, in the case of education, private schools and charter schools pro-

---

34. Conlan and Beam (2000).

35. In the economics literature, such efforts to use the political process to protect one's position are generally referred to as rent seeking. While regarded as inefficient because they channel productive energy into political agitation rather than organizational improvement, such efforts are an accepted feature of the corporate landscape. Such tactics are even more appealing to officials running public organizations that are inherently political. For a discussion of rent seeking, see Goeree and Holt (1999).

36. This passage represents an extremely oversimplified version of a point that has been a subject of extensive consideration in the sociology literature. For discussion, good starting points are March and Olsen (1987); Meyer and Rowan (1983, 1991); Meyer, Scott, and Deal (1983).

37. Hess (1999).

vide their product in a divisible fashion, while public school systems provide theirs in a collective one. The method of provision does not alter the fact that education has both public good and private good components, but it does affect the way products are consumed and the way providers market their product.

Responding to Competitors

Absent credible competitors threatening to steal customers from inefficient producers, effective competition requires producers to act as if such competitors do exist. When producers are unresponsive to an anticipated threat, the scope and the sensitivity of the competitive response will depend upon the seriousness with which existing producers regard the anticipatory threat. When existing producers are unresponsive until full-fledged competitors emerge, the changes induced by competition will develop much more slowly.

Does the introduction of school choice create a significant threat to urban public school systems? Thus far circumstance and statute have combined to ensure that in nearly all cases the threat posed by choice-based school reform is anticipatory in nature. Does the introduction of school choice mean that significant numbers of families will be able to choose among multiple providers? Only if a sufficient number of families view their school system as one provider of a divisible good, rather than the communal supplier of a collective good, will the system begin to face a truly competitive marketplace.

Current and Potential Competitors

The threat posed by school competition is a function of how many students can actually enroll in schools outside the public school system. In other words, the immediate competitive threat is limited by the capacity of the private school and charter school systems. Private schools and charter schools tend to be much smaller than conventional public schools, limiting the number of students they can absorb.[38] Moreover, although estimates are often unreliable, most observers suggest that private schools

---

38. More than 40 percent of U.S. private schools enroll fewer than 100 students, while fewer than 20 percent enroll 300 or more students. For comparison, fewer than 7 percent of public schools enroll fewer than 100 students, while 70 percent enroll 300 or more. National Center for Education Statistics (1999, p. 9).

have a relatively small number of seats available.[39] The ranks of private schools thinned during the 1960s and 1970s, particularly in urban areas, as Catholic populations moved to the suburbs and as private school enrollment declined. Once closed, schools could not be easily reopened—the schools' organizations had disbanded, the administrators and teachers had moved on, and the buildings had often been sold or shuttered.

Existing private schools are often hesitant to increase enrollment due to philosophical or financial concerns and are reluctant to take steps that might weaken a close-knit school community.[40] Private schools, especially in urban areas, are often housed in small, old buildings ill suited to expansion, and school officials rarely have the capital to renovate or expand these schools even if they were inclined to do so. Charter schooling expanded rapidly during the mid- and late 1990s, but it is not clear whether the enthusiasm and charitable giving that helped launch these schools will be available on a scale to sustain continued growth and expansion.[41] Furthermore, into the early 1990s, elementary and secondary schooling was not regarded as a particularly lucrative market by venture capitalists or entrepreneurs. Private firms in the education market emerged in the early 1990s, but their limited resources ensured that they would expand at only a moderate rate and that their effects on competitive capacity would likely be gradual.[42]

Potential Development of Competition

Competition among schools requires either that new schools open or that existing schools expand. Short of this, the public school system risks losing only a few students initially and very few thereafter. The develop-

39. Hard evidence on this question is lacking, but illustrative information from the three sample cities is presented in chapters 4 to 7. Similarly, a survey of California private schools found that, in 2000, 70 percent maintained waiting lists, almost a quarter reported being 100 percent full, and nearly 60 percent were at least 90 percent full. The president of the National Catholic Education Association commented, "The problem for us now is not demand. It's supply." See WestEd (2000, p. 2).

40. This point is discussed in chapter 8. Also see WestEd (2000, p. 3).

41. Charter schools launched thus far often relied upon charitable and foundation giving, volunteerism, public-private partnerships, and in-kind resources, which may not be available to later entrants. Wells and Scott (1999, pp. 9–19).

42. For instance, by the end of 2000 the leading for-profit education firm, Edison Schools, operated about 100 schools across the nation. Although a significant number, this figure (which includes traditional schools that Edison managed for local school districts) was still only a blip in a national system of more than 85,000 public schools.

ment of competitive capacity is limited by at least three factors. First, most choice programs are funded at a relatively low level. Per pupil funding offered by the three voucher programs considered in this volume, for instance, ranged from 35 percent to 75 percent of that received by the local school system. Funding at these low levels may dissuade many who might otherwise open new schools or expand existing ones. Second, the formal and informal strictures on for-profit school operation, especially when combined with the low level of funding for vouchers, may sharply reduce the pool of entrepreneurs and investors willing to support the creation of new schools or the expansion of existing ones. Third, most educators who want to open their own schools have a vision of the school community they want to create. They generally prefer that these communities be relatively small, and few of these education entrepreneurs evince interest in operating multiple branches or "franchising" their schools.

Other Constraints

Further, there are informational, logistical, and statutory constraints on expansion. Uprooting students from their local school to enroll them in an alternative school is not done lightly; transaction costs and switching costs are likely to be significant. While some parents are so dissatisfied with school system performance that they will seize any opportunity to enroll their child in an alternative school, it is not clear how large this group is. If only a small percentage of parents are able and willing to switch schools, the pressure on public systems may be limited. However, effective competition does not necessarily require an immense number of active consumers, so it is also unclear what number of switchers is required to provoke a significant competitive response. As Mark Schneider and colleagues note, "Competitive markets do not need *all* consumers to be informed; rather, competitive pressures can result even if a relatively small subset of consumers engage in informed, self-interested search. . . . As in any marketlike setting, these marginal consumers create pressure on all suppliers in the market to improve performance."[43]

Logistical constraints, such as transportation, may also limit the number of families able and willing to utilize alternative schools, reducing the risk that large numbers of families will exit the public school system and reducing the threat posed by competition. Conversely, it is in communi-

43. Schneider and others (2000, p. 52).

ties where information on school performance is readily available, where choice programs are simple to participate in, and where logistical support is high that competitive pressure will manifest most readily.

Statutory Limits

Competition generated by choice programs is limited by statute and policy. For instance, the Milwaukee voucher program variously capped program enrollment at between 1 percent and 15 percent of the public system's enrollment during the 1990–99 period, while the Cleveland program was capped at about 5 percent of system enrollment. When programs are touted as "pilot" programs or are produced by delicate political negotiations, public system personnel are likely to discount the implied threat. Especially in growing systems or those facing a facilities crunch, limited enrollment losses may be viewed with unconcern or even relief. Choice legislation also generally includes strictures on school operators—including mandated admissions standards, requirements regarding paperwork and service provision, and prohibitions on religious instruction—that may dissuade possible operators from participating in such systems.[44] Finally, legislators and administrative officials have a free hand to decide whether the financial implications of lost enrollment will be significant for public districts.[45]

Political and Legal Uncertainty

Political opposition and legal uncertainty can undermine the development of competitive capacity. Launching a new school or business, or expanding an existing one, requires an immense investment of resources and psychic energy. Investors and entrepreneurs who supply these expect to be materially or emotionally compensated for their efforts. When investors and entrepreneurs fear that political or legal action might negate their efforts or limit their freedom of action they may be unwilling to

44. On the other hand, as shown in chapter 7, private voucher programs are largely immune to the legal and political threats that render tenuous the year-to-year survival of public programs.

45. See Hassel (1999, pp. 134–35): "Legislative compromise might undermine competition . . . by cushion[ing] the financial blow to existing districts when students choose charter schools. . . . It would not be a stretch to say that charter schools imposed no fiscal consequences on districts" in the four states studied. Also see Teske and others (2001).

launch or expand schools.[46] The possibility that a legislature will terminate, alter, or limit a school choice program, or that a court may strike it
down, will stifle the growth of competitive capacity.[47] When political opposition is less evident, as is the case with charter schooling, entrepreneurs are more inclined to be active. Similarly, when legal issues are absent
or have been resolved, competitive capacity is more likely to expand. Privately sponsored choice programs (such as the Edgewood program discussed in chapter 7) are, of course, largely immune to such concerns and
offer a more welcoming environment for potential entrepreneurs.

The Symbolic Market

Why do urban school systems respond to competition at all? First, simple
self-interest can require some response. Although school officials and educators may not have personal incentives akin to those of their private
sector counterparts, they do have an investment in the current system:
they have position and seniority and perhaps a particular niche or com-
fort zone, which would be lost if they were forced to change jobs. School
systems—and their funding—are dependent upon popular and legislative
support. If voters or public officials expect a competitive response and if
continued backing and funding are at stake, then some response is likely.
School officials and educators also may respond out of a sense of mission.
Public educators have opted to enter a field with limited material incentives. Some of them—due to temperament, training, or professionalism—
have a deep-rooted and personal attachment to the ideal of public education
and may respond to competition, not out of the self-interest that conventionally powers markets, but out of a commitment to this ideal.

An urban school system produces a difficult-to-differentiate, hard-to-
evaluate good, making it difficult to convince the community that its
schools are effective. This means that the school system generally cannot
simply ignore the emergence of competition; communities demand a
response. As it is difficult to rapidly produce—or to demonstrate—

46. There is an extensive law and economics literature on the conditions that convince
entrepreneurs to enter risky markets. For the importance of legal and political assurances,
see Popov (1999); Flipse (1992).

47. The legal dimension is particularly relevant given the barrage of constitutional and
statutory challenges to school choice by civil rights, civil liberties, and teachers' organizations. For broad treatments of how such activity affects social policy, see Horowitz (1977);
Melnick (1994); Scheingold (1974).

classroom improvement, school officials have strong incentives to focus on broad, visible, and symbolic appeals rather than on the arduous task of enhancing performance by altering classroom practice and systemwide behavior.

Because public school systems are government-operated entities, their leadership must remain more sensitive to political support than to marginal changes in consumer behavior. Given the existent market context, system leaders are especially likely to respond to competition with symbolic measures that maintain their legitimacy or political moves that marshal support. There is a strong incentive to focus on measures such as advertising, adding new programs, or promoting particularized services. These kinds of appeal have the potential to easily and rapidly satisfy a substantial number of customers while minimizing the resulting organizational disruption.

One way to rally political support may be through emotive appeals to the community that urge support for the public schools or by decrying the invasive attacks of "extremists" or "outsiders." Such appeals are likely to be reasonably effective, as polling demonstrates a deep-seated, quasi-religious attachment of Americans to their local public schools.[48] To the degree that systems use this goodwill to discredit competitors or critics, they will have less need to attend to product quality.

Although individual schools may respond to competition in a more direct way, operating like firms that sell a distinct product (a divisible good) to individual consumers, school systems as a whole have little ability or incentive to respond in this manner.

Conclusion

Deregulation and competition are often effective in promoting long-term efficiencies, resulting in the production of higher quality products at lower prices. However, such outcomes are not inevitable. In fact, the effect of competition may depend, in often unappreciated ways, on the nature of

---

48. Moe (2001) provides an analysis and discussion of what he terms the "public school ethos." For a sense of the consistency of public support for public schooling, the best source may be the annual Gallup polls of American attitudes toward education published each fall in *Phi Delta Kappan*. A related finding is that, while 58 percent of Americans distrust federal officials and 41 percent distrust their state governor to make decisions on schools, fewer than 15 percent express such doubts about local teachers and principals. See Public Agenda (1994).

the good or service being produced and the manner in which it is provided. When it is difficult for consumers to assess the quality of a product and when the product is supplied as a collective good, producers face relatively little pressure to compete by improving product quality.

While private schools or charter schools produce a divisible good for a public with specific preferences, urban systems service troubled communities riven by disagreement about what constitutes quality schooling or how to measure it. Absent an agreed-upon outcome metric, urban systems have trouble demonstrating the quality of their performance. It is especially difficult for them to make the case to a collectivity of voters, as each voter has only a modest incentive to become well versed in the details of school system performance. Given a community relationship with its public school system that is marked by emotive attachment, communities are inclined to look favorably upon any response to competition that seems to offer evidence that the school system is improving.

In the existing urban education marketplace there are few incentives for school system leaders to radically overhaul the systems they lead. When faced with a significant threat, they are likely to concentrate on mobilizing popular sentiment or on taking marginal actions that will allay the concerns of vocal constituencies. Urban school officials add new services, publicly recommit themselves to quality and service, and seek to make better use of those committed and dedicated teachers in the system. Adding new services and launching new programs creates a sense of motion and promises improvement without forcing school leaders to confront entrenched behaviors or challenge statutory constraints.

Resources are expended with an eye toward public perception rather than to maximizing outputs, and inefficiencies are probably inevitable. At the same time, if good schools are largely a function of dedicated educators, parental commitment, and a strong sense of school community, then changes that foster such conditions are likely to have some desirable effects—whether or not they are the ones that proponents anticipate.

THREE *Urban Systems*
as Competitors

CHAPTER 2 DISCUSSES HOW the market context influences whether and how producers answer the challenge of competition. It is now time to consider the producers themselves. How will the nature of urban school systems shape the scope and nature of districts' competitive response?

The Role of Self-Interest

Just why might individual public educators bother to respond to competition? Market advocates anticipate that educators, seeking to protect their jobs and their employer, will work harder to attract and satisfy students and their parents. This "rational actor" assumption, which underlies economic theories of market effects, holds that individuals will act when they believe the benefits will outweigh the costs.

For instance, when Ford, Chrysler, and General Motors were confronted with declining market shares and profit margins in the late 1970s and 1980s, shareholders demanded that company executives take steps to protect the shareholder investment. Executives either responded to shareholder demands and were rewarded or failed to do so and were replaced. Shareholders, executives, and employees all faced pressure to act—not for the common good but to protect their particular interests. In the case of education, teachers and administrators will pursue change if they believe that the benefits of doing so are likely to outweigh the costs. However, political constraints, the design of school systems, the lack of levers at the disposal of executives, and the culture of schooling make it relatively unlikely that they will take such action.

Although educators are concerned about the possibility of losing their jobs, the threat that competition would cost urban educators their jobs was minimal in the 1990s.[1] The existing school choice programs were limited in scope and financial impact and were constrained by legal challenges. Meanwhile, urban school systems generally faced growing student populations and overcrowding, so the loss of a limited number of students was not necessarily worrisome. Perhaps most important, ongoing shortages of teachers in urban areas meant that districts needed to replace 10–15 percent of their teachers every year, so there was little chance that the loss of even a substantial number of students would result in job losses.

The Challenge of Collective Action

How individuals think about costs and benefits depends in large part on whether these are experienced collectively or individually. Competition advocates argue that urban educators are unlikely to engage in desired new behaviors unless market pressure compels them to do so. This argument is sensible, but the premise ignores the reality that public school teachers will claim little or no benefit from working to attract more students. Benefits to the system will be diffused over thousands of teachers, while the costs of any efforts will be borne solely by the teacher.[2]

Imagine an elementary teacher who responds to competition by working an extra ten hours a week on lesson plans or grading. To do this the teacher must sacrifice ten hours a week of time with family or friends. In the absence of inducements or threats, what is the incentive for the teacher to make such a sacrifice if he is not doing it already? It is clearly the hope that his efforts will improve student satisfaction and performance, boost the attractiveness of the school, and increase its enrollment, thereby enhancing his job security.

1. The same was not necessarily true in suburban systems. In those systems, where pleasant teaching conditions and relatively attractive pay produce a lower rate of teacher turnover, competition could create the risk of layoffs more easily.

2. For an elegant discussion of the collective action problem, see Olson (1971). Individuals, who share in collective benefits if everyone undertakes an action, but who incur costs if they themselves act, are unlikely to act unless compelled. In a collective action dilemma, it is in every individual's best interest that *everyone else* bears the costs of acting, while each individual seeks only his or her share of the benefits.

At most, however, the teacher's efforts will have some impact on twenty-five families out of the tens of thousands in an urban district. The decision of a few extra families to remain in the public schools rather than switch to other schools is highly unlikely to have a significant impact on the fiscal health of the district and has only the tiniest chance of enhancing the job security of any particular teacher. Consequently, on a cost-benefit basis, a given teacher has little rational incentive to throw himself into such an effort. The same challenge holds in the private sector, but private firms address it by rewarding employees individually. An accountant at Gillette does not work hard because she thinks her effort will significantly affect the company's annual performance but because she will be selectively sanctioned or rewarded on the basis of her personal efforts. It is those selective incentives that drive competitive response in large organizations—not vague links between organizational performance and individual prospects.

Public Governance: Checks, Balances, and Bureaucracy

Urban school systems, like most large public organizations, are neither designed nor equipped to respond to competition. Public organizations are designed to attend to considerations of equity and the public weal and not to focus solely on product efficiency or quality. While private firms are designed so that the leadership will focus relentlessly on profitability, public organizations are designed to accommodate multiple goals and shifting priorities.[3]

To recognize why public organizations might not respond to competition in the matter that private firms do, it is important to consider the incentives that motivate system leaders, the external restrictions on organizations, and the constraints that inhere in large public organizations. The point is *not* that public organizations will not or cannot respond to competition but that public organizations will act more slowly and less emphatically than will private firms. Similarly, large organizations, public or private, will be somewhat less constrained and more nimble than their smaller, less bureaucratized peers.

3. For a brief but useful discussion of how this plays out in schooling, see Consortium on Productivity in the Schools (1995, pp. 37–44).

The Absence of a Personal Stake

Markets are driven by self-interest. Competition promotes innovation and efficiency when it is in the self-interest of system leaders to pursue such efforts. Private firms are owned by investors intensely concerned with how the firm is faring relative to the universe of alternative investments. Investors have strong incentives to carefully weigh risks and returns before making decisions. Consequently, investors and their agents (like mutual fund managers) press executives to constantly enhance the return on equity. Executives who fail to do so are sanctioned or fired.[4]

Executives and managers who lack an analogous personal stake in their organization's market performance, as is the case at most public entities, have much less incentive to fight for wrenching change. Leadership responsiveness can be thought of as spanning a continuum, from those who are hyperresponsive to market pressure to those who are unresponsive to such pressure. Executives and board members who are ambitious, fearful for their reputations, or in more exposed positions will generally have more incentive to respond to market imperatives. Leaders who lack ambition, who are less scrutinized or less concerned about publicity, or who are insulated from popular discontent (such as school board members who are appointed or protected by a strong political machine) are less likely to feel such pressures.

Neither school board members nor top school administrators are materially compensated on the basis of competitive performance. School board members tend to be amateur politicians, generally make little or nothing for their board service, and have no political or material incentives to maximize district enrollment.[5] Top administrators currently reap no material or professional benefits for maximizing enrollment and generally have incentives only to avoid embarrassingly large losses. These administrators want to avoid the political embarrassment of "bad press" or wholesale student defections, but they have little incentive to worry about the district's competitive position per se.

---

4. This process is moderated in privately held businesses, like "mom and pop" firms, in which the investors are also the managers. In such cases the owners may opt to accept a lower rate of profitability in order to achieve other benefits (such as a relaxed lifestyle). Since investors in public firms do not share in such benefits, such trade-offs do not factor in.

5. Elected officials who are careerist in their aspirations are likely to be more sensitive to the political embarrassment produced by enrollment drops than those without such aspirations.

Paralyzed by Design

As Terry Moe observes, "American public bureaucracy is not designed to be effective. The bureaucracy arises out of politics, and its design reflects the interests, strategies, and compromises of those who exercise political power."[6] Public organizations serve multiple constituencies with an array of demands; public school administrators are pulled in several directions at once. As civil servants charged with public responsibilities, school administrators are pressed to subordinate particular conceptions of efficacy to the larger, heterogeneous demands placed on schools.[7] Unable to choose one market niche to serve, publicly governed school systems seek to juggle their various commitments. The situation is complicated by democratic educational governance and the American tradition of permeable bureaucracies, in which constituents and interest groups enjoy many possible avenues of access. This approach to educational governance encourages political actors to write their preferences into law to ensure that temporary democratic victories are lasting, a tendency that fosters rule setting and regulation.[8]

In general, by increasing the scope of an executive's responsibility while distancing her from day-to-day operations, large organizations make it more difficult for her to respond efficiently to changing market conditions. Even in small organizations, limited time, knowledge, and information keep officials from trying to maximize the benefits of every decision.[9] Instead, decisionmakers tend to "satisfice," settling for choices that seem reasonably satisfactory. These constraints bind especially tightly in large public organizations, where "government leaders can substantially disturb, but not substantially control" the many units and subordinates they have to coordinate.[10]

Large organizations confronting a changed environment often have trouble innovating and are unlikely to react in a manner likely to yield maximum benefits.[11] Innovation in fields ranging from software to adver-

6. Moe (1989, p. 267). For a trenchant discussion of the difficulties in managing public bureaucracies, see Derthick (1990).
7. See Raadschelders and Rutgers (1996) for a good survey of theoretical and historical work considering the relation of civil servants to the state.
8. See Chubb and Moe (1990). Ironically, this criticism, which the authors level in their advocacy of school vouchers, also suggests that public school systems are unlikely to respond effectively to competition.
9. For a full exploration of these ideas, see Simon (1979, 1997).
10. Allison (1971, p. 67).
11. See Allison (1971) for the classic discussion of this topic.

tising tends to be pioneered by small upstarts and then popularized by the large, established organizations.[12] In particular, the multiple demands placed upon public institutions and their murky control systems lead to standard operating procedures designed to ensure that all necessary tasks are performed as intended.[13] As a result, the ability of large public organizations to answer the competitive challenge is likely to be hamstrung by established programs and procedures.

Political Conflict and Defensive Constituencies

System officials are particularly constrained by employee unions and by civil rights organizations. In public sector agencies, the voters with the strongest interest in agency behavior are the employees themselves.[14] Consequently, in states where collective bargaining is legal, teachers' unions play a crucial role in shaping educational policy and practice. They do so both through political action and through the collective bargaining process.[15] In states without collective bargaining, the unions wield less influence, but teachers' associations are still politically influential.

Unions can play a significant role in the selection of school boards, both by working to elect members friendly to the union agenda and by working to block the election or appointment of unfriendly individuals. This is especially important because the goals of teachers' union leaders rarely coincide with those of urban school leaders.[16] Union officials are

12. Kanter (2001), for instance, explains that long-standing internal barriers and organizational conflict made it difficult for large firms to adjust to competitive changes wrought by the Internet.

13. In a classic study of the Chicago school system, Peterson (1976) finds that the school board relied heavily on its standard procedures as it addressed changing conditions in desegregation, collective bargaining, and the decentralization of decisionmaking. He observes, "Operating procedures, once established and standardized, place constraints on the problem-solving activities of an organization" (p. 113).

14. As Wilson (1989, p. 119) notes, when public employees "are numerous, well-organized, and found in many districts . . . they may have enough leverage to ensure that their benefits increase faster than their workload." However, he also notes that elected officials are hesitant to spend public funds on public employees and therefore prefer to compensate them with nonmonetary incentives. For instance, teachers' salaries may not be high, but the pay is stable, employment is secure, and employees are largely free from oversight.

15. Fuller, Mitchell, and Hartmann (2000); Stone (2000).

16. While there are instances of "reform bargaining," where unions have collaborated with districts (see Johnson and Kardos 2000; Kerchner and Koppich 2000), it is a mistake to think that this is common. Unions exist to serve their members. Union officials will make significant concessions only when it is in the members' interest to bolster the district or when offered compensation they deem equal to their concessions.

charged primarily with protecting their members' careers and working conditions, ensuring that their jobs are secure, and maximizing their salaries.[17] Because teachers have opted to enter and remain in the profession as currently constituted, a majority generally support current practices.[18] Aggressive efforts to fundamentally alter urban schooling inevitably threaten existing arrangements. Consequently, unions use contractual, legal, and political means to block such efforts.[19] Meanwhile, in order to protect their public position, union officials embrace marginal changes that they consider to be relatively unthreatening.[20]

Although their goals are different from those of the teachers' unions, civil rights organizations also use political influence to limit the operational freedom of school officials. Given America's history of racial oppression and segregation, the civil rights community is anxious to protect its hard-won gains in education.[21] As with the teachers' unions, civil rights organizations constitute a watchful constituency, with groups like the National Association for the Advancement of Colored People (NAACP) and the Urban League committed to the legislative and judicial strictures designed to protect minority students. The involvement of these groups ensures that an alert constituency lies ready to challenge any administrative decision that violates established rules or procedures regulating such matters as resource allocation or school staffing patterns. For instance, high-stakes testing and strong disciplinary measures have given rise to legal conflicts regarding their disparate racial impact. The need to abide by strict procedural directives restricts the ability of school officials to take actions they believe necessary to answer competitors. In such a set-

17. As Michael Casserly, executive director of Council of Great City Schools, observed in 1995, "A school district's inability to get rid of incompetent teachers is a major hindrance to reform. . . . In general, union contracts make it very difficult to weed out incompetent teachers because the process usually set up is so cumbersome and lengthy." Daynel Hooker, "MPS Restructurings," *Milwaukee Journal Sentinel*, December 30, 1995, p. 7.

18. Although some teachers support changing current norms, these educators are disproportionately likely to leave the profession or at least to flee urban districts, with their difficult working conditions, low pay, and organizational inertia, for more appealing educational environments.

19. At the state level unions have shaped the teaching certification process, using it to limit access to the profession and to protect their membership. See Angus (2001); Ballou and Podgursky (2000). For a wide-ranging discussion of teachers' unions and their influence, see Lieberman (1997).

20. For discussion, see Hess (1999, pp. 77–81).

21. For discussion of efforts to increase access to American public education, see Katznelson and Weir (1985); Fass (1991).

ting, proactive leadership risks triggering controversy or offending a potent constituency.[22]

Of course, private sector firms are susceptible to some of the same union-backed and race-related strictures that bind school systems. However, public organizations are more legally vulnerable to equity-based challenges, are more susceptible to active judicial intervention, and must pay more attention to the demands of motivated constituencies. The opposition of civil rights groups may make district officials hesitant to pursue changes in the status quo or may otherwise complicate their efforts.[23] The point is not only that policymakers or system administrators may be sensitive to race per se but also that they fear the political, public relations, or judicial fallout from provoking race-based or civil rights groups.

Finally, the political and legal uncertainty surrounding school choice may encourage public officials to regard choice-based reforms as transient. Especially given the complicated legal and practical questions raised by choice-based reform, public school officials have incentives to avoid unnecessary headaches and instead hope that the reforms will fade away. To the extent that choice programs overcome legal and political opposition and become institutionalized, the ability of educators to wish the programs away will diminish.

The manner in which system leaders are hired and compensated, along with the nature and structure of public sector organizations, produce school systems in which leaders have relatively weak incentives and little organizational capacity to answer market competition. These structural constraints are compounded by constraints on managerial authority and the culture of schooling.

An Empty Managerial Toolbox

School system officials are tightly constrained by the resources at their disposal and the recalcitrant nature of the systems they lead.[24] Even when they wish to act, leaders lack the tools necessary to compel cooperation

22. For instance, reform proposals are more likely to stir controversy in heavily black urban districts. See Hess (1999, pp. 147–49).

23. For discussions of the way race influences governance and reform in urban school systems, see Henig and others (1999); Orr (1999); Portz, Stein, and Jones (1999); Rich (1996).

24. For a broad overview of the leadership challenges that confront superintendents, see Johnson (1996).

from subordinates. Businesses respond to changing markets by seeking to reshape their organization, structure, and work force and by hiring experts to provide the knowledge and expertise to support such efforts.[25] When these systemic changes are intrusive, unpleasant, or threatening, they are generally met with employee resistance. Executives in the private sector overcome such resistance by firing uncooperative subordinates, by using sanctions and the threat of termination to motivate the potentially uncooperative, and by rewarding the cooperative.[26]

Educational research shows that school improvement requires classroom teachers to implement and commit to new measures if they are to have any significant effect, but administrators have few tools to produce or command such cooperation.[27] In large part this is because educational systems are loosely coupled, with officials having only limited ability to monitor or to influence the schools and classrooms for which they are responsible.[28] Urban school systems have not been constructed with much attention to efficiency, flexibility, or sensitivity to public demands.[29] Perhaps most significantly, neither state nor school district finance systems are designed to assess efficiency, reward performance, facilitate decentralized management, or fund schools on the basis of actual enrollment.[30]

Lack of Incentives and Sanctions

Urban administrators find it difficult or impossible to threaten teachers with termination. The high turnover rate among teachers and the relative undesirability of positions in urban districts mean that, in the short

25. For a depiction of such corporate reshaping and especially of the role of outside experts, see O'Shea and Madigan (1997).

26. More than 90 percent of large public and private organizations, including those in which the relationship between individual performance and outcomes is highly complex, use monetary incentives based on individual performance. See Ballou and Podgursky (2001).

27. For discussions on the importance of teachers' commitment and effort, see Elmore (1996); Fullan (1991); McLaughlin (1987, 1991). As Ballou and Podgursky (1997, p. 81) note, "We are aware of no other profession where compensation and contract renewal are so largely divorced from evaluations of performance as they are in public school teaching."

28. For the seminal discussion of loose coupling, see Weick (1976).

29. For the classic history on the evolution of urban school systems, see Tyack (1974).

30. For a review of these problems, see Odden and Clune (1998). As they point out, education finance has always been much more preoccupied with equity than with efficiency or organizational incentives.

term, there is a persistent need for teachers.[31] Only extraordinary levels of student flight will produce a credible risk of teachers being laid off. Nationally, annual turnover exceeded 8 percent in the mid-1990s, as the nation's schools sought to hire over 150,000 new teachers a year. Moreover, policymakers anticipated needing 2 million or more new teachers during the first decade of the twenty-first century.[32] In urban areas the situation was even more daunting, with annual turnover routinely amounting to 10–15 percent of the work force. Veteran teachers had no reason to fear layoffs, and the rate of turnover was high enough that teachers did not even fear being forced out of their present school due to enrollment changes. Moreover, urban teaching conditions are harsh enough that most teachers could find equally attractive jobs elsewhere if they had to.

Significantly, the context is different in suburban communities, where high demand for rewarding and relatively high-paying teaching jobs may create a much lower rate of turnover, produce much more competition for positions, and make teachers much more sensitive to the possibility of downsizing or to the potential loss of their jobs. Ironically, this suggests that school leaders might be better equipped to answer competition in those very districts where the public is most satisfied with the current condition of schooling.

Not only do administrators find it difficult to threaten urban teachers with termination, they also have little formal authority to control teachers in other ways.[33] As Decker Walker observes, administrators "cannot monitor intensively enough to verify teachers' compliance, and . . . they can do little to reward or punish teachers. They cannot, for example, give or withhold raises, promote or demote, or substantially change assignments or working conditions as an incentive."[34] The result is "the inclination of administrators to tolerate and protect, rather than confront, the incompetent teacher."[35] In such a setting, teachers have little or no mate-

31. For a detailed discussion of the nature and causes of turnover, see Dworkin (1987).

32. For an analysis of turnover and the need for new teachers, see Hussar (1998). Aggravating the problem was the high loss rate of new teachers: nearly 20 percent of teachers who began teaching in 1993–94 left the profession after three years, with attrition highest among those new teachers testing highest on achievement tests (Olson 2000).

33. For a brief overview of research on the lack of administrative tools and some potential remedies, see Odden and Picus (2000, pp. 319–21).

34. Walker (1992, p. 285).

35. Bridges (1986, p. 20).

rial interest in how administrators, parents, or students view their performance.[36]

Administrators are unable to reward or sanction teachers through salary adjustments because teachers are generally compensated according to a single salary schedule, in which they are paid solely on the basis of the degrees they hold and the length of time they have taught.[37] Such a system provides little incentive for teachers to develop their knowledge and competencies.[38] Moreover, the lack of opportunity for upward movement within teaching means that administrators cannot easily dangle, or threaten to withhold, promotions or other opportunities for advancement.[39]

Administrators rarely have the ability to grant even small perks, such as a desirable office or a key to the executive washroom. The only divisible reward that most principals can grant is to play favorites in scheduling. However, some principals are hesitant to use even that authority, since consistently assigning favored teachers to the most desirable classes is tantamount to punishing the students in the other classes. Similarly, the administrative structure is devoid of personal incentives and largely bereft of tools for tracking organizational performance. Administrators do not share in the revenues they generate and are rarely rewarded for identifiable managerial successes. Neither administrators nor faculty are punished for losing students or rewarded for gaining students.

Urban school systems have traditionally relied on centralized management of resources, with decisions guided by rigid allocation formulas. School administrators are issued teachers, personnel, and services accord-

36. Although hard data on how frequently teachers are sanctioned are difficult to come by, the anecdotal evidence is highly suggestive. For instance, a 1993 survey by the New York State School Boards Association found that pursuing the average disciplinary proceeding against a teacher cost $176,000; a review of school contracts in Washington state found only forty-two teachers whose contracts were officially terminated between 1984 and 1987; and fewer than 0.6 percent of teachers—including untenured and temporary teachers—in 141 California districts were dismissed for incompetence between 1982 and 1984. See Ballou and Podgursky (1997, p. 122).

37. See Odden and Kelley (1997, pp. 1–23).

38. This model evolved because the bureaucratic state educational systems that developed during the twentieth century built in a bias toward white, male, and high school teachers. Concern about discrimination drove efforts to pay all teachers the same, on the assumption they were all doing the same work. By 1950 nearly all urban districts had a single schedule. See Odden (1996, pp. 229–31).

39. As Lortie (1975, p. 84) notes, "Compared with most other kinds of middle-class work, teaching is relatively 'career-less.' There is less opportunity for the movement upward, which is the essence of career."

ing to these formulas or on the basis of personal pull; gaining students brings no extra resources or incentives beyond the addition of the mandated number of faculty. Conversely, losing students does not cost a principal much in the way of discretionary resources and is only problematic if the principal loses so many teachers that a favorite teacher or a hard-to-replace specialist has to leave.[40] In fact enrollment gains can lead to more crowding or larger class sizes and may be as unattractive as enrollment losses. Urban principals are typically most concerned with a *stable* school population that minimizes disruptions. Altering this preference would require creating incentives for individual performance, designing finance systems that permit a significant amount of school-controlled resources to follow student enrollment, or including enrollment change as a factor in administrative performance evaluation.

The Ambiguity of Employee Performance

Employers can usually observe or measure the job performance of assembly line workers, salesmen, and store managers, making it relatively easy to know when these employees are meeting or exceeding expectations. Such evaluations are rarely available in K–12 education, making it difficult for school officials to know whether to reward or sanction employees.[41] For instance, if a school is orderly and clean and shows improved attendance and high morale among its teachers but has flat test scores, is the principal effective?

Teachers are generally invisible in their separate classrooms, while administrative observation tends to be a perfunctory two- or three-time-a-year event. Moreover, teachers' reliance on student preparation and cooperation complicates efforts to determine whether a teacher is hardworking or effective.[42] This problem can be alleviated if districts assess teachers' performance using standardized scores, though such sys-

40. However, I did not encounter a single report of such an occurrence during the field research in Milwaukee, Cleveland, and Edgewood.

41. Moreover, the notion that educators even should be evaluated—particularly that they should be evaluated in more than a ritualistic fashion or that consequences should be attached to evaluation—is fiercely contested. For discussion, see Baldwin (1995); Duke (1995).

42. A particular problem is that teachers are most effective when their students cooperate (O'Day 1996, p. 3), but student attitudes are largely due to nonschool factors. Thus a key problem is determining the outcomes for which teachers can be reasonably held accountable.

tems are rare and raise issues of their own. The challenge is heightened in the urban school context, where teachers and principals, to be effective, must overcome severe domestic and neighborhood challenges.

Lack of Structural Capacity to Manage Information and Money

The problem of murky outcomes is aggravated by structural obstacles to monitoring performance in public schools and by the failure of most urban systems to develop institutionalized mechanisms to assess customer satisfaction or to evaluate system performance.

Most school systems have almost no information on their marketplace or on the preferences of their consumers. Business leaders generally voice dismay at the quality, frequency, and extent of the efforts that school districts make to survey parents or to assess community needs.[43] Quite simply, school systems have not yet established internal mechanisms to assess the nature or cause of customer satisfaction, have not sought to study market segmentation or context, have not created internal accounting systems to increase flexibility or efficiency in the schools or the system, and have not developed sophisticated efforts at outreach or marketing.

There is some evidence that officials are beginning to develop the capacity, either internally or externally, to collect, analyze, and use such information, although only a handful of districts have made even rudimentary progress on this front. Private sector firms have developed increasingly sophisticated ways to measure productivity and cost-effectiveness at the individual and task level, but school systems are still struggling to find reliable and agreed-upon ways to measure performance. Increased attention to concrete outcomes and accountability mechanisms suggests, however, that these conditions may be starting to change.

The Schoolhouse Culture

Not only do educational leaders have unusually weak incentives to focus on maximizing performance and few tools with which to compel desired changes, but also they lead organizations that are unusually resistant to competition-inspired direction. The significance of organizational culture

---

43. As one Cleveland executive said, "My God, I can't imagine . . . running a $500 million business" with the information the school system collects.

is heightened in organizations, like school systems, where managers have few selective incentives to motivate employees, where it is difficult to monitor employee performance, or where employees greatly value the work itself.[44] As a simplifying assumption, economic models presume that investors, executives, managers, and workers focus on maximizing their personal utility, which is usually understood as job security, income, and associated perks. This assumption generally holds, as most employees in most jobs—whether at General Motors or the local grocery—work for the material benefits it brings. Private sector managers are trained to see such measures as appropriate and significant rewards for performance. On the other hand, teachers are traditionally less receptive to the allure of such material rewards, and educational leaders are not equipped to think in terms of maximizing return to capital. The resulting culture is one in which employees are less likely to be responsive to managerial inducements than in most private enterprises.

The Allure of Teaching and the Missionary Impulse

The allure of teaching is fundamentally different from that of most other occupations.[45] Like other service-oriented professions, such as social work or the ministry, significant numbers of educators enter the field due to intrinsic motivations such as a love of the work or a desire to make the world a better place. A significant percentage of today's teaching force is motivated by a sense of community, by a love of children, and by a commitment to the ideal of public education.[46] The compensations of teaching tend not to be material but to be more ethereal; intrinsic rewards play

44. For the classic discussion of the schoolhouse culture, see Lortie (1975). For discussions of the role of culture and the manner in which it interacts with organizational characteristics, see Kreps (1990); Miller (1992); Schneider, Teske, and Mintrom (1995, pp. 147–70); Stolp and Smith (1997).

45. For the best overview of these issues, see Etzioni (1969).

46. A survey of American teachers shows that 96 percent call teaching "the work they love to do" and 80 percent say they would choose teaching for a career if they could start over again. More than 70 percent say that it "contributes to society and helps others." See Public Agenda (2000, pp. 9–10). For more textured accounts of why teachers teach and what motivates them, see Wasley (1991); Westheimer (1998). Collins and Frantz (1993) note that a major allure of the teaching profession is the chance to be around children and to feel that one is making a difference.

a large motivational role, especially for the most devoted teachers.[47] One consequence is that the rewards of a teaching career are somewhat insulated from executive decisions, which presents a problem for system leaders seeking to use sanctions and incentives—such as money, promotions, and other perks—to motivate employees.

In fields like education and social welfare, organizational cultures are shaped by notions of service, mission, and calling.[48] When service quality is hard to judge, and especially when it may not be cost effective to maximize product quality, tensions will arise between notions of mission and notions of efficiency. Given their professional ethos and the incentives that brought them into education, it is not surprising that teachers have a deep emotional commitment to the role of public education. The most energetic educators frequently express the belief that their role is to nurture all children and that schools should seek to serve all students, especially the most needy. Not surprisingly, the hardest-working teachers are almost invariably motivated primarily by such a sense of mission.[49] Public education cultivates this mind-set, tending to attract and retain teachers who frame their contribution in terms of individual children for whom they can make a difference.[50] The public school ethos rejects measures that entail sacrificing attention to individual children in pursuit of higher aggregate performance; such a notion is widely deemed appalling by public educators, even if it is sometimes inevitable. The result is that public educators may resist "necessary" competitive measures that are perceived to be harming individual students.

The Preparation of Teachers

Neither teachers nor school system administrators have even the most basic equipment to respond effectively to competition. They have no training to enable them to ascertain consumer preferences or to make use of such information. In fact schools of education generally look askance at

47. Darling-Hammond (1996); Hanushek (1997).
48. For the classic discussion, see Thompson (1967).
49. On the question of intrinsic motivation and its implications, see Darling-Hammond (1996).
50. The classic discussion of this topic is Lortie (1975). For more recent consideration of why people teach and the culture of teaching, see Fried (1995); Provenzo and McCloskey (1996); Wasley (1991).

the very notion that students ought to be viewed as consumers or that schools ought to maximize efficiency.

Principals and central office personnel are almost always former teachers who have moved up the educational hierarchy. As such it is not surprising that educational administrators are rarely entrepreneurial, generally share the cultural orientation of teachers, and focus more on pedagogy and curriculum than on productive efficiency.[51] Most school administrators are trained in schools of education, where their preparation focuses on curriculum, pedagogy, and providing mandated services to all students; on some general training in school law; and on the practical aspects of supervising a school staff and budget. Little attention is paid to staff organization, strategic management, evaluation of productivity, marketing, benchmarking, assessing market conditions and customer preferences, or other skills prominent in management training. Administrators are ill suited for the challenges competition poses: they are neither inclined nor trained to think in terms of attracting or satisfying customers.[52] In fact administrators have frequently suggested to me that thinking about education as a market good is misguided and vaguely illegitimate.

Who Stays, Who Goes, and Why

The culture of teaching is linked with the structure of the profession in a chicken and egg relationship. Education offers limited prospects for upward mobility, few prospects for recognition, little chance to exert increasing influence or to engage in more challenging tasks over time, and few opportunities for merit-based compensation or promotion. There is little room for a public school teacher to progress in professional status, authority, or responsibility unless that teacher wishes to leave the classroom and become an administrator. Employees in many private sector firms are climbing the professional ladder and assuming more challenging roles within just a few years of entering the work force; teachers rarely enjoy such opportunities. The lack of a career ladder creates a disincentive for ambitious individuals to enter or remain in the profession.

51. Sanders (1999, p. 193), in a largely uncritical account of urban schooling, notes that "there is general agreement in educational circles that a shortage of qualified candidates for school-executive positions exists."

52. A similar point has been made regarding administrative reaction to radical decentralization. Bryk and others (1997) and Hess (2000) report that most current principals appear ill equipped to operate independently or in an entrepreneurial fashion.

Public school teachers are paid according to a strict civil service–style contract, which bases pay on seniority and degrees held, a system that leaves no leeway to reward teachers who are more effective or to penalize teachers who are less effective. Again, the result is an environment in which those who seek responsibility, recognition, or compensation commensurate with their efforts pay a large premium for the privilege of teaching.[53] Public schools are thus disproportionately staffed by those attracted to the current arrangements, resulting in a school environment in which notions of competition, ambition, and selective rewards are seen as alien or threatening. Such an environment breeds support for existing policies and is unlikely to attract more entrepreneurial individuals.

A Culture of Autonomy

Like other street-level bureaucrats who staff the front lines of public agencies, teachers learn to operate autonomously and to rely on their own judgment.[54] Within their classrooms they instruct and counsel students more or less as they see fit, with only the vaguest of guidelines. Isolated in their classrooms, teachers are given little time for collegial interaction and are typically assigned to schools with little regard to philosophical agreement with present faculty.[55] Teachers thus learn to value their autonomy. Administrative efforts to limit this autonomy, to evaluate teachers, or otherwise to dictate classroom practice or policy therefore pose a grave threat. Teachers' autonomy conflicts with the preference of many teachers for a sharing and supportive school community.[56] However, given a choice between the autonomy they know and intrusive measures, even those that may foster community, teachers and their unions traditionally defend the existing structure.[57] The culture of schooling makes it more difficult for

53. Teachers themselves report being relatively insensitive to material inducements: only 33 percent say that it is essential that a job have "good opportunities for advancement," and only 30 percent that it "pay well." See Public Agenda (2000, p. 10).

54. Lipsky (1980) provides the classic discussion of the phenomenon of street-level bureaucracy.

55. This is particularly pernicious because research on school restructuring consistently finds that site control over staffing is crucial to the success of such efforts. See Wohlstetter and others (1997).

56. See for instance the discussions in Barth (1980); Westheimer (1998).

57. For a detailed discussion of teachers' attitudes regarding professional autonomy, see Provenzo and McCloskey (1996, pp. 21–49). The authors suggest that teachers particularly value the right to run a student-centered classroom, have control of subject matter, be able to create "microworlds," and be free to "reach students."

administrators to demand or obtain teachers' cooperation, making any coherent response to competition difficult.

Conclusion

Perhaps surprising is how familiar the above points are. These concerns—accountability, incentives, information systems, cultural leadership—are not unique to educational competition but are familiar to any student of effective organizational management. They also pervade every school reform effort. Motivating and empowering executives to change ineffective practices are the keys to improving any organization, whether or not markets are involved. These factors are pivotal whatever demands a school system is responding to: the threat of a state takeover, new testing standards, or the introduction of school choice.

The competition hypothesis rests on essential, but often unstated, assumptions about the nature and structure of public school systems. In particular, it presumes that school system leaders have the incentive and the desire to compete aggressively for students and revenue. In practice, the balky nature of large public bureaucracies, the political pressures that buffet school systems, the culture of public schooling, and the available tools of governance leave urban officials in a poor position to answer the call of competition.

This is *not* to suggest that public school systems cannot or will not respond to market competition, only that structural and cultural constraints will shape the nature of the response. At this juncture, market advocates may respond that markets will force urban school systems to reform themselves, making them more like successful private firms. Such assumptions may be ill founded. If public school officials faced a punishing threat and had the incentives, tools, information, and personnel necessary to answer it, such an argument would be plausible. However, these conditions do not hold, and systems continue to be hampered by structural and statutory decisions beyond the control of school officials. Advocates of competition have rarely pushed for existence-threatening levels of competition or sought to grant urban school system officials the wherewithal to pursue systemic change. Markets are not magic—they drive change only when producers have the motive and the means to make the change.

Even as school culture proves resistant to systemic change, the schoolhouse culture helps to inspire small-scale change. The same ethos that makes it difficult for administrators to compel teachers to work harder or to improve also inspires some teachers to make extraordinary efforts without material incentive. These teachers seize upon any relaxation of rules and strictures to effectuate their vision of schooling. Some act merely because they finally have an opportunity to forge the schools they have always wanted. For others an abiding commitment to the ideal of public education impels them to make heroic efforts. Such educators operate not out of extrinsically motivated self-interest but out of intrinsic motivation and spiritual commitment. (These fascinating issues are considered more fully in chapters 8 and 9.)

Clearly, although not all of the constraints discussed can be readily altered, many can. The implications of such change are discussed in chapter 9.

FOUR   *Milwaukee, 1989–95:*

Prologue

In seeking to understand the effects of choice-induced competition in an urban public school system, Milwaukee is the logical place to start. Home to the nation's first and longest-running urban voucher program, Milwaukee has been the epicenter of the nation's school choice debate since the launching of the Milwaukee Parental Choice Program (MPCP) in 1990.[1] Milwaukee offers a chance to see how the extended existence of school choice influenced the development of public school governance, educational politics, and school system management. Moreover, significant alterations in the school choice program, the passage and subsequent amendment of state charter school legislation, and the involved role of the courts offer an opportunity to observe how Milwaukee and the Milwaukee Public Schools (MPS) reacted as the threat posed by school choice alternately rose and subsided.

Milwaukee's story is dramatic, with national publicity, oversized personalities, political skullduggery, hundreds of public and private schools, and five full-time superintendents in the 1990s alone. It is not possible to do justice to all of the twists and turns that have shaped the context and consequences of competition in Milwaukee in two chapters. Instead, I try

1. The Milwaukee voucher program was preceded by long-standing measures in Maine and Vermont in which those states funded private school tuition for some students in isolated areas. However, these policies were never designed as systemic or targeted initiatives, prompting most observers to think of the Milwaukee experiment the nation's first voucher program.

to illuminate the major elements of the story and the key lessons to be learned from the first decade of Milwaukee's experience.

It is probably best to think of the Milwaukee Parental Choice Program as encompassing two distinct programs. The first stage was a tiny pilot program that the state approved in 1990, was limited to 1 percent of the MPS population, and provided vouchers only to students attending nonsectarian schools. The second program began in 1995, when the legislature radically expanded the size and scope of the voucher program, permitting up to 15 percent of MPS students to receive vouchers and making religious schools eligible to receive vouchers.

Especially after 1997 Milwaukee was also the site of a potentially far-reaching charter schooling initiative. Wisconsin first passed charter school legislation in 1993 and later amended the legislation to enhance its scope. Among the key amendments adopted in 1997 was one that permitted three new bodies, most significantly the city of Milwaukee and the University of Wisconsin–Milwaukee, to authorize charter schools in Milwaukee.

Background

Like many other cities of the industrial north, Milwaukee's economic position eroded dramatically between 1960 and 1990 as employers and the middle class fled the city. Between 1960 and 1985 the city lost more than 40 percent of its manufacturing jobs, and by 1985 just 40 percent of the metropolitan area's population and employment were located in the city. Between 1970 and 1990 the city's poverty rate doubled, from 11 percent to 22 percent, and the share of MPS students qualifying for a free or reduced-price lunch quadrupled, from 15 percent to 60 percent. Meanwhile public school enrollment grew steadily during the 1980s and 1990s, from more than 80,000 students in 1980–81 to more than 90,000 in 1990–91 and topping 100,000 by the late 1990s. Moreover, MPS officials had known throughout the 1980s and 1990s that enrollments would continue to increase into the early twenty-first century, because the number of births in Milwaukee also rose steadily, from less than 10,500 in 1976 to more than 12,500 in 1990.[2]

2. Milwaukee Public Schools (1998b).

Milwaukee's population had been less than 2 percent black in 1940 but was more than 30 percent black by 1990. Inner-city Milwaukee, just 8 percent black in 1950, was 87 percent black by 1985. These changes resulted both from an increase in Milwaukee's black population—which grew from 62,000 in 1960 to 155,000 in 1985—and from an absolute decline of 241,000 in the white population over the same period.[3] Although Milwaukee remained more than 50 percent white throughout the 1990s, the MPS African American population grew steadily, from 25 percent of students in 1970 to 60 percent by the late 1990s (see table 4-1). Having a majority-white population govern majority-black schools proved to be a source of continuing tension.

Race and the Milwaukee Public Schools

Educational competition in Milwaukee played out against a history of racial inequity. Milwaukee's desegregation fight started with a lawsuit filed in 1963.[4] However, the trial did not begin until 1973, and it was not until 1976 that U.S. District Court Judge John Reynolds ordered the city to begin desegregation efforts. The public school system was ordered to ensure that nearly all schools were between 20 and 60 percent black (the MPS population was 34 percent black).[5] At the time of Reynolds's ruling, just 14 of Milwaukee's 158 schools met the judge's guidelines.[6]

In the 1970s, many MPS educators lived in the predominantly white suburbs. Responding to court demands that the MPS take steps to desegregate its teacher work force, a teacher residency requirement was implemented in 1978 after contentious negotiations.[7] In 1976, seeking to promote voluntary desegregation, the legislature enacted Chapter 220, which provided generous state funding to encourage surrounding subur-

3. For an overview of the Milwaukee context from 1960 to the late 1990s, see Levine and Zipp (1993); Milwaukee Public Schools (1998b); Witte (2000, pp. 36–42).

4. For excellent accounts of Milwaukee's history of desegregation, see Stolee (1993); Dougherty (1997).

5. A few schools were exempted because they housed special programs or had large Hispanic populations.

6. Nicholson (1990).

7. Although the agreement grandfathered current MPS teachers, the residency requirement, as well as race ratios bargained into the union contract in the late 1970s, would inhibit administrators' attempts to alter MPS staffing patterns and would exacerbate the teacher shortage of the 1990s.

Table 4-1.   *Milwaukee Public School Enrollment, 1990–99*

Year	Total enrollment	Percent African American	Percent white
1990–91	97,789	55.1	30.8
1991–92	93,519	56.2	29.1
1992–93	94,301	57.1	27.5
1993–94	95,271	58.1	25.9
1994–95	96,773	58.9	24.2
1995–96	98,380	59.8	22.3
1996–97	101,110	60.6	20.7
1997–98	101,963	61.1	19.6
1998–99	100,525	61.4	18.5

Source: Milwaukee Public Schools, "Third Friday" September enrollment count.

ban school districts to accept MPS students and to send some of their (predominantly white) students to the city's schools. Internal MPS documents report that outmigration from the MPS to the suburbs grew slowly. In 1976, 323 students participated in Chapter 220. By 1981, 1,034 students, or less than 2 percent of MPS enrollment, participated.

After a 1984 suit charged state officials and twenty-four Milwaukee suburbs with conspiring to contain black students in the MPS, Chapter 220 was expanded in a voluntary 1987 desegregation agreement. In 1988 more than 4,000 MPS students attended suburban schools. By 1990, 112 of Milwaukee's 138 schools were officially deemed integrated.[8] Participation in Chapter 220 would peak at 5,918 students in 1993, before beginning a precipitous decline.

Despite the growth in Chapter 220 participation, black student performance showed no improvement. Meanwhile, busing, specialty schools, and other programs to enhance racial balance were blamed for undermining neighborhood schooling and accelerating white flight.[9] White enrollment in the MPS fell by more than half between 1970 and 1980, while black enrollment grew steadily. By 1989 Chapter 220 had cost more than $335 million, had not improved the performance of MPS minority students, and had resulted in a "dual system of schools . . . [composed of] a system of traditional schools on one hand and specialty and suburban schools on the other."[10] By 1990 more than half of Milwaukee's residents

8. Nicholson (1990).
9. For a good overview, see Fuller (1985, pp. 9–10).
10. Mitchell (1989, p. 4).

wanted to abolish the desegregation guidelines.[11] A handful of black leaders grew frustrated with the disappointing educational results of desegregation and held the white-dominated MPS bureaucracy responsible for the slow progress. These activists would prove essential to assembling the provoucher coalition.[12]

Throughout the early 1980s, MPS superintendent Lee McMurrin and both major local newspapers—the *Milwaukee Journal* and the *Milwaukee Sentinel*—maintained that the MPS was performing adequately in light of the challenges it faced. Defenders of the MPS pointed out that the system was struggling to educate a student population in which a majority of students were low income and roughly a third changed schools each year.[13] Such excuses angered some black community leaders, who saw the system's low expectations as racist.

In 1984, at the urging of Howard Fuller, a member of the governor's cabinet and an influential Milwaukee black community activist, Governor Tony Earl appointed the Study Commission on the Quality of Education in the Metropolitan Milwaukee Schools. The commission was chaired by George Mitchell, a Milwaukee businessman. It hired John Witte, a professor at the University of Wisconsin–Madison, to lead the research team. The commission spent approximately $350,000 and in 1985 issued a series of ten reports.

The reports, a scathing indictment of the performance of the MPS, struck a chord in the community, which had been lulled by McMurrin's reassurances and a lack of data on MPS performance. The school dropout rate in the city was twice the state average and five to six times that of most surrounding districts. The longer they remained in school, the further MPS students fell behind national averages. The only high schools with grade point averages above a C were the two citywide specialty schools.[14] One

11. Gretchen Schuldt, "Desegregation Guidelines Opposed by Whites, Hispanics in MPS Poll," *Milwaukee Sentinel*, September 22, 1990, p. 1.

12. For a more detailed account of the racial dynamics of Milwaukee schooling, see Fuller (1985).

13. Grover (1990–91) provides a good look at many of these contextual data in the course of an article that opposed the Milwaukee voucher program.

14. The reports cited several factors hampering MPS administration, notably the need to make hiring decisions based on projected enrollment and with incomplete information on planned teacher resignations. During the first five months of 1984–85, for instance, the school system had to hire 427 new teachers. Infrequent teacher evaluation and a lack of attention to professional development were also cited as problems.

observer recalled, "For the first time, the system could no longer deny what was actually happening."

The reports triggered a demand for action among the leadership of Milwaukee's black community. However, four years later little had changed. A 1989–90 legislative study found that one-third of high school students were habitually truant and almost half of MPS high school students dropped out before graduation, with black students faring particularly poorly.[15] In 1987 the national dropout rate for black males was 6.2 percent; the MPS figure was 19.3 percent. Black students were also in trouble more frequently than whites. Between 1978 and 1985 more than 90 percent of students expelled from the MPS were black, and in 1988–89, 17 percent of black students were suspended at least once.[16] By 1988–89 a Wisconsin Policy Research Institute survey found that Milwaukee citizens were almost three times as likely as other Wisconsin citizens to view the public schools as fair or poor.[17] Frustration with MPS performance and with desegregation efforts fueled demands for radical approaches to reform.

The Milwaukee Public Schools and Reform

John Norquist, a staunch Democrat, was elected mayor of Milwaukee in 1988 and reelected repeatedly in the 1990s. As he explains in his 1998 book, *The Wealth of Cities*, Norquist believed the city's future depended on luring middle-class families back to the inner city.[18] He saw good schools as essential to attracting these families and argued that competition would improve schooling. Norquist's support for school choice would provide visible, local Democratic backing for choice-based school reforms.

In the late 1970s and during the 1980s the MPS had launched a number of reform efforts, including specialty programs at individual schools; magnet schools and citywide specialty schools; Project Rise, a program to improve children's reading, math, and language skills; the Children at Risk program, which allowed the public school system to contract with certain

15. Rogers Worthington, "Judge Halts Program in Milwaukee That Links Aid Cuts to Teen Truancies," *Chicago Tribune*, July 11, 1990, p. 3M.

16. Kevin Johnson, "A Bold Experiment for Educating Black Males," *USA Today*, October 11, 1990, p. 4D; Jean Merl and Eric Harrison, "Schools Reach out to Blacks," *Los Angeles Times*, December 28, 1990, p. A1.

17. Black (1989).

18. Norquist (1998).

private "partnership" schools to provide for the education of a limited number of at-risk high school students; Project Care, a program to create a climate of success for ninth graders; and a school-based management program providing for site governance councils at participating schools. The initiatives produced some individual successes but no evidence of systemic improvement.[19]

In a controversial 1983 governance reform, the fifteen-member school board was recast as a nine-member body, with eight members elected by district and one elected citywide.[20] All members served four-year terms. Throughout the 1990s general election turnout for board elections tended to be about 7 percent when school board elections were the only race on the ballot and 20–25 percent when school board elections were held in conjunction with other races. Low turnout meant that an organized and intensely concerned voting bloc, like the teachers' union, could have a major impact on outcomes.[21]

Of the reforms launched during the 1970s and 1980s, the 1985 Children at Risk program would later prove to be the most significant in terms of the future voucher program. It created a framework for providing "public" education through local private schools. With the support of Governor Earl and then–state senator John Norquist, the Children at Risk program passed over the opposition of the Wisconsin Department of Public Instruction and the Wisconsin Education Association Council (WEAC).[22]

19. For a survey of the political and organizational changes in the MPS during 1960–85, see Cibulka and Olson (1993); for a discussion of Milwaukee's reform efforts and their disappointing results, see Mitchell (1994).

20. The old board configuration, under which each of the fifteen board members was elected districtwide to a six-year term, was widely remembered, in the words of one former member, as "an unruly mess."

21. For a full discussion of the MPS school board and for summary data on district voting, see Milwaukee Public Schools (1998a).

22. The director of one of the first partnership schools recalled the factors that fed the push for partnership legislation in the early 1980s. "I started to hear from students how they were pushed out of the traditional schools. At that time in Wisconsin when you were sixteen years old you could sign a waiver and waive out of school. I had literally hundreds of students tell me that the day they turned sixteen an administrator met them at the school door with a piece of paper saying, 'If you sign this, you don't have to come to school anymore.' They were pushing kids out of the system, artificially keeping the dropout rate low because kids who waived out weren't considered dropouts. Meanwhile, it was difficult for us to stay open, even though we were faring well with these students. Since we were providing a nonsectarian free education, it seemed that public education dollars ought to be coming to our program to educate those kids."

An observer involved in the creation of the program recalled, "The union was against it because it allowed contracting for programs like ours, where the teachers would not necessarily have to be union members." As was the case with Chapter 220, contract schooling helped to make school choice more familiar and acceptable to the public. By 1992 the MPS was contracting with eighteen partnership schools. A 1992 report evaluated the performance of the eleven schools with more than two years of participation in the program. Overall, the schools were reported to be highly effective, although concerns about crowding, dirty buildings, fire and building code violations, and academic assessment were noted.[23] By 1998–99 approximately two dozen partnership schools were serving roughly 2,000 students a year.

In 1987, frustrated with the system's failure to improve the plight of black students, Howard Fuller and fellow activist Mike Smith drafted the "Manifesto for New Directions in the Education of Black Children," advocating a separate, nearly all-black, school district in the northern portion of the city.[24] A black community activist recalled, "We pushed for a separate school district because we [in the black community] did not feel that anybody was listening to us and we couldn't get people to pay attention to our concerns." In 1988 Democratic state representative Polly Williams, who represented an all-black, low-income Milwaukee neighborhood, submitted a bill to create a separate district in north Milwaukee.[25] The proposal passed the Wisconsin Assembly on a sixty-one to thrity-six vote but was defeated in the Senate. Opponents, including the WEAC and the educational establishment, argued that creating a "black" district could set a dangerous precedent. The fact that the controversial bill made it as far as it did was interpreted as a searing critique of the

23. Dan Parks, "Alternative Schools Scrutinized," *Milwaukee Sentinel*, October 10, 1992, p. 5.
24. The manifesto followed an earlier document, "A Call to Action for Positive Change in the Education of Black Students in the Milwaukee Public Schools," issued in 1986 by the Black Educators for Positive Change in Education. This group, which included ten MPS principals, argued that black children were ill served by the public schools and called for decentralized school control and more attention to helping all black children learn.
25. Williams served as state chairwoman for Jesse Jackson's presidential campaigns in 1984 and 1988 and enjoyed the active backing of Howard Fuller and several other black Milwaukee leaders. For a brief overview of Williams' beliefs regarding education and politics, see McGroaty (1996, pp. 55–61). Williams and Fuller were longtime friends, having attended MPS's North Division High School together decades earlier. In the late 1970s they both fought for preserving neighborhood schools.

MPS.[26] An observer noted that the effort was "substantive but also symbolically important. The message sent by the African American community was 'We want to take our marbles and go home.' It was after that, after we lost on creating the separate school district, that the effort for choice really started."[27]

The Milwaukee Public Schools and the Milwaukee Teachers Education Association

Critics argued that MPS performance was hampered by an inefficient central administration and by teachers' union influence over policy and practice. Headquartered one block down West Vliet Street from the MPS administration building, the Milwaukee Teachers Education Association (MTEA) is a powerful, active union that enrolls about 95 percent of MPS teachers.[28] Between the mid-1960s and the mid-1990s, the MTEA institutionalized protections for faculty by limiting the discretion of MPS administrators through an increasingly complex contract, which grew from 18 pages in 1964 to 174 pages in 1995. The contract substantially curtails the managerial freedom of administrators. As is typical, teachers' salaries are solely a function of experience, degrees, and credit hours. The contract also features rigid rules regarding school staffing, teachers' discipline, and teachers' termination. In fact the contract includes an MPS acknowledgment that contract language trumps district policy in the event of a conflict.

The agreement requires that the school administration have "just cause" to discipline teachers and guarantees teachers the right to appeal disciplinary actions to arbitrators. One principal explained that, to pursue a

26. For a sense of the fallout, see Dan Allegretti, "Black School District Voted, Defeat of Budget Amendment Expected in Wisconsin Senate," *Chicago Tribune*, March 19, 1988, p. 3C.

27. For an extensive history of the school system's social context and its experience with reform, see Carl (1995).

28. The MTEA, like other urban teachers' unions, has not always been powerful. Historically, urban teachers across the nation were ill treated, poorly paid, and without a voice to defend their interests. The Milwaukee Teachers Association (formed in the late 1950s) became the MTEA in 1963 when it merged with the Milwaukee Secondary Education Association. It negotiated its first collective bargaining agreement in 1964 and only then began to influence MPS policy. For an even-handed history of the MTEA, see Kritek and Clear (1993, pp. 176–87). The union's role is discussed at length in Fuller, Mitchell, and Hartmann (1997); for a concise version, see Fuller, Mitchell, and Hartmann (2000).

case, a principal must have "the will, the time, and the tenacity. You've got to be almost invincible."[29] Not one of the 6,000 teachers in the system between 1985 and 1990 was fired for poor teaching, and not one of the 1,000 teachers hired between 1985 and 1990 was denied tenure.[30] When administrators tried to get tough with teachers for misconduct, their efforts were often foiled in arbitration. Between 1990 and 1995, in eleven of seventeen cases appealed all the way to binding arbitration, arbitrators either threw out or reduced the punishments sought by MPS administrators. MPS policy required a central office conference for teachers receiving negative performance evaluations. From 1986 to 1996 there were twenty-six such conferences, or just over two a year. The conferences produced eighteen resignations or terminations, or one and a half a year, in a work force of nearly 6,000.[31] Examples of the limits on administrative authority are plentiful.[32]

A former MPS superintendent explained, "Teachers see the union as protecting their wages, hours, and benefits, and very few are going to go against the union no matter what they may think about the union leadership." When MTEA executive director Don Ernest departed in 1994, the *Milwaukee Journal* editorialized that the MTEA had "alienated a good deal of the community during Ernest's five-year tenure" and that "Ernest's brand of unionism was breathtaking for its rigidity, and at a time when the school administration was seeking flexibility to effectuate desperately

29. An MTEA official justified the union's strictures, explaining, "We are protecting our teachers by making sure the administration is not haphazard in saying someone is not a good teacher and firing them."

30. John H. Fund, "Can Competition Save America's Failing School Systems?" *San Diego Union-Tribune,* September 9, 1990, p. C-7.

31. Fuller, Mitchell, and Hartmann (1997, p. 62).

32. Steve Shultze and Mary Zahn, "Kids Take Second Place in Discipline System," *Milwaukee Journal Sentinel,* November 20, 1995, p. 1, review some misconduct cases to illustrate the teacher behavior that went undisciplined. The cases illustrate just how limited the control of administrators often is. In one case, in 1994, Bruce Harr placed a dunce cap on the head of a thirteen-year-old mentally retarded boy and led students in throwing wastebaskets and other objects at the boy. Harr explained he had done this to punish the boy for fighting. The arbitrator overturned the system's effort to fire Harr, giving him instead a thirty-day suspension and a transfer to another school. In a 1989 case Richard Housfeld engaged in what he termed an act of "very poor judgment." He punished a fifth-grader for fighting by plunging the boy's head into a toilet that—according to the boy—contained "dookie and pee." Housfeld did not allow the boy to wash his head before boarding his school bus. School administrators sought to fire Housfeld, but the board opted for a one-year suspension, and the arbitrator reduced the punishment to eighty-one days without pay. Housfeld was transferred to another school.

needed reforms. . . . Rather than propose or support educational changes, MTEA generally used the prospect of reform as a bargaining chip. Thus the union has been one of the biggest stumbling blocks to the rescue of the Milwaukee Public Schools."[33]

A high rate of teacher turnover created a persistent need for teachers, ensuring that MPS teachers had little to fear from even a significant loss of enrollment or the resultant downsizing. In the late 1990s the school system was hiring 600–1,000 teachers a year, or about 10–20 percent of its teaching force. Meanwhile, due to the system's residency requirement and the relatively low pay for new teachers, young teachers frequently departed for more comfortable suburban districts.[34]

Wrestling the MPS Administration

In August 1988, shortly after the controversy over the black school district, Robert Peterkin was hired to replace Lee McMurrin as superintendent. Peterkin, formerly the superintendent of the Cambridge, Massachusetts, schools, was Milwaukee's first black superintendent. He brought with him his deputy, Deborah McGriff, who became the highest ranking black woman in MPS history. The pair recognized that their first steps would involve gaining control of the unwieldy MPS administration. Central administration, headquartered in a two-story building on West Vliet Street, housed hundreds of employees in dozens of departments. Tenured into their position after three years, administrators lacked a personal investment in the superintendent's agenda or success. One veteran administrator noted that the school system "doesn't directly fire many principals and assistant principals . . . Instead . . . they remove people from the building, assign them to central office, and bury them. And they get entrenched there, just waiting for each new superintendent."

The board that hired Peterkin was dominated by moderate reformers that included Jeanette Mitchell, David Cullen, Mary Bills, and Joyce Mallory. Recalled one, "We were looking to hire a superintendent who had been part of educational reform and had some success in . . . educating minority students." Peterkin was quickly hailed as a local hero, was

33. "Teachers Get a Chance for Change," *Milwaukee Journal,* April 1, 1994, p. A10.
34. Between 1993–94 and 1998–99 resignations due to the residency requirement accounted for about 8 percent of the teachers who left the school system.

named Man of the Year by the *Milwaukee Times* in 1989, and proved popular with MPS employees and the board.[35] During 1988 and 1989 Peterkin launched several initiatives, reforming the system's entrenched bureaucracy, implementing a school choice program, and decentralizing the administration by dividing the MPS into six service areas.[36] This last initiative was warmly received by the community, but participants felt their authority was largely illusory, and some school principals complained that the new structure confused responsibility and added a layer of bureaucracy.

When Peterkin arrived, the school system was dominated by a coterie of several dozen long-serving senior administrators. A former board president remembered, "When we hired Bob, we had in mind that he would cut back the administration at Vliet Street. At the time, the district was very centralized, and everyone in administration was a company man." Veteran MPS employees recalled Peterkin forcing out dozens of experienced administrators, using demotion or threatening an undesirable transfer to prompt resignations.[37] Peterkin enjoyed some success in this effort, trimming the number of budgeted central administration staffing positions by almost 10 percent, from 342 to 312, between 1988–99 and 1991–92.

Peterkin also championed a "controlled choice" plan that would allow parents to choose from among the district's traditional public schools. The plan encountered opposition from black activists, who did not want to integrate the city's all-black schools; advocates of neighborhood schools; and middle-class parents worried about the fate of the specialty schools.[38] In 1991–92 a relatively weak three-choice school selection plan was implemented. The timing of the three-choice plan—it was initially proposed while school vouchers were being debated in the state legislature—might foster the impression that it was a response to the Milwaukee Parental Choice Program. However, key participants from that time unanimously dismiss that notion. An observer involved in hiring Peterkin recalled, "The 'three choice' plan was something that Bob had brought from Cambridge.

35. Walters (1991).

36. Nicholson (1990).

37. Recalled a veteran administrator, "Bob had no choice. . . . He was from outside and he wasn't going to get anything done so long as those folks were still sitting where they were and doing what they were doing."

38. Robert A. Jordan, "Don't Count This Integration Plan Out," *Boston Globe,* August 12, 1990, p. A19. An observer said, "The plan got all of the specialty schools parents mad and . . . it started touching on this whole integration thing."

It was not a response to vouchers, which weren't really a threat to us." A Peterkin deputy agreed, "Bob brought the public choice plan from Cambridge in '88. The voucher program had nothing to do with it."

By fall 1990, although Peterkin had begun his job with wide support and had compiled a record of active leadership, there was growing impatience with his inability to change the culture of the system or to visibly improve its performance.

Vouchers Emerge

In 1989, spurred by the failure of her 1988 "black district" proposal and by the plight of several financially strapped Milwaukee private schools, legislator Polly Williams introduced a bill proposing a school voucher program.[39] More limited than a proposal that the Republican governor Tommy Thompson had put forward in 1988, Williams's proposal called for Wisconsin to issue vouchers to a number of low-income MPS students for use at nonreligious private schools. Williams's bona fides as a Democrat, a black single parent, and a Milwaukee resident blunted criticism that the proposed parental choice program was a conservative assault on Milwaukee by an upstate Republican governor.[40]

The MPCP was a highly restricted version of Thompson's proposed 1988 voucher legislation. That bill, 1987 Assembly Bill 816, had outlined a program that would not cap the number of participating students, would not impose admission requirements or school standards on participating schools, would include religious schools, and would allow current K–6

---

39. Polly Williams turned to vouchers after the MTEA resisted Peterkin's efforts to have the school system enter into "partnership school-style" contracts with four established, nonsectarian community schools: Urban Day, Harambee, Highland Community School, and Bruce Guadalupe. The arrangement, largely an effort to keep these established institutions from folding, enjoyed broad community support but failed when the MTEA demanded that the school system control which students would attend the schools. A participant in the negotiations said, "It was when those discussions fell through that Polly came to us and said, 'What do you think about a choice program that you all can be involved in where the money will bypass MPS?'"

40. Later, Williams would break with Thompson and the Milwaukee voucher coalition, arguing that the MPCP had been "hijacked" by advocates less focused on helping poor inner-city children and complaining that other advocates had not shown her the proper respect at ceremonial occasions.

private school students to receive vouchers.[41] Whatever its substantive merits, Thompson's proposal would clearly have presented a much more credible threat to the MPS than did the voucher program proposed by Williams and enacted by the legislature. Thompson's initial program, with its large number of potential recipients and its lack of constraints, would have encouraged private school expansion and posed a much more immediate financial threat to the MPS.

In the face of a Democratic legislative majority, however, the Thompson proposal had gone nowhere. In 1989 Thompson amended his proposal so that students attending religious schools would no longer be eligible for vouchers, but he soon dropped that bill in favor of Williams's more restrictive Assembly Bill 601, which would provide vouchers only for use at nonsectarian schools and only to students whose family income did not exceed 175 percent of the federal poverty line (in 1990 the poverty line for a family of four was $13,359). Even with these compromises and with bipartisan sponsorship in both the Assembly and the Senate, the bill did not pass until additional amendments limited the size of the program to 1 percent of the MPS population, limited the amount of each voucher to less than $2,500, made current private school students ineligible for vouchers, required schools to use a lottery to admit students, and mandated that no more than 49 percent of a school's population could consist of voucher students.[42] The program posed little immediate or future threat to the MPS, as the strictures on participating private schools, the exclusion of religious schools, the low level of funding, and the limits on the number of eligible students all made it unlikely that many students would depart or that the private system's capacity would grow significantly.

The voucher program was to be funded by state aid taken from the MPS. This decision was in part due to the reluctance of upstate legislators to subsidize MPCP schools at the expense of their own districts, but it

41. Howard Fuller and George Mitchell had spoken to the new governor, Tommy Thompson, in early 1987, advocating a pilot school voucher program in Milwaukee. A meeting participant remembered Thompson being enthusiastic: "Why just do a pilot program? I'm tired of pilot programs. If we're going to do it, let's do the whole thing." In the end Thompson agreed to settle for a pilot program.

42. For complementary accounts of the creation of the voucher program, see Carl (1995, pp. 291–303); McGroaty (1996, pp. 73–80); Peterson and Noyes (1997, pp. 126–36); Witte (2000, pp. 43—44). The narrative here is factually consistent with these prior accounts, though there are variations in the interpretation of events. These works offer substantial additional detail beyond that provided here.

was also explicitly promoted as a way to compel the MPS to compete. Even if loss of students did create a potentially significant loss of funds for the MPS, however, enrollment-driven changes in Wisconsin state aid are softened because they are phased in over three years: in the first year the school system retains 67 percent of state aid for each student it loses. Conversely, if a district gains students, state aid is initially only 33 percent of the usual per pupil amount. In its first year, 1990–91, the MPCP cost approximately $740,000 for the 337 participating students, or less than 0.1 percent of the MPS's $584.5 million budget (see table 4-2).

The impact of the MPCP was further weakened by the reluctant manner in which officials at the Wisconsin Department of Public Instruction (DPI) administered the program. Herbert Grover, the superintendent of public instruction, termed the program a "disgrace" and actively opposed it.[43] The DPI issued a series of decisions that created paperwork for choice schools and required schools not only to guarantee compliance with an array of statutory provisions but also to provide services for "exceptional education" children.[44] Choice advocates accused the DPI of "harassing" voucher schools and undermining the voucher program.[45] State officials responded that they were obliged to see that all publicly funded schools met state-determined criteria.

From the beginning the MPCP was bedeviled by court challenges, which dramatically lessened the threat it posed to the public school system, since neither the legality nor the shape of the program was ever entirely certain. In May 1990, immediately after the passage of the MPCP legislation, the Wisconsin Educational Association Council and other parties filed suit to

43. For discussion and a detailed account of the conflicts that swirled around the role of the Department of Public Instruction in administering the program, managing the data on student performance, and contracting for an official evaluator, see Mitchell (1992).

44. On the department's administrative actions to frustrate and dissuade choice operators, see McGroaty (1996, pp. 85–90); Mitchell (1999).

45. For a description of the displeasure with which DPI officials greeted vouchers, see Amy Stuart Wells, "Milwaukee Parents Get More Choice on Schools," *New York Times,* March 28, 1990, p. B9. Voucher advocate Daniel McGroaty provided one of the more biting reviews of the state's efforts: "For many proponents of school choice, it amounts to an article of faith: Vouchers will exert a healthy catalytic effect, forcing public schools to compete to keep students. That theoretical faith . . . however, could not withstand the ground-level realities of a public education system under siege. The education establishment's strategy was clear—and the rules of engagement were not to be some sort of Marquis of Queensberry quest for educational excellence. Rather than summon up the effort to outcompete Choice schools by serving students better, the Wisconsin public education establishment adopted a different strategy: It deployed its considerable powers to strangle the Choice experiment in its crib" (1996, p. 85).

Table 4-2. *The Milwaukee Parental Choice Program, 1990–99*

Item	1990–91	1991–92	1992–93	1993–94	1994–95	1995–96	1996–97	1997–98	1998–99
Dollar amount of voucher	2,446	2,634	2,745	2,985	3,209	3,667	4,373	4,696	4,894
September enrollment	337	504	591	718	786	1,320	1,606	1,501	5,830
Number of schools	7	6	11	12	12	17	20	23	88[a]
Total value of aid (millions of dollars)[b]	0.74	1.35	1.63	2.10	2.46	4.61	7.07	7.03	28.4
School operations fund in MPS budget (millions of dollars)	536.5	563.7	586.6	612.2	646.8	674.0	704.1	735.1	776.0
State and federal categorical aid (estimated) (millions of dollars)	48.0	31.5	59.1	61.2	76.9	82.8	90.9	104.8	97.5
Total educational spending (millions of dollars)[c]	584.5	595.2	644.7	673.4	723.7	756.8	795.0	839.9	873.5
MPCP aid as a percent of total educational expenditures	0.09	0.23	0.25	0.31	0.34	0.61	0.89	0.84	3.25

Source: All values in the first four rows from the Wisconsin Department of Public Instruction, www.dpi.state.wi.us/dpi/dfm/sms/histmem.html. Numbers in rows five and six from "Amended Adopted Budget Books," figures provided by Milwaukee Public Schools Office of Research.

a. Including three distinct schools run by Seeds of Health.

b. This number does not equal September enrollment times voucher value, because the money paid to the MPCP is based on per-pupil enrollment each month.

c. Excluding construction and recreational programs.

stop the program.[46] The courts first upheld the MPCP and then struck it down in a stayed decision. In March 1992 the Wisconsin Supreme Court, in a four-to-three ruling, finally declared the program constitutional, noting that "local" bills were routinely written into the budget and that, although this was in technical violation of the state constitution, the practice did not constitute grounds for striking down the program. This ruling, however, would not end the challenges to the MPCP. Later efforts to expand choice would provoke new legal skirmishes.[47]

Partners Advancing Values in Education

Local school choice in Milwaukee expanded in 1992, when business and religious organizations responded to the MPCP's exclusion of religious schools by establishing a private scholarship program. Partners Advancing Values in Education (PAVE) grew out of the Milwaukee Archdiocesan Education Foundation, which had long provided financial support to the city's Catholic schools. PAVE scholarships could be used at any private school in Milwaukee, including religious schools. The program was intended as a stopgap measure, offering educational options to low-income families, stabilizing enrollment at Milwaukee's secular schools, and cultivating a political constituency for the voucher program, while proponents sought to expand the MPCP to include religious schools.[48] PAVE's director explained that the program "was never envisioned as a long-term solution. It was a way to get the ball rolling."

Utilizing Milwaukee's large network of religious schools, PAVE quickly enrolled more students than the MPCP, even though PAVE's scholarships were less generous. In 1993–94 an MPCP student received $2,984 for tuition (the equivalent of state aid for each MPS student), while PAVE scholarships paid 50 percent of tuition up to a maximum $1,000 for el-

46. The plaintiffs claimed that the legislation violated the state's public purpose doctrine of education and the Wisconsin constitutional provision that schools be as uniform as practicable. For a discussion of the legal issues and the court fight, see Underwood (1991).

47. For discussion, see Petersburs (1998, pp. 128–46).

48. Concerns about the sustained viability of Milwaukee's private schooling were based in part upon a decline in private school enrollment: 23 percent of local students attended private schools in 1989–90, down from 27 percent in 1989–90. See Milwaukee Public Schools (1998b, p. 17). There was particular concern about the viability of the local Catholic school system. The Milwaukee diocese, which serves the greater Milwaukee area, saw a drop in elementary enrollment from nearly 94,000 in 1960 to less than 34,000 in 1990. See McLellan (2000, p. 25).

ementary and middle school students and $1,500 for high school students.[49] In 1993–94 PAVE received about 3,500 applications (see table 4-3), while the MPCP received 970. In both the 1992–93 and 1993–94 school years, the number of students receiving PAVE scholarships was more than three times that of the MPCP, and by 1993–94 PAVE scholarships were used at 102 of Milwaukee's 108 private schools. This disparity was largely due to the fact that PAVE awarded nearly half of its scholarships to students already enrolled in private schools. PAVE's impact on the MPS was thus much smaller than the enrollment numbers might suggest.[50]

Fuller's Superintendency

In November 1990, shortly after the launching of the MPCP, Peterkin announced that he would leave the superintendency the following June, opening the door to a fierce succession fight. Peterkin's deputy, Deborah McGriff, was an obvious choice. Other prominent candidates included Robert Jasna, an associate superintendent and lifelong Milwaukee resident; local black activist and public official Howard Fuller; and Thomas McGinnity, one of Peterkin's six area superintendents. With three incumbent school board members choosing not to run in the April 1991 elections, the board postponed a decision until the new board was seated.[51] During this period, Governor Thompson unveiled a proposal to split the MPS into four districts, spurring board members to accelerate their search for a strong superintendent who could fend off state incursions.

The campaign preceding the April school board elections was deemed low key. The candidates were described as "disappointing."[52] The two incumbents, Joyce Mallory and Jeanette Mitchell, faced only token competition. The *Milwaukee Journal* endorsed both, as well as the MTEA-backed candidates Christine Sinicki and Sandra Small. In the race for the at-large board seat, David Lucey, the son of a former governor, faced

49. However, PAVE families could earn 185 percent (rather than the MPCP's 175 percent) of the federal poverty level; the 185 percent figure is used by the federal government for qualification for its free and reduced-price school lunch program.

50. For an account of PAVE's early activities, see Beales and Wahl (1995).

51. During this delay McGriff, frustrated by the board's indecision, accepted the superintendency in Detroit.

52. Priscilla Ahlgren, "Big Bucks Being Spent in School Race," *Milwaukee Journal*, March 31, 1991, p. 1.

Table 4-3. *The PAVE Program, 1992–99*

Item	1992–93	1993–94	1994–95	1995–96	1996–97	1997–98	1998–99
Scholarships awarded	2,089	2,450	2,654	4,303	4,201	4,371	846
Schools participating	86	102	103	106	106	109	112
Students on waiting lists	. . .	1,093	1,036	[a]	. . .	. . .	. . .
Total value of scholarships (dollars)	1,278,932	1,704,007	1,954,257	n.a.	n.a.	4,100,000	1,052,000
Total funds contributed (millions of dollars)	2.4	1.5	2.0	2.2	3.7	4.2	5.6
Private foundations contributing	10	18	21	49	65	77	95

a. No waiting lists after the 1994–95 school year.

former board member Kathleen Hart. With Mayor Norquist's support, Lucey spent about $15,000 on an unprecedented, "full-blown" campaign, which surpassed all such previous efforts.[53] Mallory, Mitchell, Sinicki, Small, and Lucey all won.

During the spring, while the board considered its options, a groundswell of support built for the controversial but popular Howard Fuller.[54] In May 1991, after a seven-to-two vote, the board offered Fuller a three-year contract. As Fuller leapt onto the stage of the Vliet Street auditorium to shake their hands, board members understood the path they had chosen. Recalled a MTEA-backed board member, "We all knew Howard was going to generate sparks. . . . We knew he'd rock some boats and were even willing to deal with the whole choice and charter issue with him." Fuller remembered matters somewhat differently. While the board did promise to support an ambitious reform agenda, he recalled their telling him that they would not back any voucher-related proposals.

Fuller had grown up in Milwaukee, gaining notice as a basketball star at North Division High School. After working as a community organizer in other cities, he returned to Milwaukee in 1977 and served in such roles as secretary for the Wisconsin Department of Employee Relations and director of the Milwaukee County Department of Health and Human Services. Fuller's 1979 fight for community schooling increased his visibility in Milwaukee's black community. He believed that the city's emphasis on desegregation had distracted attention from the needs of black children, and he became an ardent backer of reform. By the late 1990s private polls showed Fuller with local name recognition of more than 90 percent and overwhelmingly positive personal ratings. However, despite his stature, many wondered whether Fuller would be an effective manager of the system.

Fuller's ascendance marked a new and heated stage in the system's politics. If anyone was going to change the MPS significantly, it was this credible, fiery, hard-charging reformer. A known quantity hired to pursue a radical agenda, he enjoyed gubernatorial backing and benefited from Peterkin's earlier effort to reshape Vliet Street. When Fuller was bogged

53. Priscilla Ahlgren, "Board Rejects Charter Schools," *Milwaukee Journal,* December 19, 1991, p. 1.

54. Fuller held an Ed.D. from Marquette University but lacked the state-required superintendent's certification. At the urging of Fuller's supporters, the Wisconsin legislature passed a bill exempting the MPS superintendent from certain certification requirements. Governor Thompson, Fuller's frequent ally, signed the bill in April 1991.

down by administrative inertia, the temporizing of the board, and union opposition, many critics saw evidence that the MPS could not be reformed from within. As one ally commented, "When Howard ran into the brick wall of the union and the administration, people started to see just how impregnable the status quo really was. That's when a lot of civic leaders started to take a good look at the choice program."

Fuller's aggressive 1991–95 superintendency coincided with the beginnings of the MPCP, but observers unanimously agreed that neither Fuller's initiatives nor the responses to those initiatives had much to do with that program.[55] Fuller, himself an architect of the MPCP and a staunch advocate of vouchers, ridiculed the notion that choice influenced his decisions. "The voucher program was a little too small to have had any effect [during my superintendency]. . . . They talked about vouchers because they didn't want them around, but realistically, to be blunt, a thousand poor kids leaving at $2,900 [each] meant squat. . . . Vouchers had nothing to do with what I did or what I was able to do."

The school board generally supported reform proposals dealing with district organization, enhanced accountability, strengthened discipline, and other traditional concerns but was cautious about Fuller's more ambitious reform proposals. Peterkin's three-choice selection process, permitting parents to rank order the three schools they would like their children to attend in the coming school year, was implemented in 1991–92. However in December 1991 the MPS board refused to create MPS "charter schools" that would be free from most district regulations. This proposal was part of a legislative package, endorsed by Fuller and opposed by the MTEA, that requested the authority to close failing schools and to reassign teachers and administrative staff from such schools. The vote on charter schools failed four to four, with opposition from Jared Johnson and MTEA-backed board members Lawrence O'Neil, Christine Sinicki, and Sandra Small. The measure was backed by the moderate reform bloc of Mary Bills, Joyce Mallory, Jeanette Mitchell, and David Lucey. The board also opposed the inclusion of Milwaukee in a statewide open enrollment proposal and the governor's proposal to expand the MPCP. In 1991, in his first budget proposal, Fuller had offended the teachers by not calling for a wage boost. Again, the board had not backed him, including a salary increase in its final budget.

55. A report by a leading voucher proponent illustrates how minimal the impact of MPCP was in its early years. See Mitchell (1992).

In June 1992, frustrated by his string of setbacks, Fuller wrote a letter to the board stating that he would not continue as superintendent without more substantial support. The following week, the board met in closed session with Fuller for nearly four hours. The meeting was perceived to be successful, and at a press conference following the meeting five board members wore t-shirts expressing support for Fuller.[56] Also in June, the board approved Fuller's proposal for a $366 million school construction and maintenance referendum. However, the referendum quickly encountered opposition, as Mayor Norquist voiced concerns and critics warned that Fuller's desire to use the revenue to promote neighborhood schools would reverse desegregation efforts. After a fierce campaign, the referendum was defeated by a crushing three-to-one margin in February 1993.[57]

Fuller and the Milwaukee Teachers Education Association

While the MPCP did not have substantive effects on the MPS during Fuller's superintendency, Fuller himself proved a threat to the established MPS culture and to the MTEA. The response illustrated the manner in which the school board, the MPS administration, and the MTEA would later respond to vouchers. Particularly illuminating was Fuller's exploration of the use of outside contractors to govern some of the MPS schools.

Fuller assumed the superintendency with the intention of refocusing the school system's priorities and clarifying expectations for teachers and principals. Among his first personnel moves, Fuller nominated the system insider Robert Jasna to serve as deputy superintendent and hired the consultant Susan Mitchell, a longtime friend, to help reorganize the administration. He discarded the subdistricts that Peterkin had created, eliminated eleven central office positions, and mandated tougher disciplinary standards.

Fuller soon found himself stymied by the collective bargaining agreement and concerted MTEA opposition, obstacles he was unable to overcome. Three months into his reign, Fuller attempted to fire three teachers and a principal for misconduct. A student had sneaked a video recorder into school and produced footage that showed, as one former administra-

56. Paula A. Poda, "MPS Board, Fuller Apparently Progress," *Milwaukee Sentinel*, June 11, 1992, p. 8A.

57. Paula A. Poda, "Mayor Puts Conditions on Fuller Plan," *Milwaukee Sentinel*, March 11, 1992, p. 11; Dan Parks, "Barbee Had Ten-Year Desegregation Fight," *Milwaukee Sentinel*, January 2, 1993, p. 8A.

tor recalled, "a teacher reading a newspaper while the kids are shooting craps in the back of the room, another teacher saying 'I'll slap your mamma,' and kids walking in and out of the class." The television show *Exposé* ran the footage, while guests—including Fuller and MTEA's executive director Don Ernest—viewed it for the first time. Fuller announced on the air that those involved would be fired, but suffered rapid and resounding reversals.[58] The board reduced the sanctions to one-year suspensions, and even these were overturned by arbitrators, who reinstated the teachers with back pay.[59]

Another clash occurred when Fuller sought to increase the percentage of black faculty at the new black immersion schools (Martin Luther King Jr. Elementary and Malcolm X Academy).[60] Fuller wanted a greater percentage of black teachers than was allowed under the union contract, believing that black teachers would help further the immersion schools' focus on black history and culture. Fuller recalled, "There were seven openings, so no white teachers were going to be axed, we were just going to fill the slots with seven African American teachers who volunteered. But the desegregation settlement limited the percentage of African American teachers in a school." The union was hesitant to give Fuller the necessary waiver, "So, in August I said, 'I'm going to do it anyway.' So I did, and they took me to court, and we lost . . . because it was a violation of the damn contract."

Another clash was provoked by Fuller's April 1992 decision to fire North Division High School's principal and appoint an advisory committee of teachers, alumni, parents, and business leaders to oversee the school. The MTEA held that Fuller's plan violated labor regulations and was a unilateral action taken without union involvement. The union and the

58. Fuller recalled that "right away, all of the staff in the back of the room were trying to tell me no, I couldn't fire them. I was under the illusion that I was the damn superintendent, that I could actually do something. Meanwhile, I'm thinking, 'This is on national television. You think I'm going to sit here and say, This is terrible but we can't do anything about it because of the contract?' So we went through the whole process and tried to fire them."

59. Curtis Lawrence, "Taking up the Gauntlet," *Milwaukee Journal Sentinel*, November 21, 1995, p. 7.

60. For the black immersion schools and the MTEA's reaction, see Paula A. Poda, "Teachers Will Make Home Visits," *Milwaukee Sentinel*, June 4, 1991, p. 1; "Immersion Schools Selected," *Milwaukee Journal*, February 11, 1991, p. 4.

administration eventually replaced Fuller's committee with one that they jointly selected.[61]

Frustrated by his limited authority, Fuller began a long-running effort to convince the state legislature to expand the superintendent's powers. He wanted the power to close "failing" schools, to remove their principals and teachers, to create independent charter schools, and to relax the restrictions on partnership schools. Except for a weak charter school bill that the state enacted in 1993, his agenda met with little success during his tenure.

Fuller's Contracting Threat

As in 1991, the 1993 school board election was a quiet affair, dominated by the MTEA, whose candidates easily won three of the four races.[62] The MTEA suffered its only defeat when incumbent Mary Bills won 56 percent of the vote in her reelection bid. In the other three races, MTEA-backed candidates David DeBruin, Larry O'Neil, and Jared Johnson all carried their districts with more than 80 percent of the vote. Frustrated in his efforts to get his reform proposals accepted by the board, Fuller sought other opportunities to change the status quo. His most dramatic proposal was his decision to explore the possibility of hiring private vendors to manage some of the Milwaukee public schools. In February 1993, on the heels of the defeat of his $366 million building referendum, the MPS received a bid from the for-profit company Education Alternatives Inc. (EAI) to manage fifteen schools. EAI, based in Minneapolis and headed by David A. Bennett, a former MPS deputy superintendent, was managing nine schools for the Baltimore public school system. Fuller announced that the MPS was not negotiating with EAI but that three school principals were exploring alternative management strategies, including using EAI.[63] Mayor

61. Curtis Lawrence, "Union Vows Change but Clings to Old Ways," *Milwaukee Journal Sentinel*, November 21, 1995, p. 1.

62. Priscilla Ahlgren, "Bills Clinches Third Term on School Board," *Milwaukee Journal*, April 7, 1993, p. 8A; "MTEA Endorses Bills' Opponent," *Milwaukee Sentinel*, February 4, 1993, p. 13A.

63. Karen Herzog, "Firm Hopes to Manage Fifteen Schools," *Milwaukee Sentinel*, February 25, 1993, p. 1A.

Norquist backed EAI's bid, arguing that the city needed new models of education, and Governor Thompson supported exploring the idea of outside management. A Fuller deputy recalled,

> We brought in Edison and EAI and talked to them. It was strictly to get information. We were trying to see what we could do because we'd kept saying that we wanted to decentralize . . . and every year we would drop even more money into the schools. So we invited some principals and others to come to those meetings about Edison. Some people really looked at this as an entrepreneurial opportunity. . . . Others saw it as a tremendous threat, they saw it as someone who is going to come in and take our money.[64]

Although the MTEA worried that private management would adversely impact educational practice, teachers' autonomy, and teachers' job security, in August 1993 Fuller offered EAI and the New York–based Edison Project an opportunity to present their management proposals to the school board. The board chose not to pursue the matter in the face of MTEA hostility and general apprehension about for-profit schooling. Instead, during the winter of 1993–94, the board pushed ahead with Sandra Small's proposal to create "innovative schools," public schools that would, in partnership with the MTEA, apply for innovative status. The MTEA would grant these schools memoranda of understanding freeing them from particular elements of the collective bargaining agreement—especially the provision requiring that all MPS schools hire staffs on the basis of seniority—while the district would free them from many of its rules and regulations. In April 1994 the board adopted a resolution governing the innovative school application and approval process. In June it adopted an official policy, established the Innovative Schools Committee, and called for the launching of the first schools in 1995–96.

In the end, Fuller was able to push the MPS to create innovative schools, contemplate charter schools, and expand public choice, and the MTEA to offer a series of memoranda of understanding that relaxed the strictures in the union contract on a case-by-case basis. He used private contracting to force system change, hoping that outside operators would be able to

---

64. Fuller said that critics who suggested that he was trying to force private contracting onto the school system distorted the truth. "I set up a broad-based committee to listen to the EAI and Edison proposals, and that committee said we should go forward with Edison because they liked the design. . . . We then held sessions for parents, [administrators], teachers, and [union officials] . . . so it wasn't like I was trying to sneak them in here."

circumvent existing constraints or that the threat would scare MPS officials and the MTEA into action. Recounted a board member, "The for-profit companies were essentially his leverage to make both the administration and the MTEA do something. And that really worked."[65] However, the effort cost Fuller political capital and foundered when the contracting threat receded. A board member remembered that, although the for-profit issue defeated Fuller politically, "it certainly shocked [the MTEA] into making some concessions that they had never been willing to make before." When superintendents have to generate a visible threat on their own, the exertion can be politically exhausting. Later, in 1998 and 1999, vouchers and charters would provide a threat and promote a political coalition that the superintendent could leverage more readily and with less professional risk.

The Noneffects of Voucher Competition

Between 1990 and 1994 the MPCP drew intense attention both locally and across the nation. However, even with the complementary presence of PAVE, the voucher experiment's structure, its tiny size, its limited prospects for growth, and the continued growth in public school enrollment kept the program from presenting any substantive threat to the MPS. A school board president from that period explained, "Basically, the initial choice legislation held MPS harmless. It did very little and only took a very small amount of children." No school-level actions from that period can reasonably be termed a consequence of choice-induced pressure.

In fact, although school administrators and teachers regarded the MPCP negatively, they had little understanding of just what the program entailed or what kind of threat vouchers posed. A veteran MPS teacher recalled, "I don't think any of us had a strong sense of what vouchers or charters were. Though there was this notion among at least a segment of us, starting in '93 or '94 or so, that there's going to be this thing where you can start a new school if you're not happy." Another former teacher remembered, "Even a lot of board members didn't understand charters. They'd lump charters with vouchers, or say we're already giving money to these community-based organizations, or that charters are going to go

65. A former principal recalled, "Fuller felt that if we didn't make major changes and open up public schools, that we were going to be someone's breakfast. It turns out that he probably was correct. He was desperately trying to get people to do new things and include the real people in decisions."

off and do whatever they want—the bull you hear from people who aren't clear on the provisions."

On the heels of the Wisconsin Supreme Court's 1992 ruling for the MPCP, Governor Thompson proposed increasing the maximum number of students who could participate, from 1 percent to 2 percent of MPS students. In 1993 compromise legislation boosted the cap to 1.5 percent for the 1994–95 school year, increasing the number of eligible students to about 1,450. Voucher schools would be permitted to enroll up to 65 percent of their students through the MPCP, up from 49 percent. The cost of the MPCP to the MPS increased slowly during Fuller's tenure, growing to just under $2.5 million in 1994–95, though even that figure represented less than 0.5 percent of the $724 million MPS budget.

The Wisconsin legislature also passed its first charter school law in 1993. In his January 1993 State of the State address, Thompson called for charter legislation that would free such schools from many of the regulations that applied to traditional district schools. After heated wrangling, a weak charter law was included in the state budget. The bill permitted no more than two charter schools per district, capped the statewide total at ten charter schools, required that the schools be sponsored by the local school district, and permitted no existing private schools to become charter schools. Fuller chose not to apply for charter schools under the legislation, explaining that the weakness of the law meant the district would gain nothing.[66]

Meanwhile, state elections had a significant impact on the fragile choice program, particularly since the MPCP's fate turned heavily on statutory interpretation and legal decisions. The April 1993 election for superintendent of the DPI was won by John T. Benson, a WEAC-backed local superintendent. Benson, who opposed the voucher program, defeated a pro-

---

66. Observers disagreed about Fuller's motives in the matter. One MPS veteran and Fuller supporter explained, "The initial legislation made the schools instrumentalities, so the full union contract was in effect. Fuller said, 'Let's not even bother.' He said the state regulations aren't our problem, the problem was the union contract . . . that said we have to hire by seniority, stop[ping] us from creating schools where like-minded teachers can come together. Fuller wanted to wait until we could go back to Madison and get a stronger law." Fuller's critics, on the other hand, saw his actions as politically motivated. A union official said, "We supported the 1993 legislation and encouraged the system to seek charters for some innovative district options. But Fuller absolutely refused, even though he kept saying he wanted to expand parental choices. . . . If MPS charter schools were successful it would have undercut his effort for a more radical charter law. So he chose not to do anything."

MPCP primary opponent and a general election opponent backed by Governor Thompson. Benson's win ensured that the DPI, as it had under Grover, would continue to look at choice with a skeptical eye.

The MPCP had little competitive impact during the 1990–94 period, either initially or after Governor Thompson pushed the slightly strengthened version through the legislature in 1993. It was not until 1995 that observers reported plausible evidence that the MPCP had any impact at all on the MPS.

Why was the early MPCP so ineffective in producing change in the MPS? In large part, it was because the program was so limited. However, consideration of the question in light of the preceding chapters may clarify just why the program failed to produce bulldozer-style competition.

First, MPS enrollment continued to grow during the period. In fact, given the facilities concerns that prompted Fuller to push for a massive building referendum, the MPCP may have been a blessing in disguise. In 1990–91 the public schools enrolled 92,789 students, with another 5,582 students in the Chapter 220 program. By 1994–95 enrollment was 98,380, with another 5,296 in Chapter 220. In fact, as one principal recalled, "The [choice] program really wasn't at all bad from our point of view. I mean, we were and are hurting for space as it is." Under such circumstances, a possible loss of enrollment did not pose much of a threat at all.

Second, the program's small scope ensured that its competitive effects were nonexistent. The former director of the administrators' union spoke for both choice critics and choice supporters when he observed, "Because it was such a small population, it didn't have much effect. It had more of an emotional impact than an actual impact." With religious schools excluded from the MPCP, participating schools never had the capacity to enroll even the permissible 1 percent of MPS students. In 1990–91 there were just twenty-two nonsectarian private schools in Milwaukee. By 1994–95 there were still only twenty-three such schools. In 1990–91 there were just 406 available seats in the seven participating schools—room to accommodate less than 0.5 percent of MPS enrollment. Primarily due to the decision of five additional private schools to participate in the MPCP in 1994–95, capacity increased to 982 students. That figure was still less than 1 percent of MPS enrollment and nearly 500 students below the amended 1.5 percent enrollment cap.[67] Restricting MPCP schools to secu-

---

67. Generally small and located in old, cramped facilities, most private schools lacked the space or funding to make expansion a viable option. Regardless of statutory restri-

lar institutions substantially weakened the threat posed by the MPCP. Throughout the 1990s, religious schools made up 80 percent or more of all private schools in Milwaukee. A 1993–94 census of schools counted 108 private schools, of which 85 were religious.

Third, the schools participating in the program were accepted community schools with track records, long-standing community ties, and respected leadership, factors that blunted the perceived threat—though not the philosophical and political hostility to vouchers. These schools were integral elements of Milwaukee and enjoyed friendly working relationships with MPS personnel. The administrators of MPCP schools were not viewed as outsiders or amateurs. Recalled one school administrator, "These were schools we knew, people we had worked with. Before they tried to include the religious schools, this really wasn't all that different in size or nature from the partnership program, which we were used to."

Fourth, legal challenges and political opposition from local Democrats and Democratic legislators meant that the fate of the MPCP was never certain. This insecurity discouraged educators from opening new voucher schools or expanding existing voucher schools, and families from making the effort to apply for vouchers or change their children's school.

Mixed findings on the merits of the voucher program, whatever the relative technical merits of the reports, also threatened to undermine political support for the MPCP and encouraged MPS leaders to view it as a tentative pilot program rather than an established threat. John Witte, the University of Wisconsin professor who oversaw the 1985 study that helped trigger demands for reform of the Milwaukee Public Schools, served as the official program evaluator of the voucher experiment. In a series of reports issued during 1991–95, Witte found that choice students did not do significantly better on reading and math tests than did their MPS counterparts. In 1993 Harvard University professor Paul E. Peterson started to challenge Witte's methods and findings, arguing that the evidence in fact suggested that MPCP students outperformed MPS students.[68] This high-profile disagreement turned ugly, creating a political firestorm that left the public confused, increased the stakes for researchers and foundations,

---

ctions, the lack of available private school capacity blunted both the actual and the potential threat posed by vouchers. Meanwhile, it was very difficult for existing private schools or potential new schools to secure either the property for construction or the money to support such efforts. This last point is discussed in chapter 7.

68. For brief discussions, see Mitchell (1992); Morken and Formicola (1999, pp. 230–31); Witte (2000, pp. 132–36).

and offered advocates on both sides research that appeared to support their positions. Regardless of the technical points at issue in the research debate, the dispute muddied the waters regarding the consequences of vouchers and made clear that academics would not be able to offer conclusive findings either to cement or to undermine the program's political support in Madison.

Fifth, the reputation of MPCP schools was tarnished by the widely publicized closure of four participating schools between 1990 and 1996.[69] Regardless of what these closures said about the actual benefits and risks of voucher schools, the attendant publicity permitted critics to attack the reliability of these schools.

Innovative Schools

In May 1994 the school board approved a radically decentralized governance model for the Hi-Mount Community School, in June a formal policy on innovative schools was adopted, and in December the first innovative school was approved.

The Hi-Mount proposal created a faculty-governed school with a community focus and an emphasis on technology. Responding to the demands of its principal, Spence Korte—who was regarded as a highly effective maverick—the board agreed to a sweetheart funding deal that gave Hi-Mount hands-on control of 85 percent of the per pupil allocation. During Fuller's discussions with private contractors, Korte recalled that one for-profit firm "had accountants at Price Waterhouse digging through the system books, but they couldn't figure out the actual costs for MPS. So they settled on 85 percent simply because they'd figured that about 75 percent was the break-even point, and then upped it by 10 percent." He continued, "We . . . said, 'Look, if you're going to make a deal with for-profit organizations to take schools, we want to run our own school. We'll take the same financial deal, only . . . we'll take what would've been the profit and plough it back into instruction.'" Korte got his deal not because he was especially beloved by the MPS hierarchy but because he had

---

69. The Juanita Virgil Academy, plagued by administrative and educational problems, closed in February 1991. Exito and Milwaukee Preparatory would close during the 1995–96 school year. The directors of both schools were later charged with fraud and with mishandling public funds. During summer 1996 the Milwaukee Waldorf School closed. For a discussion of these closings, see Witte (2000, pp. 106–09).

a plan of action. In fact, he recalls, "There were a lot of [employees] in central administration who would disappear into doorways when they'd see me coming down the hallway. They didn't want to have to deal with me." Hi-Mount was frequently used by the MPS to showcase the system's progress. A school board member later recalled that "the innovative schools resolution was passed because . . . charter school issues were coming up and there was talk about expanding vouchers and there were all kinds of things going on."

The 1995 Board Elections and Fuller's Departure

In the spring 1995 board elections, driven by its distaste for Fuller, the MTEA mounted an unusually aggressive effort.[70] The MTEA slate won four of the five elections, prompting Fuller to tender his resignation. MTEA-backed incumbents Sandra Small and Christine Sinicki easily won their first reelection bids, former teacher Joe Fisher won the District 1 seat that Jeanette Mitchell had vacated in 1994, and former board member and union ally Leon Todd overcame an election petition scandal to win the seat formerly held by Joyce Mallory. The election of Todd, an old Fuller adversary and an aggressive critic of school choice and privatization, was a fierce blow to the embattled superintendent. MTEA-backed candidates spent $132,897 in the five races, while their opponents spent $58,331, less than half as much. The MTEA alone spent $62,886 on behalf of its candidates, exceeding the combined total of all non-MTEA candidates.

Although the union lost only one race, that loss would prove critical. The outspoken voucher advocate and labor organizer John Gardner defeated three antivoucher candidates to win the high-visibility at-large seat that David Lucey was vacating. Gardner, forty-five years old, a bass-voiced New York transplant with a master's degree in history, favored expanding the school choice program, supported Fuller's contracting efforts, and stridently called on the board to "unleash Dr. Fuller."[71] Confrontational and often abrasive, Gardner attacked the MPS as a failed system plagued

70. Figures are from a private summary compiled in October 1995.
71. Gardner's most formidable opponent was Rose Daitsman, a director at the University of Wisconsin–Milwaukee who opposed vouchers and Fuller's contracting initiative. Daitsman was backed by the MTEA and the Administrators Supervisors Council (the MPS principals' union).

by bureaucratic "duplicity, dishonesty, and deception."[72] Gardner had the support of Mayor Norquist, the Metropolitan Milwaukee Association of Commerce, and the *Milwaukee Journal Sentinel*. The race marked the first time a coherent provoucher coalition had assembled to challenge the MTEA, and Gardner's candidacy provided a flag around which critics of the MTEA and the MPS could rally.

After the election, energized MTEA-backed members ruled the board in place of the fragile coalition upon which Fuller had relied. Fuller announced his resignation just two weeks after the spring elections.[73] An MTEA-allied board member recalled, "The school board election in April '95 marked the end for Howard. When the big turnover came, it was very obvious to Howard and to many others that there was no way he could effectively do his job."[74]

In July 1995 Fuller was replaced by Bob Jasna, his deputy and a veteran MPS insider.[75] In August 1995 Fuller accepted a faculty position at Marquette University in Milwaukee, where he founded the Institute for the Transformation of Learning.[76] Fuller's efforts to build an infrastructure to support the choice movement would prove critical, as he helped assemble the expertise and resources to develop charter school and pri-

72. For interesting discussions, see "Gardner Takes on Status Quo," *Milwaukee Community Journal,* February 15, 1995, p. 1; Curtis Lawrence, "Way beyond Bulldog," *Milwaukee Journal Sentinel,* August 11, 1996, p. 1. Several more articles on Gardner and his race are available, as the colorful Gardner tended to attract coverage.

73. A former MPS superintendent commented, "The way these boards work, it only takes two or three members to tip the balance. You don't have to have a majority change to create a situation where, even though you win, you feel like you've lost and have to spend all your time trying to get five votes. . . . Your power is much more limited than people think, so a key . . . is how the bureaucrats perceive your relationship with the board."

74. The MTEA-allied board member continued, "The union is extremely active in school board campaigns and, even then, was much more active than usual in '95. For instance, I was out of town for a few days during my campaign. I got home and it turns out while I was gone the MTEA put up four massive billboards throughout my district supporting me, which I didn't ask for and did not want. I do believe it was the union's goal to get rid of Howard Fuller. They didn't like Howard's overall philosophy. The union was stuck in their ways; they don't like change, and Howard represented change."

75. On the day he resigned as superintendent, Howard Fuller remarked, "Today is the first day of the rest of my struggle." See Alan J. Borsuk, "Contracts for Teachers, Brown OK'd," *Milwaukee Journal Sentinel,* September 24, 1998, p. 1.

76. Fuller launched the institute with backing from several donors, including the conservative Bradley Foundation. His contacts helped him to build a research and service infrastructure to support school choice. He set up the institute in a converted house on 14th Street, just blocks from Marquette. By 1998 the building also housed PAVE, the Charter School Resource Center, and the Center for Parent Alternatives.

vate school capacity, combat legal challenges, and make the political case for choice.

In its 1995 session the Wisconsin legislature passed three significant initiatives for which Fuller had long fought. The initiatives, which gave Fuller's successors a much stronger hand, were included in the budget bill over the heated opposition of the teachers' unions. One measure gave the MPS the authority to close and reconstitute failing schools, allowing it to staff them without regard to the seniority rights of existing faculty. A second measure amended the charter school law to allow the conversion of existing private schools to charter schools. A third allowed the school board to contract with any nonprofit, nonsectarian school. The MTEA quickly filed against the three measures, charging that including specific Milwaukee legislation in the larger budget bill was unconstitutional.

An Unusual Alliance

By 1994 a broad coalition had begun to assemble in support of vouchers. Including black, Democratic, and business community leaders, the movement enjoyed substantial success in countering claims that vouchers were a racist, conservative assault on Milwaukee. Recalled one leader in the prochoice coalition,

> I think one of the significant things that people miss about Milwaukee is that this coalition was not a right-wing think tank. This was not a bunch of conservatives riding into town and saying, 'This is good for you guys, you ought to do this.' This was really a group of strange bedfellows, because I can't think of another issue where you could get all these people in a room [to work together].

While the practical impact of the choice threat on the MPS was minimal, vouchers provided a banner under which anti-MTEA and proreform sentiment could coalesce.

Key school choice supporters included Mayor Norquist and his staff, Michael Joyce and the Bradley Foundation, Governor Thompson, Howard Fuller, the PAVE leadership, and members of the initial choice schools.[77]

77. Recalled an official with Wisconsin's Charter School Resource Center, "A coalition of people who couldn't be painted as dupes of big business were responsible for the continued success of choice. People like Howard Fuller, Zakiya Courtney, Mayor Norquist, John Gardner . . . gave us legitimacy. . . . Chamber support was also key; they really bankrolled the effort and made it their number-one priority in Madison."

In early 1995 the business community backed away from its traditional support for the MPS and began to support the efforts of the voucher coalition. The director of the MMAC traced that decision to the business community's frustration with the 1995 MTEA election board victories and to Fuller's subsequent resignation. As an MMAC official recalled,

> The membership, which mostly lives in the suburbs, is leery of being seen as hostile to the city's public schools, but there was growing concern that MPS was not getting the job done and was unable to really reform itself. That's why Fuller's departure was so important— it led some members to argue that no one was going to turn this thing around without radical changes. And that's when we starting to really support [choice].

Important also to the provoucher alliance was Milwaukee's deep-pocketed and conservative Lynde & Harry Bradley Foundation.[78] The Bradley Foundation helped fund the researchers, activists, and consultants making the case for school choice. A voucher advocate argued, "The sale of the Bradley Corporation created the financial footing for the voucher coalition."[79] Between 1986 and 1995 the foundation gave away more than $200 million, including more than $2.7 million to PAVE.[80] By the late 1990s the Bradley Foundation was awarding more than $30 million in grant support each year.

Conclusion

Between 1991 and 1995 the primary impact of school choice was to stir political conflict, provoke the MTEA to heightened activity, and spur the formation of an unusual coalition for school change. The voucher program was largely overshadowed in the early 1990s by Fuller's aggressive

---

78. In 1985 the Bradley Corporation had been purchased by Rockwell International Corporation for $1.65 billion. The sale boosted the Bradley Foundation's endowment from $14 million to more than $400 million by the early 1990s.

79. A leading voucher critic agreed, noting, "Bradley's played a very significant role . . . they have a huge amount of money and have targeted that money to direct the public policy debate."

80. The Bradley Foundation was a chief funder of PAVE, contributing $500,000 a year for the program's first three years. See Beales and Wahl (1995). For additional discussion of the foundation and the role it played in Milwaukee, see Katherine M. Skiba, "Bradley Philanthropy," *Milwaukee Journal Sentinel*, September 17, 1995, p. 1; Carl (1995, pp. 266–77); Miner (1994).

superintendency. While Fuller tried a number of unorthodox strategies, from considering the possibility of hiring for-profit management firms to pushing the MPS to launch its own charter schools, institutional and political resistance meant that his efforts never produced much real change. However, in 1995 Wisconsin moved to radically strengthen the voucher program and in 1997 it did the same to the state's charter school legislation. These changes would provide new openings for the political coalition for change that had emerged in Milwaukee. This coalition would provide support to future board members and superintendents willing to challenge the MTEA contract, district routines, and the entrenched MPS administration.

FIVE

Milwaukee, 1995–99: Hints of the Pickax

THE EXPERIENCE OF 1990–94 offered little evidence that small-scale school choice would prompt a competitive response from the Milwaukee Public Schools (MPS) or that even an aggressive reform effort campaign could significantly change the system.[1] The 1995–99 period would teach somewhat different lessons. The radical expansion of the Milwaukee Parental Choice Program (MPCP) in 1995 would produce a slightly more substantive systemic response from the school board, the upper reaches of the administration, and the Milwaukee Teachers Education Association (MTEA). However, both the MPS and the union would take proactive steps only when their political and legal efforts to fight school choice appeared to be faltering.

The scope of the MPS and union responses increased markedly after June 1998, when the Wisconsin Supreme Court ended the persistent legal challenges to the MPCP by declaring the 1995 expansion of the voucher program to be constitutional. The end of the MPCP's legal difficulties and the presence of a rapidly expanding charter sector combined to create the first semblance of a real market threat in Milwaukee.

The 1995 MPCP Expansion

In January 1995 Governor Thompson proposed a dramatic expansion of the MPCP, calling for the inclusion of religious schools and the eventual

1. This assessment is not meant as an indictment of school choice. As proponents argue, vouchers and charter schooling may aid participating families regardless of competitive effects. For a powerful depiction of how vouchers affected individual Milwaukee families, see McGroaty (2000, pp. 7–48).

lifting of the program's enrollment cap.[2] With Republicans controlling both houses of the state legislature, a slightly amended version of Thompson's proposal passed over fierce union opposition in late June 1995.[3] The amended bill increased the enrollment cap to 7 percent of MPS enrollment (or about 7,000) students for 1995–96 and to 15 percent (roughly 15,000 students) thereafter.[4] The legislation also increased state expenditure for the program from $2.3 million in 1994–95 to $14.7 million for 1995–96 and $27.5 million for 1996–97. Crucially, the expansion allowed religious schools to participate in the MPCP, dramatically increasing the number of available seats. The changes meant that in spring 1995 the MPCP ballooned from an insignificant program costing the MPS less than 1 percent of its educational budget to a program that potentially could cost tens of millions of dollars within two years.[5]

In its 1995 session the legislature also expanded the scope of charter school legislation. Most significantly, all school districts in Wisconsin were granted the authority to charter schools, and the statewide limit of twenty charter schools was eliminated.[6] The legislature also moved to permit the MPS superintendent to shut down and "reconstitute" failing schools (allowing him to replace faculty without regard to seniority) and expanded

2. The 1995 effort was greatly aided by the growing strength of the Milwaukee voucher coalition. In 1994 an MMAC-supported group coordinating community efforts worked to identify a core group of parents to advocate for choice expansion. Within sixty days, the group had 4,000 parents enlisted. In October 1994 a rally at the Milwaukee Area Technical College (MATC) was attended by 750 parents and children, in addition to the governor and other political leaders. Reportedly, the size of the October rally prompted Thompson to make expansion of the MPCP a priority.

3. Supporters tucked the law into the budget bill because that was the easiest way to win passage. Their earlier legal triumph on the "local" bill issue led them to believe the courts would permit the maneuver.

4. Polly Williams, the sponsor of the initial MPCP legislation, was cool on Thompson's 1995 expansion proposal. Williams sought to distance herself from Thompson and business leaders, saying, "We have our black agenda and they have got [their own] agenda. I didn't see where their resources really were being used to empower us as much as it was to co-opt us." See Curtis Lawrence, "Rift Seen in Support of Choice," *Milwaukee Journal Sentinel*, September 10, 1995, p. 1. By June 1998, Williams was accusing Thompson and other conservatives of "hijacking" the choice program and shifting its focus from poor children. In truth, Williams had become less significant to the voucher coalition as it gained political strength. See Felicia Thomas-Lynn, "School Choice Pioneer Chafes at Her Status," *Milwaukee Journal Sentinel*, June 29, 1998, p. 1.

5. For a more detailed discussion of the MPCP expansion, see Witte (2000, pp. 162–70).

6. For more detail, see Wisconsin Department of Public Instruction (1999, p. 2).

the ability of the MPS to contract with partnership schools for at-risk students.[7]

The Milwaukee Public Schools and the 1995 MPCP Expansion

During Bob Jasna's tenure as superintendent MPS enrollment continued to grow. The system's third-Friday count in September 1995 was 98,380, an increase of more than 1,500 students from the previous fall. The school system had to scramble to locate enough certified new teachers to replace the hundreds of departing or retiring faculty. The notion that choice had an impact on school-level advertising, school outreach efforts, or teacher recruitment during 1995–97 was routinely dismissed by educators and informed observers. Much of the choice and charter debate remained an abstraction, touching teachers only through the critical media attention the school system received in the course of the choice debate. Discussing whether there had been any school-level changes that might be linked to the MPCP, Partners Advancing Values in Education (PAVE), or charter schooling, one school system insider reflected the general consensus when he said in 1999, "I haven't noticed any evidence at the school level that things have changed due to choice."[8] When asked whether their schools had been compelled to change practices or revisit core tasks, principals said that choice had no impact on the daily business of teaching, running a school, or interacting with the central administration.[9]

If choice had no systemic impact on individual public schools, it did have significant effects on the behavior of the system's most visible and politically sensitive actors. Those behaviors, in turn, produced new opportunities, which entrepreneurial teachers and principals were able to seize. As with Fuller's flirtation with school contracting, the size and drama of the MPCP expansion temporarily shocked the school board and the

7. By 1997 the MPS Division of Alternative Programs listed twenty-four participating programs for students in grades five through twelve.

8. The closest to a report of a school-level response came when a few principals said that they had slightly increased outreach efforts during 1995–97 by making an additional effort to visit junior high schools or to print t-shirts with their school's name. The principals, however, suggested that the effort was due more to the evolution of Peterkin's three-choice system than to the MPCP or administrative pressure.

9. One principal reflected the view of many when she said, "You've got to understand, in just trying to run a good school I've already got a full plate. There's not a lot of time to worry about things like vouchers."

MTEA into relaxing many of the routines that previously constrained unusual ideas, radical teachers, and eccentric principals. A voucher proponent serving on the school board recalled:

> The nervousness about choice expansion really started in February or March [of 1995], when it became pretty clear that [expansion] was going to pass. . . . Board candidates supported by the MTEA, and the MTEA itself, suddenly made noises about all the reforms they were going to do and, probably more significantly, the reforms they were not going to oppose. . . . [Reformers] within the teachers' union and . . . the public school system . . . been interested in making changes long before the choice threat, but they'd been unable to pull it off. Choice brought external pressures so [that] the MTEA Executive Committee and the system's not-terribly-entrepreneurial administration began. . . . 'Okay, we'll let you do it to show that we're doing something.'"

Teachers, union leaders, and their allies responded to choice primarily through legal and political means. Believing choice to be antithetical to the mission of public schooling, opponents focused on attacking choice and choice supporters rather than on seeking to meet the educational challenge.[10] One business leader observed, "At one level there's been a very visceral response to choice, and that is to attack back [against] a threat to the public school system. . . . At least that's the way they express it. They say that [choice proponents] don't care about kids, that [they] are a bunch of white guys from the suburbs."[11] Between spring 1995, when it became clear that the Wisconsin legislature was likely to expand the MPCP, and February 1996, when the Wisconsin Supreme Court followed a series of lower court injunctions with a decision that effectively neutralized the

---

10. The head of one antivoucher organization explained, "Vouchers are primarily a distraction from what we could be doing in the system. There's always politics . . . but there's an inordinate amount of politics when you've got all this going on."

11. The reaction of many antivoucher leaders was expressed by an NAACP official: "It concerns me when I see Tim Sheehy [director of the MMAC] and the Metropolitan Milwaukee Chamber getting involved with black kids. I want to know why Michael Joyce and the boys care about black kids. Not that they shouldn't. But I want to know why, because they've never cared about any racial issues. It was Joyce and the Bradley Foundation that funded [the book] *The Bell Curve*, which said these black kids are racially inferior. I'm saying they're involved now because there's money here. The MPS budget is about $800 million, and they want to control that money."

expansion, the school system faced a significant threat.[12] This was the period (previous to 1998) that voucher proponents most often cited as supplying evidence of a competitive response.[13] Although there is little to suggest there was significant change in educational practice or in the public school system during that period, the school board and the MTEA did take five significant actions.[14]

First, and most significant, the expansion pushed the MPS to increase its offerings, particularly by approving a number of new schools under the innovative schools program. Although the program predated the expansion of the MPCP, the board's interest in approving innovative schools and the MTEA's willingness to relax the collective bargaining agreement so as to help launch these schools were evident only when expansion appeared likely. The board had approved the first innovative school, the Grand Avenue Secondary School, in December 1994. When expansion loomed, it rapidly approved four additional innovative schools—in February and March 1995.[15] In spring 1995 it opened two new specialty schools, the Hayes Bilingual School and the Frances Starms Discovery Learning Center, and in October 1995 it approved four more innovative schools for the 1996–97 school year.[16]

The explosion of innovative schools was a case of energetic and atypical teachers and principals popping through cracks, rather than a consequence of deliberate board or administrative action. I interviewed most of the founders of these schools. Almost without exception, they had launched

12. In February 1996 what the Wisconsin Supreme Court actually did was refuse to lift a lower-court injunction against the expansion. However, the effect was to derail expansion for more than two years.

13. See, for instance, John Gardner's unpublished five-page 1997 memo, "How School Choice Helps Public Education."

14. A board member recalled that the threat posed by the MPCP reached its height in August 1995, becoming "palpable when the implementation rules were promulgated and, in a period of about seventy-two hours, almost six thousand poor kids signed up. That scared the living daylights out of MPS from top to bottom." While the actual number of students who signed up was closer to 3,000, the board member's recollection was indicative of the prevailing mood in summer 1995.

15. The schools ranged from the Wisconsin Conservatory of Life-Long Learning (launched by MPS principal Sally Brown and designed to eventually enroll 800 and become Milwaukee's first K–12 school) to the 100-student Milwaukee School of Entrepreneurship (started by MPS teachers in leased facilities on Appleton Avenue).

16. These included the Congress Extended-Year School, a year-round elementary school, and the Milwaukee School of Languages, a grades six-through-twelve school that extended the language immersion elementary program into middle and high school. For a comprehensive look at the innovative schools program, see Milwaukee Public Schools (1997).

their schools for one of two reasons: they "had wanted to do this for awhile and . . . finally had the chance" or they weren't "going to stand by . . . and just watch these zealots beat up on the public schools." The founders of these schools, who could expect neither promotion nor monetary compensation for their efforts, described numerous unpaid weekends and evenings spent scratching together the plans they submitted to the board.[17] The degree to which first Fuller and then the threat of expansion were responsible for the school system accepting some experimentation is illustrated by the fact that the innovative schools process ground to a halt in 1996. Remembered one MTEA-backed board member, "It was choice and vouchers that encouraged the board to pull together with the union to create innovative schools. Suddenly you have a union that said, 'Yeah, we like this idea, let's do it.' They were protecting their own butts. . . . Once the takeover threat was no longer there and choice was pretty much a done deal, they went back to their old ways." After spring 1996 the MTEA did not approve another memorandum of understanding allowing innovative schools to waive the seniority hiring process, essentially making it impossible to launch a new school with a faculty of like-minded educators.[18]

The MPS had long faced demands for increased Montessori programs but had moved only slowly to address them. In the fall of 1995 the board approved expansions of both existing Montessori schools, and in January 1996 it decided to open a third school in the fall. In early 1996 the system also took steps to add hundreds more early-childhood slots. In June 1996 the school board approved Highland Montessori as the system's first charter school.[19] However, no additional charters were launched in that pe-

17. Recalled one MPS teacher, "Our basic line was, 'Look . . . there's all of these teachers doing incredible things. Why don't we really use the innovative schools process here in the city, where people can [offer new programs].' . . . We were saying, 'Why don't you look at the people who have done stuff here, at the people who are trying new things in MPS?'"

18. The issue came to a head over Fritsche Middle School in April 1996. The principal had told Jasna he intended to negotiate with the MTEA for site-based management in the manner provided for by the contract. A senior administrator recalled, "The union let that sit. It became a joke at meetings. We'd be saying, 'Well, how are we going to deal with this?' Finally, the union turned down the request, even though the school staff said they wanted it. When the union turned that down, that was a real blow." The MTEA's refusal to issue additional memoranda of understanding effectively brought the innovative school program to a halt.

19. Highland Community School, a small Montessori school launched in 1968, enrolled sixty-eight students in 1994–95. For a detailed account of Highland and the challenges the Highland community had to overcome, see Williams (1997).

riod, as the MTEA filed suit to stop the district from chartering and the board chose not to press the issue.

Second, the effort to financially decentralize, which had been pursued intermittently since 1988, made some progress in late 1995. Between September and December the board pushed the administration to proceed with the pilot decentralization of funding at nine schools. The system trumpeted the change as a major shift in authority from Vliet Street to the schools, although neither administrators nor system data suggest any concrete change ensued.[20]

Third, graduation requirements were visibly strengthened. In September 1995, at the height of the expansion furor, the board passed a resolution sponsored by Mary Bills, Lawrence O'Neil, and Christine Sinicki that directed the administration to consider higher standards for graduation. The board received the administration plan in January 1996 and enacted it in February.[21] The concerns that had plagued Fuller's earlier efforts to raise standards and to demand algebra of all students were barely evident postexpansion.

Fourth, the MPS "report card" system for school accountability was dramatically toughened and made more visible, clear, and comprehensive. Before 1996–97 the report cards were unimpressive and somewhat sporadic.[22] After exploring the issue during 1994–95, in June 1995 the board approved a more comprehensive report. But it also loosened the definitions for "improving" and "high-achieving," ensuring that more schools would be rated positively.

Fifth, the most visible response to expansion was the sudden presence of slogans expressing the system's commitment to parental choices and high standards. Orange and black banners proclaiming "High Standards

20. For an explanation of why the effort produced little change, see Alan J. Borsuk, "Red Tape Revolution," *Milwaukee Journal Sentinel*, November 23, 1995, p. 1.

21. The new requirements called for students to demonstrate mastery of mathematical reasoning, scientific reasoning, communication, and community membership. The new standards were truly challenging, especially for an urban district. For instance, students were expected to study three years of math beyond algebra I and to have three years of study in the physical, biological, and chemical sciences.

22. John Gardner had been concerned about the quality of the data produced by the MPS since he joined the board. When the Legislative Fiscal Bureau issued a 1995 report on the fiscal effects of choice that contradicted the information supplied by the MPS, Gardner blasted the staff as "irresponsible," saying, "Consistently, the numbers being fed to us from our own staff are just wrong." See Joe Williams, "Choice Would Help MPS, Reports Say," *Milwaukee Journal Sentinel*, September 21, 1995, p. 1.

Start Here" were omnipresent.[23] A banner proclaiming "MPS, Milwaukee's First Schools of Choice" was hung behind the board members at their meetings (it would later be replaced with "High Standards Start Here"). The board also made the slogan "First Choice within MPS" its planning and budget priority for 1995–96. It is important not to overestimate the practical impact of this effort, however; in fact, some administrators involved in running the program privately disparaged the effort.

The MTEA and the 1995 Expansion

Some voucher advocates suggest that, after the expansion of the MPCP, the school system felt compelled to bargain more firmly with the MTEA. However, there is little evidence of significant union concessions. The union did agree to a number of memoranda of understanding related to innovative schools, but it was careful to keep that permissive language out of the collective bargaining agreement. Meanwhile, the MTEA maintained an aggressive legal campaign against the choice, charter, and reconstitution legislation. The union agreed to some single-school measures that it previously would not have considered—and that it would reject once expansion was held up by a court injunction—but the agreements tended to be grudging and incremental.

The MTEA claimed to be receptive to reform during the negotiations of the 1995–97 contract—as demonstrated by gestures such as its acceptance of the Hi-Mount model—but it refused to contemplate changes in seniority rules, residency requirements, school closing criteria, and evaluation provisions.[24] A former official in the school administrators' union

23. A senior administrator recalled that in late spring of 1995, when expansion was on the front burner, "We felt that we needed something to really get out and show what we're doing." The district brought in a consultant, who argued that high standards are integral to boosting minority student performance. Recalled the administrator, "It was then that we actually sat and said, 'Here are going to be our goals.' . . . That's how High Standards and that whole push came up." Another senior administrator remembered, "When the whole High Standards Start Here thing first came out, it was an empty phrase, just because everyone was beaten down. But [by 1998] I think it's actually starting to mean something." One principal strung High Standards banners from all the light poles at his school. Recalled another system veteran, "Once the banners started getting out, everyone starting calling us and saying, 'Where's my banner?'" The result was that the orange and black High Standards Start Here banners were an unavoidable part of the Milwaukee cityscape by 1998–99.

24. John Stanford, "MTEA, School Board Must Put Kids First," *Milwaukee Journal Sentinel*, November 26, 1995, p. 6.

cautioned not to make the mistake of viewing small concessions as evidence that the expansion produced significant changes in the MTEA. "Through that 1995 to 1997 period," he said, "neither choice nor charter legislation had any real effect on contract negotiations or on any agreements reached." For instance, even as it used memoranda of understanding to give individual alternative schools more flexibility on hiring, the union continued to resist reforms that would allow schools to interview all applicants for posted positions. A former school board member aligned with neither the MTEA nor the provoucher faction noted that the union would grant memoranda of understanding but would never put them in the contract, "which means that they're always playing the gatekeeper."

The union was not monolithic in its opposition to change. The incremental acceptance of reform provisions was partially the consequence of an internal union conflict between the dominant traditionalist wing and a smaller "progressive" faction. Sam Carmen, the MTEA executive director, was forced to bridge this divide with symbolic gestures. For instance, at a September 1995 meeting, in the midst of the postexpansion furor, Carmen told MTEA members that the union needed to "change the way we operate" even as he and the executive board proposed a two-year ban on further contract concessions modifying the seniority system.[25] In August 1996, after an eighteen-month negotiation, the school system and the union settled the 1995–97 contract. The union agreed to a new peer evaluation process but held firm on seniority and other traditional concerns.[26] By fall 1996 the MTEA had filed suit to block choice expansion, to block the district from "reconstituting" schools and moving teachers out of targeted schools without regard to seniority, and to block Highland Community from becoming a charter school and the MPS from contracting with partnership schools to educate at-risk students. The union offensive triggered an angry response from board president Mary Bills, an ardent voucher foe. Bills fumed in August 1996, "The MTEA makes the Teamsters look enlightened."[27]

25. Curtis Lawrence, "Taking up the Gauntlet," *Milwaukee Journal Sentinel*, November 21, 1995, p. 7.

26. Daynel L. Hooker, "MPS, Union Reach Agreement," *Milwaukee Journal Sentinel*, August 14, 1996, p. 1.

27. In all cases, the MTEA primarily challenged on the grounds that "local" legislation was passed as part of the budget bill rather than as separate legislation and that the measures hindered its ability to bargain with the district. For discussion, see Daynel Hooker, "Suit Seeks to Block Charter School," *Milwaukee Journal Sentinel*, August 7, 1996, p. 1.

PAVE and the 1995 Expansion

Between 1995 and 1997 PAVE played a critical role in maintaining the momentum of choice. When the courts stopped MPCP's expansion to religious schools in fall 1995 and again in fall 1996, PAVE raised millions of dollars for an emergency fund to help the students planning to enroll in religious schools attend the school of their choice. Nearly half of the two-year total of $6 million was provided by the Bradley Foundation.[28] Observed one voucher critic, "Bradley . . . has help[ed] create and expand the constituency for vouchers. . . . In effect, the Bradley Foundation is very cleverly . . . buying a constituency." In 1995–96 MPCP enrollment rose to 1,115 students, and more than 4,000 students were enrolled in religious schools through PAVE. By 1996–97 the MPCP figure reached 2,500 and the PAVE figure was 4,300. However, public school enrollment also grew—to 101,110—exceeding system projections by nearly 2,000 students. In 1997–98, system enrollment grew to 101,963, again exceeding the MPS projection.

The Evolving Politics of the Milwaukee Public Schools

To the frustration of the voucher critics, John Gardner used his at-large school board seat as a bully pulpit to push for radical restructuring, decentralization, and school choice. Gardner was not a lone voice for long. In December 1995 he gained an ally when Warren Braun, a Catholic church official and former state senator, was elected to fill the vacancy left by David DeBruin's resignation. The special election could have given the MTEA a fifth vote and control of the board, but its candidate, James Buss, failed to even make it out of the primary. In April 1996 former MPS teacher Joe Fisher was elected board president by a five-to-four vote; Braun was named vice president by the same margin. The votes reflected the increasing division on the board. In 1993, when the board last chose a president, Mary Bills was elected without opposition. Fisher and Braun were backed by an odd coalition of MTEA-backed members (Fisher, Leon Todd, and O'Neil) and pro-MPCP members (Gardner and Braun). Gardner reportedly supported Fisher in the belief that he would be a weak president. Given Fisher's MTEA-endorsed opposition to Jasna's effort to reor-

---

28. Jay Purnick, "Metro Matters; In Milwaukee, School Choice with Caution," *New York Times*, October 24, 1996, p. B1.

ganize six failing schools, MPS administrators were afraid that his ascendance to the board presidency might prompt Jasna to retire before his contract expired in 1997.

Voucher opponents—including the leadership of the NAACP, the American Civil Liberties Union, and the MTEA—rallied to defend the school system in the community and in the courts. One voucher critic noted, "Most observers would say this is the most contentious school board in the last twenty or twenty-five years, and it's pretty much vouchers that have done that." When she left office in spring 1997, Mary Bills worried that the board had become "an ideological playground, with a tug of war between the [teachers'] union and City Hall."[29]

The 1997 School Board Elections

The April 1997 school board elections left the board polarized into two blocs, with six MTEA allies and three voucher sympathizers. Both sides gained support during the election cycle, as a retirement and a successful challenger eliminated the last unaligned members. Whereas urban school board elections are generally ambiguous affairs, with the teachers' union the clearest voice in a murky and factionalized environment, Milwaukee's school board politics was evolving into a two-party system.

The key contest was the race to replace Mary Bills, who was retiring after three terms. The election marked the departure of the last member of the troika (Mary Bills, Jeanette Mitchell, and Joyce Mallory) that, in the late 1980s and early 1990s, had maintained its distance from both vouchers and the MTEA. The general election for Bills's seat matched businessman Gregory Coffman, who was supported by both Bills and the MTEA, against Bruce Thompson, a professor of engineering, the president of the Downtown Montessori School and Child Care Center, and the campaign manager for Gardner's victorious 1995 campaign. Coffman opposed both the MPCP and MPS contracts with private firms; Thompson supported both. The *Milwaukee Journal Sentinel* endorsed Thompson for his boldness and his expressed willingness to challenge the bureaucracy and the union, although its editors questioned Thompson's support for the inclusion of religious schools in the MPCP.[30] In the April

29. Alan J. Borsuk, "Former President Leaving This Week," *Milwaukee Journal Sentinel*, April 21, 1997, p. 1.

30. John Stanford, "Thompson, Aljuwani Best Picks for MPS," *Milwaukee Journal Sentinel*, February 14, 1997, p. 18.

election Thompson won 54 percent of the vote, handing the MTEA its third defeat in two years. The soft-spoken and professorial Thompson provided the board's provoucher faction with another, gentler spokesman to complement the abrasive Gardner.

One MTEA-backed candidate, Charlene Hardin, managed to defeat an incumbent board member, winning Jared Johnson's seat by a handful of votes. Johnson, regarded as a marginal and inconsistent board presence, was the first incumbent defeated since the 1980s. Hardin, a staunch defender of traditional MPS practice, was harshly critiqued by the *Journal Sentinel* for not grasping "the urgency of drastic reforms in a school system where last year's graduating class was a third the size it was in its freshman year."[31] In the two other elections, incumbents Lawrence O'Neil and Braun won handily, Braun with 80 percent of the vote and O'Neil with 55 percent.[32] O'Neil, an MTEA ally who had served on the board for eighteen of the past twenty years, defeated college student Paul Gessner 55 to 45 percent in a contest marked by similar platforms and in which both candidates denounced school vouchers.

During this period the evidence regarding MPS performance was mixed, with both the system's defenders and its critics pointing to isolated figures or occurrences to support their claims. School officials noted that the official high school dropout rate fell from 17.4 percent in 1992–93 to 12.8 percent in 1994–95 and that 81 percent of seniors had passed the mathematics proficiency test required for graduation. Critics, however, suggested that there was little evidence that the school system was improving its practices or student performance in any systematic fashion. In a widely circulated June 1997 memo, Gardner calculated that, in 1995–96, the city's fifteen public high schools graduated just 2,434 students, even though 6,874 freshmen had entered in 1991–92. In a February 1997 letter, Jasna addressed parental concerns about locker theft, a "freshman kill day" at a high school, R-rated movies shown in classes, smoke-filled school bathrooms, fighting and foul language in school, and drug and handgun sales and possession on school grounds. A month earlier Jasna had been confronted with complaints from board member Todd about drug dealing,

31. Multiple recounts and a court challenge followed Hardin's razor-thin victory, during which negative reports emerged regarding questionable expenditures on behalf of Hardin by the MTEA. See John Stanford, "Thompson, Aljuwani Best Picks for MPS," *Milwaukee Journal Sentinel*, February 14, 1997, p. 18.

32. For a summary of the 1997 election results, see Alan J. Borsuk, "Milwaukee Public Schools, Recount Expected," *Milwaukee Journal Sentinel*, April 2, 1997, p. 1.

gang influence, racially inflammatory curricula, and violence against teachers and students.

A Restructuring Effort

Efforts in 1997 and 1998 by Bills and Gardner to cut administrative spending were either rebuffed by the board or, in a few cases, simply not implemented by the school administration. In April 1997, after the local Public Policy Forum noted an increase in central administration jobs and busing costs in the 1997–98 MPS budget and a decline in instructional spending, the board voted seven-to-one to produce a blueprint for a radical restructuring of the school system's administration by October. It also adopted a Sinicki amendment that directed the school superintendent to trim $6 million in central administration expenditures. None of the changes materialized. Jasna recalled of the 1997 effort, "We had the budget meetings, where I would be the one that would say, 'We're going to cut this. You're going to cut X and you're going to cut X.' And the people there would just say to me, 'Well, you know we can't.'" The failed effort would be cited in 1999 as another case of the school administration resisting change.[33]

Charter School Expansion

In 1997, frustrated that the 1995 amendments to the Wisconsin charter law had produced no new schools in Milwaukee, Governor Thompson urged the legislature to again revise the charter law. The existing law, which required that charter schools be approved by the local school board, had yielded just one charter school (Highland Community) in the city.[34] More than a dozen schools had expressed interest in chartering with the MPS in 1995 and 1996, but the proposals had gone nowhere. The governor now proposed that the city of Milwaukee, the University of Wisconsin–Milwaukee (UWM), and the Milwaukee Area Technical College

33. For an in-depth discussion of the challenges in reforming the MPS administration, see Joe Williams, "MPS Officials Spurn Plan by School Board," *Milwaukee Journal Sentinel*, February 4, 1999, p. 1.

34. The dearth of activity was due primarily to the union's lawsuit challenging the 1995 charter legislation, though several MPS critics also asserted that the school board and the school administration showed no inclination to move aggressively into approving charter schools.

(MATC) be authorized to approve charter schools.[35] The Wisconsin Education Association Council (WEAC) lobbied bitterly against the proposal, to no avail.[36]

The MATC, an institution with strong prounion sympathies, exhibited no interest in using its charter authority. However, UWM began its planning process during 1997–98 and looked to open its first schools in fall 1999. The city of Milwaukee, the first municipal government in the country to have the authority to charter schools, moved promptly. Mayor John Norquist appointed Howard Fuller to chair the city's Charter School Review Committee, which would make recommendations regarding charter approval.[37] The city approved its first charter schools during 1997–98 and launched its first three schools, with a combined enrollment of 300, in fall 1998. A fourth school, Bruce Guadalupe Community School with nearly 500 students, had declined a city charter.

There were no income restrictions on participation in the program, and the state formula ensured that charter schools would receive a much more generous per pupil allotment than voucher schools. Interest in charter schooling thus grew rapidly among both parents and potential charter operators.

The Alan Brown Appointment

Superintendent Bob Jasna announced his resignation in January 1997, triggering a search that would stretch into September. After numerous stops and starts, the board settled on the Waukegan, Illinois, school superintendent Alan Brown over the Fuller-affiliated Jasna deputy Barbara

35. Charter opponents were particularly leery of what the city government headed by Mayor Norquist—an avowed advocate of privatization and vouchers—might do. Consequently, opponents were able to insert legislative language that prohibited the city from chartering with "for-profit" firms. One observer noted, "That was directed at Howard [Fuller] and Deborah [McGriff], due to a fear they'd work with the mayor to create a new private system with all the schools run by Edison." McGriff, the former deputy superintendent under Robert Peterkin, was a vice president at the Edison Project—a for-profit education firm—and was married to Fuller.

36. For a discussion of the introduction of local chartering authority in Milwaukee, see Mead (2000).

37. Howard Fuller remained active and central to events during 1995–99. He advised Tommy Thompson on the 1997 legislation and backed a friend-of-the-court brief lobbying the state Supreme Court to uphold the constitutionality of the expanded MPCP. Striking a blow at the MTEA, in 1997 he coauthored a report that argued that the MTEA-MPS collective bargaining process had hurt student achievement.

Horton. In early September 1997 MPS officials had announced that Horton, an African American who had been acting superintendent since Jasna's June departure, and Brown were the finalists for the superintendency. Brown, an advocate for shifting more responsibility and authority to the schools, had helped to put in place one of the first public school choice programs in Illinois.[38] Unaffiliated with Howard Fuller or the MPCP, unlike Horton, Brown was the preferred choice of the MTEA-backed board members.

In a closed session on September 17, 1997, the board hired Brown by a five-to-four vote, with the five votes provided by the five union-backed members. The MTEA president, Paulette Copeland, denied that the union influenced the vote, saying, "We weren't included in the process at all. I didn't even know they were taking a vote."[39] The MTEA-backed board members Sandra Small and Charlene Hardin also rejected suggestions of union influence. Such disclaimers were regarded skeptically, even by one MTEA-backed board member who voted for Brown: "Sandy Small is so entrenched in union politics that she doesn't make a move without talking to the union. Same thing with Charlene Hardin."

Brown's hiring prompted intense criticism both because of the nature of the search process and because of widespread support for Horton.[40] At a public meeting a week after the hiring, the board followed custom by unanimously endorsing Brown, provoking hisses from the packed auditorium. Black community leaders were dismayed that three black board members had backed the white candidate—Brown—over the black candidate—Horton.[41] Alderman Michael McGee, a leader in the black community, shouted "coon," "Aunt Jemima," and "sellout" from the third row, while other members of the audience threw raw eggs at black board members Hardin and Fisher.[42]

38. For an overview of Brown's background and experience in Waukegan, see Daniel Bice, "Likely Superintendent an Innovator," *Milwaukee Journal Sentinel*, September 24, 1997, p. 1.

39. Joe Williams, "Out of the Frying Pan," *Milwaukee Journal Sentinel*, September 20, 1997, p. 1.

40. For a description of the heated dispute, see Joe Williams, "MPS Given Two Years, or Else," *Milwaukee Journal Sentinel*, January 21, 1997, p. 1.

41. The three board members were Joe Fisher, Charlene Hardin, and Leon Todd.

42. For contemporaneous accounts, see Eugene Kane, "Vote Is Typical When It Comes to MPS," *Milwaukee Journal Sentinel*, September 23, 1997, p. 1; Daniel Bice, "Likely Superintendent an Innovator," *Milwaukee Journal Sentinel*, September 24, 1997, p. 1; Joe Williams and Felicia Thomas-Lynn, "Board Picks Brown amid Eggs, Insults," *Milwaukee Journal Sentinel*, September 25, 1997, p. 1.

The significance of Hardin's narrow victory over Johnson in the school board elections became apparent as Brown, with support from the five-vote bloc of MTEA-allied board members, sought to reverse several changes initiated by Peterkin, Fuller, and Jasna. In contrast to their earlier decentralization efforts, Brown called for an "aligned, districtwide curriculum" and for "learning teams," made up of central office administrators, to guide improvement efforts at specific schools.[43] Brown's stance marked a reversal of the April 1997 Bills resolution that called for a dramatically scaled-down central office; in contrast, Brown's plans called for no central office staff reductions. During the first year of Brown's reign, the board also showed signs of moving to dissolve its ties with the increasingly provoucher business community.

Brown occasionally sided with the Gardner, Thompson, and Braun bloc, but he quickly became identified as the agent of the status quo. In August 1998 the entire board publicly criticized Brown's five-year reform plan as inadequate.[44] Nonetheless, the board approved a two-year extension of Brown's contract during the summer. Observers suggested that the extension was awarded largely because both the MTEA-allied faction and the provoucher faction feared that the other would control the board after the spring elections. Gardner—who had backed Horton over Brown—blamed the board for many of Brown's difficulties, saying, "I'm not giving him rave reviews. I'm just saying it's very difficult to judge a CEO when he's working for a demented board."

Governor Thompson's Takeover Threat

In January 1998 the whole question of vouchers was thrust to the sidelines for five months as the MPS confronted a much more immediate and direct threat. Governor Thompson—citing continued unacceptable performance—called for a state takeover of the city's public school system unless the MPS met specified performance goals in the course of the next two years.[45] If it failed to deliver the mandated improvements, Thompson

43. For more detail on Brown's efforts, see Daniel Bice and Joe Williams, "Brown's MPS Plan Is Modest in Tactics," *Milwaukee Journal Sentinel*, June 17, 1998, p. 1; Joe Williams and Daniel Bice, "Brown Says MPS Will 'Teach to the Test' to Avoid Takeover," *Milwaukee Journal Sentinel*, April 10, 1998, p. 1.

44. For a detailed account, see Joe Williams, "Ministers, Labor Hold Vigil to Seek Changes in MPS," *Milwaukee Journal Sentinel*, April 29, 1998, p. 6.

45. The goals included improving graduation, attendance, and dropout rates and closing the gap between the city's average and the state average on reading tests. See Joe Will-

proposed that the MPS be dissolved and the system be turned over to a three-person commission to be run as a charter school system.[46]

The superintendent responded to Thompson's announcement by arguing that the school system's problems had been exaggerated and that efforts to boost MPS achievement should focus on improving curriculum and teacher preparation, not on altering governance structure.[47] Brown attacked Thompson's proposal, saying, "The governor hasn't said anything about the kids learning more. What he said was he wanted higher test scores. There's a difference," the superintendent said, between instituting "long-term strategies to really help these kids" and "higher test scores." To improve test scores, Brown said the district would need to teach test-taking strategies and give practice tests even if "some people would say" that teaching to the test "is immoral or wrong," because school funding depended on how well students test.[48] The governor and several legislators criticized Brown's comments as symptomatic of the system's bureaucratic and inflexible mind-set. The exchange highlighted the difficulty of forging agreement over what constitutes school improvement and how it should be measured.

Milwaukee's African American community attacked the governor's proposal as an effort by upstate Republicans to seize control of a mostly black school system, with the Democratic representative Johnnie Morris-Tatum saying, "We don't need lily-white faces telling us what to do."[49] Milwaukee's black ministers formed the Minority Ministerial Alliance and ran an aggressive radio and newspaper campaign to fight Thompson's proposal. Numerous observers alleged that the teachers' union was behind the alliance and the ad campaign, and the *Journal Sentinel* charged that the alliance was a pawn of the WEAC. Teachers' union leaders and

---

iams, "MPS Given Two Years, or Else," *Milwaukee Journal Sentinel*, January 21, 1998, p. 1.

46. Statewide concern over the MPS had been reinvigorated by two studies released in September 1997. A study prepared by Morris Andrews, the former executive director of the WEAC, called for neighborhood schooling and site-based management. A second study, prepared by Howard Fuller and two associates, blasted the MTEA as an impediment to progress. Following the Andrews report, State Superintendent Benson announced a reform package. When the Benson proposal died, Thompson put forward his plan.

47. Joe Williams, "MPS Has Trouble Spots but Isn't in Crisis, Brown Says," *Milwaukee Journal Sentinel*, February 26, 1998, p. 1.

48. Joe Williams and Daniel Bice, "Brown Says MPS Will 'Teach to the Test' to Avoid Takeover," *Milwaukee Journal Sentinel*, April 10, 1998, p. 1.

49. Daniel Bice, "Race Raised as Issue during Hearing about State Threat to Take over MPS," *Milwaukee Journal Sentinel*, April 22, 1998, p. 1.

other labor representatives were visible at alliance events and helped shape the proposal the ministers offered as an alternative plan.[50] During the five months between January and May, when the legislature finally defeated Thompson's heavily amended proposal, the conflict dominated discussion about Milwaukee schooling and preoccupied the MPS leadership. It was only in late May that the MPCP and charter schooling again attracted much local concern. Within a month, however, the MPCP would be more threatening than ever to the city's public schools.

MPCP Expansion Revisited

The competitive environment changed radically in June 1998, when the Wisconsin Supreme Court ruled four-to-two that the MPCP expansion was constitutional. Observers remember Brown and the MPS administration as "shell-shocked" by the ruling. The decision became even more important in October, when the U.S. Supreme Court declined to review the case, ensuring that the ruling would stand for the foreseeable future. Once the future of the MPCP was secure, the interest expressed in choice by parents and potential school operators rapidly grew.

The new threats posed by charter schools and expansion triggered a wave of responses by the school board and the superintendent's office, just as they had in 1995. Early in spring 1998, after Norquist launched the city's charter school push, Brown and a few key lieutenants sat down with the directors of the partnership schools to hear their concerns and to appeal to them to stay with the public school system. Brown reportedly told the directors, "We think that you're doing a good job. We want to keep you working with us," and asked, "How can we make our relationship better?" The most common answer was that the schools wanted partnership contracts that provided more stability than the current one-year agreements. However, according to the school administrators, such an arrangement was not feasible given the structure of the MPS budget. Several meeting participants were disappointed by the overall effort. Commented one partnership school director, "I have not been happy with the follow-up."

50. For more detail on these allegations and the related events, see Joe Williams, "Ministers, Labor Hold Vigil to Seek Changes in MPS," *Milwaukee Journal Sentinel*, April 29, 1998, p. 6; Joe Williams, "Pastors Decry Claim That They Were Used," *Milwaukee Journal Sentinel*, May 24, 1998, p. 3.

Another significant change was the school system's aggressive court-ship of the Bruce Guadalupe Community School after the city offered that school a charter. As a charter, the school would receive $6,100 per pupil. However, the school's director, Walter Sava, was concerned about legal uncertainly regarding the school's obligations to provide potentially costly services for students with special needs. Brown offered the school a contract that would pay $5,000 per pupil but would ensure that the school—as part of the larger public school system—would not be required to enroll students with disabilities. The deal got snagged on MTEA concerns and was eventually settled when the school system and Sava agreed to a one-year arrangement, ensuring that the school's enrollment would be included in official MPS enrollment figures.

The effects of the expanded voucher program struck home in September 1998, when the number of students enrolled in the MPCP nearly qua-drupled over the year before, rising from 1,501 to 5,830.[51] The number of participating schools grew from twenty-three to eighty-eight. The explosion was largely accounted for by the inclusion of religious schools, which compose roughly 80 percent of Milwaukee's private schools. At the same time, public school enrollment dropped for the first time in the 1990s. It fell from 101,963 to 100,525, a drop of more than 1 percent, even though the system's forecast (known for its consistent accuracy) had projected an increase of 629 students. An administrator involved in enrollment management termed the numbers a "shock" and said that the drop forced the school system to trim dozens of elementary teaching slots and to "hedge its bets on everything." For the first time, the MPS faced the loss of enrollment and funding.

The impact of the enrollment losses on the system's budget was a topic of heated dispute. The Institute for Wisconsin's Future, known as hostile to the MPCP, claimed that the voucher program cost the school system about $22 million in state aid in 1998–99 (out of a budget of $874 million).[52] Voucher proponents Fuller and Mitchell disputed such claims as "erroneous" and argued that state aid to the MPS rose by $8 million (1.4 percent) from 1997–98, even as the system's enrollment fell.[53] Regardless of the relative merits of these claims, the salient point for the present study

---

51. In 1998–99 a family of three could qualify for an MPCP voucher if its yearly income was $28,788 or less.
52. Moore (1998).
53. Fuller and Mitchell (1999).

is the reluctance of voucher proponents to forcefully argue that the MPS *ought* to be financially penalized for losing students. The mere fact that provoucher voices found it necessary to challenge claims that the public system was suffering revenue losses made clear how hard it was to establish a market that actually disciplined the MPS. Neither the voucher proponents nor the state legislators were inclined to the requisite callousness, ultimately undermining their ability to launch a market regime that would drive systemic change.

Given that the public schools needed to hire more than 650 new teachers in 1998–99 and roughly 900 teachers in 1999–2000, the loss of even hundreds of teaching slots would have little direct impact on school personnel. A prominent MTEA official explained in fall 1999 that the voucher issue had not affected teachers, "at least not that we have been able to detect. Enrollments have gone up each year until this year. . . . This year we still hired over 700 new teachers. Last year it was about 850. . . . Vouchers and choice and charter schools," according to this source, did not reduce the need for teachers, "so thus far it hasn't adversely affected us." Faculty turnover was high enough, and loss of students small enough, that not one principal or teacher interviewed recalled any teacher being forced out of a school due to enrollment changes by fall 1999. Because of the system's inability to track students' reasons for leaving a given school, the high rate of student mobility, and the fact that enrollment losses had only a small effect on school-level resources outside of faculty allocation, no one in the school system knew which schools were losing dissatisfied students or had much reason to do anything about it.

The school system did, however, mount two responses to the enrollment drop at the district level. First, in December 1998, weeks before the annual three-choice school selection process, Brown announced—with much fanfare and an advertising budget of at least $10,000—a "reading guarantee" program. Any second-grade student who had attended a Milwaukee public school from kindergarten through second grade and had a 90 percent attendance record but was not reading at grade level would receive extra tutoring at the school system's expense. Observers noted that the program was partly a marketing move to encourage parents to start their children in public school from day one. In the second visible resonse, during the winter of 1998–99 the school system agreed to share the governance of the new Milwaukee Tech Vocational School with a consortium of local organizations. The MTEA agreed to allow much of the school's faculty to be nonunion teachers and to waive several contract elements. These concessions were driven by the threat that a local philanthropist would otherwise have funded the school as a charter school, independent of Milwaukee Public Schools and the union.

The MTEA Contract

In September 1998 the school system and the MTEA ended a prolonged negotiation over the union's 1997–99 contract after Joe Fisher, board president and MTEA ally, personally took over the negotiations in August. The result was widely characterized as a massive union victory.[54] By December 1998, however, the U.S. Supreme Court's decision not to hear the challenge to the MPCP, growing interest in charter schooling, and the burgeoning voucher coalition campaign for the school board changed the negotiating context. The result was that in January 1999 the MTEA leadership opted to make a number of dramatic concessions it had previously refused to consider.

The new environment empowered Paulette Copeland, the MTEA president and head of the union's "reformist" faction, to argue that the union had to appear cooperative or risk reversals in the board elections and in the state legislature.[55] The results were evident in the 1999–2001 contract, settled in January 1999. Negotiating while voucher coalition school board candidates were using the terms of the September agreement to attack MTEA-backed board members, the MPS and the MTEA reached a tentative contract just four months after penning the September 1998 agreement. The new agreement marked the first time in three decades of collective bargaining that the two entities had come to terms before the previous agreement expired. The contract was promptly endorsed by 92 percent of MTEA's membership.[56]

54. The contract settled in 1998 granted the MPS a few minor but symbolically attractive concessions. It allowed schools, in select circumstances, to hire new faculty members on the basis of merit. Traditionally, staffing was based on seniority. The contract also created a weak school reconstitution process, under which the superintendent could require that low-performing schools develop a comprehensive plan for raising student achievement. In return, teachers received a boost in health insurance, pension benefits, and salaries.

55. Paulette Copeland, leader of the "reform faction" opposed to the traditional MTEA leadership, had narrowly won the union's presidency in 1997 in a 3,221-to-2,710 vote. However, Copeland's supporters remained a minority of the MTEA executive board, where the "traditionalist" majority distrusted her willingness to relax contractual protections that the union had struggled to win in the 1970s and 1980s.

56. The actual vote was 3,984 votes for ratification and 362 against.

Most significantly, the union yielded substantial ground on procedures governing staffing. The language that the union had agreed to on a case-by-case basis for innovative schools was now in the contract, freeing a school from the obligation to accept incoming teachers based on seniority if it elected to participate in one of several programs. Copeland said, "This takes away some of the power of the union and gives it to our members, and that's the way it should be."[57] This concession significantly loosened the procedural strictures that made it difficult for principals to attract a like-minded staff, while posing a real threat to the culture of teacher autonomy. Seniority would no longer provide its traditional protection. The union and the school administration also agreed to settle the union's long-running lawsuits against measures such as increased contracting and MPS charter schools. Union-supported board members wanted to demonstrate their independence from the union, while the MTEA wanted to negotiate with a board controlled by allies rather than risk dealing with the new board, which would be elected in April.

An Evolving Market and Capacity Constraints

In December 1998 the city's Charter School Review Committee approved four applications for charter school status, but just two of the schools were scheduled to open in fall 1999. UWM approved two other charter schools for fall 1999, both to be managed by the for-profit Edison Project. Edison's prospective involvement in local education infuriated teachers, school administrators, and local opponents of for-profit education, prompting threats that UWM's ties with the school system and with MTEA members would be severed. In the end the UWM process bogged down, and the planned opening of the schools was pushed back to fall 2000. The emergence of a radicalized school board in spring 1999 shifted the locus of action to the school system, which approved two charter schools for fall 1999 and aggressively moved to create new options.

As the need for PAVE scholarships evaporated with the approval of the full MPCP expansion, PAVE enrollment plunged (from 4,371 in 1997–98 to 846 in 1998–99). The program then shifted its focus from providing scholarships to supporting the opening of new schools or the expansion of existing ones. Such assistance was desperately needed by private schools

57. Joe Williams, "Teachers Union Gives Ground on Seniority," *Milwaukee Journal Sentinel*, January 19, 1999, p. 1.

Milwaukee, 1995–99 / 129

and charter schools as they sought to add capacity. Internal PAVE documents show that as of May 1999, twenty-nine schools planned to add classrooms and four sought new locations that would permit expansion. Support from the Bradley Foundation and the MMAC was pivotal in helping PAVE launch its effort to support capacity growth. Capacity constraints, however, continued to limit the threat posed by choice.[58]

A Political Revolution

By late 1998 a rough approximation of a two-party system characterized local school politics. In place of the eclectic campaigns that characterized school board elections before 1995, a unifying campaign theme emerged. The MTEA, the employee unions, and the defenders of traditional public schooling mobilized behind one slate; the choice coalition behind the other, though it should be noted that not every member of the "provoucher" slate actually supported the MPCP.[59]

Drawing on professional campaign organizers, Mayor Norquist's pollster, local choice groups, and the MMAC, Gardner coordinated a carefully orchestrated campaign in 1999. He alone spent $190,000—more than triple the previous record for a board campaign. He raised much of the money in large donations from national school choice backers. Each of the other four coalition candidates—Jeff Spence, a parent activist and public employee; Don Werra, a retired police captain; Ken Johnson, an electrician; and Joe Dannecker, a lawyer—spent $15,000 to $20,000, and the MMAC is thought to have spent tens of thousands of dollars more in support of the coalition slate. The *Journal Sentinel* endorsed four of the five coalition candidates, neglecting only Dannecker, who ran against the MTEA-backed economist Stephen Latin-Kasper for the sole open seat. While the MTEA claimed to have spent just $47,000 on the elections,

58. A 1998–99 survey of local private school capacity found that the city's 140-plus private schools could support a total K–12 enrollment of 25,319. Of that figure, 5,620 seats were unfilled. About 1,700 of the available seats were at non-MPCP schools, meaning that MPCP schools had a total of 3,953 available seats. That figure (which amounted to 3 to 4 percent of MPS 1999–2000 enrollment) was heavily dependent on the participation of religious schools in the MPCP, as nonsectarian schools accounted for only 1,159 of the available MPCP seats. Meanwhile, in 1998–99 just three charter schools operated in Milwaukee, enrolling fewer than 200 students. Choice options were starting to proliferate, but still served only small numbers of students.

59. The language of the debate illustrates the stark division between the two sides. For instance, the MTEA newsletter, the *Sharpener*, took to referring to the provoucher coalition as the "privatization machine."

observers estimated the figure at closer to $400,000.[60] The National Education Association (NEA) contributed $75,000 to the WEAC and to the People for the American Way to finance the union slate. It appears that each side spent at least a quarter of a million dollars, shattering all previous records in a board election of unprecedented expense, scope, and coherence.

Stunning nearly all observers on both sides, the voucher coalition swept the April elections. In an easy victory—unforeseen even on the morning of election day, when supporters thought his race would be a tight one— John Gardner bested Theadoll Taylor by a 60-to-40 percent margin. Union-backed incumbents Leon Todd, Sandra Small, and Joe Fisher were all defeated by Gardner allies. Not since the board was reformed in 1983 had Milwaukee seen an election in which more than one incumbent was defeated. After the smoke cleared, the Gardner-Thompson-Braun bloc included seven of the nine board members. The MTEA and the defenders of traditional public education had been routed.

The new board members signaled an intention to approach business differently when they opted to be sworn in at Garden Homes School, one of the city's top-performing public schools, rather than at the conventional locale, City Hall. The board installed the professorial Bruce Thompson as president, replacing Joe Fisher, a move that allowed reform members to put forward a temperate face, even as Gardner continued to play the role of lightning rod and provocateur.[61] The board initially showed some inclination to retain Brown as superintendent, but—encouraged by Howard Fuller and several other leaders of the voucher coalition—the four board freshmen determined that they wanted to bring in a fresh, visionary leader.

In late April the school board opted to buy out the remainder of Brown's contract, and in early May it hired the maverick Hi-Mount principal Spence Korte as the new superintendent.[62] Korte, an aggressive missionary who

60. Joe Williams and Alan Borsuk, "Issue Advocacy Lets MTEA Avoid Reporting Extensive Campaign in School Races," *Milwaukee Journal Sentinel*, April 6, 1999, online. However, because much of the spending escapes disclosure, these figures are based largely upon confidential information.

61. Gardner had initially pushed Braun, as a senior statesman, for the position of board president. However, Thompson, who had played a pivotal role in recruiting the victorious challengers, quickly assembled five votes for his presidency.

62. For a review of these events and a good depiction of local reaction, see Alan J. Borsuk and Joe Williams, "Brown's Goodbyes Begin," *Milwaukee Journal Sentinel*, April 30, 1999, online.

shrugged off concerns of political viability and professional advancement, immediately pushed for radical decentralization as a way to create more opportunities for entrepreneurial educators within the school system. The board took other aggressive and symbolic steps: at its first meeting it approved a structure for creating charter schools; in May it approved an administration plan to increase contracting; also in May Gardner pushed through a motion to revise school district accounting to facilitate significant decentralization; and in June the board approved the school system's second and third charter schools.

As the 1999–2000 school year began, seven charter schools were operating in Milwaukee with an enrollment of about 2,000 students. Meanwhile, ninety private schools were set to enroll about 7,500 MPCP students. Sixty-seven of the participating schools were religious; forty-one of those were Catholic schools. Of the schools participating in the MPCP, thirty-four (or over a third) had opened since 1990, and nearly half of those were opening their doors for the first time. In short, as the legal threat receded, there was evidence of a significant and growing expansion in competitive capacity.[63]

Ironically, just as leadership willing to pursue systemic change took power, the Republican legislature passed legislation softening the threat posed by competition. Legislators did so in reponse to pleas from Korte and several board members that they not undercut the system just when reformers had taken control. The state would henceforth deduct from the MPS general aid payment only about half of state support for students enrolled in the MPCP and Milwaukee charter schools, with the rest of the cost coming from the state's general aid pool.[64] As a result, though the measure was more complicated than this description suggests, in practice the potential monetary loss to the MSP from enrollment lost to choice programs was significantly reduced.

The Effects of Choice

Although the actions discussed above caused a great stir at the level of the school board, the MPS administration, and the state legislature, they had little or no impact on MPS classrooms and schools. When asked how

63. For a detailed look at these statistics, see Public Policy Forum (2001).
64. A good discussion of these financial design questions is available in Public Policy Forum (2000).

competition had affected their schools between 1990 and 1999, teachers typically commented, "You need to understand, many teachers are unaware of this," or, "Teachers . . . have too much on their hands to worry about vouchers and charters." No more than one in ten teachers interviewed could think of even one substantive effect of competition. One recalled that an additional faculty member was being shifted to the third grade to help boost reading scores at her school, another mentioned an increased focus on teaching to the state tests—but then seemed to attribute the focus on testing to threats of reconstitution.

Teachers felt besieged and unappreciated, while demonstrating confusion about the choice programs and a sense of being helpless to do anything educational that might affect competitive outcomes. In general, most teachers implied that the whole notion of "competing" for students was alien and somewhat unsavory, while explaining that they were already overburdened and doing all they could. In the words of a member of the MTEA board, "Choice had a negative effect on morale, as part of the general assault on the public schools that voucher advocates launched. As part of their fight for school choice [voucher proponents] sought to do everything they could to discredit the public schools." For the 1995–99 period the only school-level activity that respondents consistently mentioned was a spate of school advertising in 1997 and 1998, most noticeably in the aftermath of the Wisconsin Supreme Court decision. A few schools aired radio and newspaper advertisements to attract students, while many schools increased their outreach efforts through additional parent information nights or a greater effort to distribute flyers and handbills. One teacher described her school's outreach effort, which drew notice for its proactivity: "Our principal has formed a committee to meet with the community . . . we've got kids getting involved in making a video, and there are t-shirts [we're distributing]." Such an effort pales in comparison to the targeted niche marketing and aggressive customer recruitment pursued by dollar-conscious private universities or for-profit educational providers, like Stanley Kaplan and Sylvan Learning Systems, which live or die based on their success at attracting customers.

In 1999 the principal at the middle school for the arts perfectly captured this ambivalence, expressing both a cheerful enthusiasm for good-natured marketing and a reluctance to engage in any efforts that might upset educational routines or priorities. He related how his school sought to attract positive publicity and maintain its enrollment by working harder to contact elementary schools and Chapter 220 districts, seeking publicity, refining ads for the school's production season, and producing lithographs on a poster-making machine with the assistance of a parent volunteer:

> We're putting this stuff up all over the city—we've never done that before. We're new at marketing, and we're probably marketing to the wrong audience, but we're trying and we're learning. . . . We're not visiting the elementary schools because taking the band would mean taking about ninety kids out of school to go to an elementary where we might get three students, so it's not worth it. But we will have to target schools at some point and work to attract those kids.

In general, observed a pro-MPCP board member, MPS employees "are just not marketers. For instance, parents of four-year-olds are always telling me that they haven't heard anything from the schools. I suggested the schools ought to buy a mailing list of these families, [but] they just don't think that way. Partly it's ideological. They think, 'We're the schools. You're lucky that we're here to provide this service.'" Educators appeared to merely dabble in outreach and advertising, seeming to view it primarily as a sporting endeavor. However, absent pressures and incentives that make such efforts a necessity, there is little reason for them to approach such tasks any differently.

The school board and the school administration also lacked information on which schools students were leaving the MPS, why they were leaving, or where they were going. The school system was good at counting heads, because the state had always required it to do so. However, it never had cause to develop a capacity to gauge its market or to anticipate consumer needs. Consequently, decisions were generally made with little regard for what consumers wanted or needed. Despite a decade of commitment to decentralization, the system's budgeting capacity made no allowance for disaggregating costs on a unit basis.[65]

The muddiness of the figures and the lack of per pupil accounting meant that the system was unable to easily or directly penalize schools when

---

65. For instance, while Hi-Mount, with control of 85 percent of its budget, was supposed to buy its services from the central administration, school administrators were uncertain how much to charge and would often simply fail to bill the school for services provided.

they lost students. Similarly, schools that were gaining students did not immediately receive all the implied resources.

There was in fact little significant change before Korte took office. In 1997 and 1998 the MPS continued to drag its feet on proposed reforms for decentralization and budget cutting, with administrators sometimes simply reporting to the board that the system could not implement directives. Korte, however, purged several high-ranking officials and aggressively pushed efforts to decentralize the system and to remove structural impediments to entrepreneurial energy. He took these steps not because he was seeking to "compete" per se, but because these were moves he had long advocated. The pickax of competition did provide the radical Korte an opportunity to rise to the leadership of this system, but Korte's specific goals and actions were not fundamentally different than they would have been in the absence of choice.

As of 1999, observers generally agreed that there were no more than fifteen or twenty entrepreneurial leaders among the 150-odd principals in the MPS. A leader of the union that represents MPS administrators estimated that there were "no more than five real tigers in MPS." Most of them, he noted, had been regarded as "oddballs" or "pain[s] in the ass" and had traditionally been made suspect by their entrepreneurial energy. These leaders were rewarded for their efforts with increased responsibilities but no additional pay or resources. They operated out of a messianic commitment to the ideal of public schooling, a joy in hands-on school leadership, and a desire to run a school in the manner they deemed appropriate.

On paper, by 1999–2000 the local opportunities for entrepreneurs were impressive, with charter schooling, contracting, and the MPCP. However, by mid-1999 no more than a handful of local individuals appeared to fully grasp the financial implications of these varied arrangements. The few who did understand the funding rules and mechanisms, the impact of enrollment changes on the public schools, and the state rules on school operation were primarily voucher advocates and choice school operators rather than public school educators. Most entrepreneurial MPS teachers and principals sought an opportunity to work in a rewarding educational environment and to escape bureaucracy. They did not want to manage a small business, had no desire to make sense of state regulations and funding formulas, and had even less interest in wading into ongoing legal conflicts. Consequently, even entrepreneurial educators made little effort to explore the available options.

Conclusion

Through the beginning of the 1999–2000 school year, short-term market forces had not bulldozed away inefficiencies in the Milwaukee Public Schools, but competition had shown significant signs of chipping away at the barriers to entrepreneurship. Entrepreneurs operating on the outskirts of the system were sometimes able to obtain resources and freedom from an administration that needed to use them to make a statement (a point discussed in chapters 8 and 9). The most significant effects of competition were the political changes that allowed entrepreneurs within the MPS to emerge. Meanwhile a coherent political coalition challenged the MTEA's interest in preserving accepted procedures, which protected teachers and their autonomy. The partisan divide made it easier to hold school board members accountable for their positions and gave the board's governing bloc the ability to provide consistent direction.

The presence of limited competition had not refocused teachers or principals or changed the manner in which they approached their jobs. It produced some new efforts to raise standards, increase choices, and open new schools, but little evidence that these moves affected classrooms. At times of obvious potential threat, choice and charters provoked active symbolic reactions from MPS and MTEA leaders. These symbolic responses created the potential for meaningful change by permitting new schools to form unencumbered by many of the constraints on existing urban schools.

There was no guarantee, however, that these changes would be permanent. In fact, in the spring 2001 school board elections the voucher coalition suffered significant setbacks. Bruce Thompson was unseated by an MTEA-backed opponent, shrinking the board's voucher bloc to five members. Further, in spite of efforts by Milwaukee's voucher bloc, its experience did not seem to be replicable in other cities. It may be that the historic roots of choice in Milwaukee, the key role of African American and Democratic leaders, and the resources of the Bradley Foundation, and other Milwaukee-specific elements produced a unique political dynamic.

The Milwaukee experience shows that the effects of a choice program on the public school system is dependent upon the degree of competition posed by the program, and in Milwaukee the degree of competition depended upon key program design elements and the participation of religious schools. Further, the changes that can be produced by a pickax response are dependent on the willingness of union leaders to relax procedural strictures, of system leaders to push for change, and of entrepreneurial educators to take advantage of any proffered openings.

The experience in Milwaukee from 1995 to 1999 illustrates the real effects that the pickax response can produce even over a relatively short time period. The next two chapters consider two other programs, where such effects were less evident.

Cleveland, 1995–99:
Muffled by the Din

THE CLEVELAND VOUCHER EXPERIENCE offers a vivid contrast to that of Milwaukee. Although the Cleveland program's 1995 launch was also met with heated national attention and a burst of legal challenges, in most other ways the story was very different from the one played out in Milwaukee. In Cleveland, vouchers met with lukewarm union opposition, gave rise to tepid political conflict, and sparked little if any visible response by the Cleveland Public Schools (CPS) leadership. The differences were due both to the construction of the programs—the Cleveland voucher program bore a strong resemblance to the early, ineffectual Milwaukee Parental Choice Program (MPCP), in place from 1990 to 1995—and to the context in which the programs operated. This chapter focuses on the effects of the first years of the Cleveland voucher program, from 1995 through fall 1999.

Like other large cities, Cleveland was the site of nearly continuous educational reform throughout the 1990s. The number and variety of reforms make it difficult to draw precise conclusions about the consequences of any particular reform, including school vouchers and charter schooling. As with the case of Milwaukee, the analysis should therefore be regarded as suggestive rather than definitive.

Struggling with Urban Adversity

Entering the mid-1990s the CPS operated in a context not much different from Milwaukee's. While CPS student enrollment was slightly smaller than that of the Milwaukee Public Schools (MPS), Cleveland's population was similar in that it was also poor, heavily black, and highly mobile. Enrollment grew slightly during the 1990s, from 70,760 in 1989–90, to 72,728 in 1993–94, to 73,312 in 1997–98.[1] During the decade, the CPS operated roughly 120 schools. As of 1998–99 the school system continued to project climbing enrollment, anticipating it would have more than 78,000 students by 2002 and more than 80,000 by 2006.[2] The steady growth produced a facilities squeeze, aggravating Cleveland's existing financial problems that were a consequence of its declining tax base. The strain on the public school system had also increased as enrollment in Cleveland's private schools declined precipitously after 1960.[3]

In 1998–99 the CPS employed more than 8,400 full- and part-time employees, including nearly 4,800 teachers. Total district employment increased by more than 400 employees from the previous year.[4] The 1998–99 CPS budget was $539 million, a 7 percent increase from the 1997–98 budget of $504 million, and per pupil spending was over $8,100, with just under $4,500 spent on services directly related to instruction and the rest on support services and noninstructional expenses. Those numbers were up markedly from 1994–95, the year before voucher legislation was enacted, when the CPS spent more than $7,100 per pupil, of which just over $4,000 went to instruction.[5]

Teacher turnover was consistently in the 6–10 percent range throughout the 1990s. By fall 1999 an increasing rate of retirement resulted in 500 teacher vacancies, positions that the CPS was often hard-pressed to fill with certified teachers. The district anticipated a growing wave of retirements in the coming years, both because more than two-thirds of CPS teachers had ten or more years of experience and because CPS teachers' salaries were slightly below the average in neighboring school systems. CPS employees are heavily unionized, with about 98–99 percent of class-

1. For these figures, and a wealth of additional information on the financial state of the Cleveland Public Schools, see the *Comprehensive Annual Financial Report* by the Cleveland City School District (1998, pp. S14–S15).

2. For growth projections, see "Message from Barbara Byrd-Bennett." *BEST News: Building Excellence and Success Together* 1 (1999).

3. For instance, elementary enrollment in the Cleveland diocese, which served the greater Cleveland area and schooled most Cleveland students not in CPS, dropped from nearly 110,000 in 1960 to just over 50,000 in 1990. See McLellan (2000, p. 25).

4. Cleveland Public Schools (1998, p. vii).

5. Cleveland City School District (1998, p. S15).

room teachers in the Cleveland Teachers Union (CTU), an affiliate of the American Federation of Teachers (AFT).

Some school choice was available in the state before the passage of the Cleveland voucher plan. In 1990 Ohio became the fifth state in the country to pass statewide open enrollment. The law, which took effect in 1993–94, required public schools to accept any district student if the school had available space. Students were also allowed to transfer between school systems, with the state's share of per pupil funding following them to their new school. By spring 1999 interdistrict open enrollment was in effect in more than half of the state's 600 school districts, though the number of participating students was relatively small.

The Role of Race

Cleveland's troubled history of desegregation shaped the context in which the CPS reacted to school choice. When blacks migrated to Cleveland during 1910–40, the vast majority settled on the city's east side. A system of segregated housing soon emerged, producing a system of segregated schools.[6] In 1973 the National Association for the Advancement of Colored People (NAACP) sued to force Cleveland to integrate its schools, and in 1976 Judge Frank Battisti found the city and state guilty of "intentionally and deliberately operating a racially dual public school system in Cleveland." Battisti required the CPS to pursue desegregation through an extensive system of busing. In 1978 Battisti ordered a number of additional educational changes.[7] White communities strongly opposed busing, with groups such as Citizens for Neighborhood Schools and Parents against Busing springing up across Cleveland.[8]

For years, school officials resisted the court orders on desegregation, arguing that black and white communities were naturally divided by ge-

6. For a careful discussion of the history of black migration to Cleveland, the evolution of the city's race relations, and the CPS's desegregation battles, see Jefferson (1991). For a concise overview of the desegregation fight, see "Cleveland Looks at Desegregation Case" (1992).

7. These improvements dealt with reading, counseling, extracurricular activities, student rights, expanded testing, and community education and were designed not only to improve the schools for minority students but also to encourage middle-class, predominantly white, families to keep their children in the public school system.

8. For a good contemporaneous account of CPS desegregation in the early 1990s, see Evelyn Theiss, "Schools Case at Twenty," *Cleveland Plain Dealer*, December 12, 1993, p. 2B.

ography (specifically the Cuyahoga River) and that full-fledged busing would cause white families to flee the CPS. In 1980, after a six-week investigation of the CPS desegregation plan, Judge Battisti found the board and top administrators in contempt of court. Having acceded to two previous board requests to postpone desegregation, Battisti now criticized the board's "procrastination," "aimless administration," and "lack of will to desegregate" and appointed an administrator to oversee desegregation efforts.

The desegregation fight and the ensuing busing did spur white families to flee the public schools for private schools and the suburbs, radically reshaping the demographics of the CPS student population. In the twenty years after court-ordered busing began, CPS enrollment dropped from 125,00 to about 73,000 and changed from mostly white to more than 70 percent black. As in other cities, the social tensions produced by forced busing left the community bitter and divided. In this context, many civil rights activists viewed school vouchers and other school choice reforms with suspicion, worrying that they constituted a backdoor effort to resegregate the CPS.

A Troubled School System

The effect of choice-based reform must be understood in the context of Cleveland's economic difficulties, poor educational track record, and history of racial antagonism. Over the years, the school board was assailed for micromanagement, bureaucratic rigidity, and a lack of coherent leadership.

The school board was repeatedly criticized for centralizing decisionmaking and reducing system flexibility and accountability. One scholar noted that "over the years, the Board . . . placed itself in the midst of day-to-day decisionmaking. It has served as a court of appeals . . . and has taken steps such as approving individual purchases and personnel moves."[9] In 1985 the popular and respected superintendent Frederick D. Holliday committed suicide in the hallway of one of the schools. His suicide note said he was "sickened by political battles with the school board." The tragic event, which received extensive press coverage, was a poignant symbol of the problems that plagued the CPS. The CPS leadership was char-

9. Butler (1997, p. 46).

acterized by tremendous instability, cycling through fifteen superintendents in the thirty-year period between the late 1960s and the late 1970s.[10]

Turnover in the superintendent's office and the administration, and the continuing struggles between the state and the city and between the mayor and school officials made it difficult for community members and educators to know who was in charge or for those in charge to gain control of budgeting, personnel, and policy. A union official noted, "We've had so many changes in leadership, it's like the right hand doesn't know what the left hand is doing. . . . We never knew who we were dealing with, whether it's the governor or the mayor, the city or the state. . . . You don't know who you're negotiating with and who's calling the shots." Organizational confusion and the district's wealth of troubles reduced the likelihood that key public school actors would respond to the coming voucher threat in any concerted fashion.

The school system was also plagued by corruption. A 1987 levy raised $60 million; by the 1990s all but $6 million had been spent with no evident capital improvements. Throughout the late 1980s and into the mid-1990s, the CPS suffered through a large standing debt, declining revenues, and increasing operating expenses. One result was that the district succeeded in passing only one property tax increase between 1970 and 1995.

In 1991 Mayor Michael White backed an ambitious reform slate known as the Four L slate, so named because all four members had last names that began with the letter *L*. The slate swept to victory, claiming four of the seven school board seats. In 1992, seeking to put its stamp on the system, the board hired respected superintendent Sammie Campbell Parrish from North Carolina. By 1995, however, the board itself had experienced great turnover and controversy, Parrish had departed, and only one of the original Four Ls remained on the board. Mayor White answered this setback by initiating a public struggle with the unions and the superintendent's office for control of the school system.[11]

By the mid-1990s the CPS was widely thought to be in crisis: per pupil expenditures were relatively high, yet student achievement, as measured by standardized tests, and graduation rates were poor and getting worse. Just 9 percent of CPS twelfth graders in 1997–98 passed the five Ohio proficiency tests required for graduation. The problems were equally se-

10. See Butler (1997) for a full account of the challenges that beset the CPS board and administration.

11. See Butler (1997, pp. 126–42) for discussion, including reflections of former board members.

vere at the elementary level, where just 8 percent of sixth graders passed all five tests.[12] The system also had a high attrition rate, with declining enrollment in the higher grades. In 1996–97 less than 28 percent of the 6,281 students who had entered the system as ninth graders in 1992–93 graduated as seniors. The school system faced a $29.5 million budget shortfall, and as many as twenty-five school buildings were judged beyond repair. In 1994 the system failed in two attempts to secure additional operating funds by passing levies.[13]

One observer said that by 1995 the CPS was in "disarray, financially and academically. A new superintendent would come in and he or she might be able to bring in a couple people, but the same old entrenched, dysfunctional bureaucracy was in place. The same old folks who knew how to undermine and keep power and financial control . . . would not allow any forward movement."[14]

The 1995 Reform Push

The CPS entered 1995 reeling from failed levy efforts and the unexpected resignation of Superintendent Parrish in early 1995.[15] The 1994 efforts to pass levies failed, despite campaigns that each spent more than $350,000. A 1994 agreement providing for Cleveland's 1997 release from court supervision called for the city to raise $275 million and required

12. See "Message from Barbara Byrd-Bennett," *BEST News* 1 (1999), pp. 1–2. for these statistics. The five required tests covered writing, reading, math, citizenship, and science. A sixth test, for science, was added for 2000–01.

13. Buckeye Institute (1998b).

14. Jeff Archer, "Obstacle Course," *Education Week on the Web*, June 9, 1999. A somewhat more optimistic assessment was presented in the 1995 report card of the CPS Reform Task Force, which concluded that the district had made progress during the 1991–95 period. The task force hailed changes that included the hiring of a new administrative team, the purging of several high-profile "worst offenders" in the bureaucracy, the elimination of more than $100 million from the operating budget, the formation of the Vision 21 plan for school improvement, and progress in negotiating a desegregation settlement. Continuing challenges highlighted by the task force included the loss of the new superintendent and his top administrators, the quiet continuation of some practices of the departed "worst offenders" in the bureaucracy, the failure to formulate an implementation plan for Vision 21, and a return to litigation after failing to implement the student assignment portion of the desegregation agreement. See Citizens League of Greater Cleveland (1995).

15. In her account of the affair, Butler (1997, p. 140) observes that "Parrish's resignation in February stunned the district and the community. An attempt was made to keep the district running in spite of the loss, but all concerned began to sense that disaster was looming."

that the levy remain on the ballot until approved by voters. On February 28, 1995, the school board pulled the proposed levy off the May 2 ballot, fearing its likely defeat. On March 3 Judge Krupansky turned control of the CPS over to the state. Amid the concerns cited by Krupansky was the district's staggering debt-to-revenue ratio of 25 percent and concerns that the CPS had failed to comply with court requirements in the ongoing desegregation lawsuit.[16]

The State Takeover

Calling the CPS "a ship without a rudder," Judge Krupansky ordered the state to assume control of its management. The school system was in a "state of crisis," he said, and "internal dissension, management problems, and a crippling budget deficit had undermined the district's ability to carry out its educational program." The state immediately installed Richard "Dick" Boyd as deputy state superintendent for Cleveland. The judge ordered the CPS to close at least fourteen schools that were in major disrepair and to prepare an operating levy for voters. Meanwhile, Boyd moved to assemble a new strategic blueprint, launched a decentralization effort (which made only minimal progress), and initiated an accountability system. During the period of state control, the city's elected school board continued to operate, albeit without any significant decisionmaking power.

The takeover and resultant media attention generated a flurry of activity. Several actions taken by the CPS were cited by some observers either as evidence of genuine reform or as a response to the imminent voucher threat. In the summer of 1995 the CPS closed eleven dilapidated and underperforming schools, transferred more than 1,200 teachers and staff, fired 161 teachers, and slashed the system's overall budget. Two of the system's worst schools were also closed under what was called "reconstitution."[17]

Upon further inspection, however, these reforms offer surprisingly little evidence of substantive change. The only element that appeared to work

16. For information on the levy fights, see Patrice Jones, "With Levy Dead for Now, VA1 City Schools Face Cuts," *Cleveland Plain Dealer*, March 1, 1995, p. 1A; Patrice Jones, "School Levy Campaign Missing $880," *Cleveland Plain Dealer*, April 4, 1995, p. 2B; Patrice Jones and Scott Stephens, "School Levy Heads for Second Defeat," *Cleveland Plain Dealer*, November 9, 1994, p. 1A; Patrice Jones and Scott Stephens, "State Takes Control of City Schools," *Cleveland Plain Dealer*, March 3, 1995, p. 1A.

17. Cleveland Teachers Union (1995).

as intended was the plan to shut down underperforming schools. While significant, this effort was more limited than reformers had desired and was due primarily to explicit language in the court order. The layoffs of teachers proved hollow. Almost all of these teachers were hired back in the fall, both because of a successful legal challenge by the union and because the system had more teaching vacancies than it could fill.

The attempt to "reconstitute" two schools encountered similar problems. The new principal of one of these schools explained that initially the entire staff was laid off, but that the Cleveland Teachers Union protested and sued. Ultimately one-third of the previous staff returned. The remainder of the new faculty were transfers from other CPS schools (many of whom had reportedly been squeezed out of their old schools because they were poor teachers) and inexperienced new hires. The CPS had promised greater financial and administrative flexibility to the school, but the principal reported that this never materialized. The union's collective bargaining agreement remained a major "restraint" to improving the school, he said. The CTU opposed the principal's request to have grade-level teams meet regularly to develop curriculum and assessment strategies, and the contract limited his ability to hire, fire, reward, or discipline teachers. The details of reconstitution illustrate the system leadership's limited ability to push fundamental change even in Cleveland's worst public schools.

In what was proclaimed a major initiative to improve accountability, the union agreed in the 1996 contract negotiation to the creation of academic achievement plans (AAP) at each school. By writing these plans into the contract, however, the CTU controlled them and ensured they would include no significant sanctions. The union's newsletter noted that "all power for developing the AAP's for each school is now legally in the hands of teachers at that school. . . . The AAP cannot change contractual agreements covering compensation, fringe benefits, the grievance procedure, due process requirements, union organization, evaluation, transfer, seniority, layoff/recall, or any contract provision not related to the Academic Achievement."[18] The union also agreed to school governance councils, starting with eight schools in 1998–99. The union's leadership was comfortable with these measures because the CTU exercised control over how they would be implemented. In interviews at least two CTU officials pointed to these reforms as union "wins" and chuckled at the notion that they could be termed union givebacks. Due in large part to the positive

18. Cleveland Teachers Union (1996).

public relations produced by the union's "flexibility," the CPS succeeded in passing the court-ordered levy in November 1996. The levy promised to generate about $67 million a year in additional school funding.

Throughout the 1995–97 period the elected board pursued legal challenges to state control of the CPS in the courts, muddying the question of where authority lay and who was responsible for CPS behavior and performance. In 1997 Boyd passed control to Jim Penning, a key deputy and CPS veteran. However, angry with provisions in Penning's contract, Mayor White quickly removed Penning. In September 1998, when the state officially returned control of the CPS to the city of Cleveland, the mayor appointed New York City area superintendent Barbara Byrd-Bennett as the system's new chief executive officer.[19]

The Emergence of Vouchers

In October 1993 two Republican legislators, Representative Michael Fox and Senator H. Cooper Snyder, announced their plan to introduce Ohio's first voucher bill. The State Board of Education joined a number of organizations (including the Ohio School Boards Association and the state Congress of PTAs) in opposing the Fox-Snyder Ohio Scholarship plan, which proposed a two-year pilot voucher program in eight urban school systems (including Cleveland). From the start, Cleveland was central to the debate, due to the problems plaguing the city's schools. (Interest in Cleveland would grow after the March 1995 state takeover of the CPS.) Although defeated by fierce opposition from Democratic and black leaders, the bill sparked much debate and put vouchers on the state agenda.

In October 1994 two important black Democratic leaders in Cleveland—Mayor White and Councilwoman Fannie Lewis—announced their support for vouchers. Lewis said she supported vouchers because Cleveland's public schools had been unresponsive to her constituents. Nonetheless, in 1994 vouchers died in the General Assembly Education Committee.

The turning point for vouchers came in January 1995, when a Republican majority assumed control of the General Assembly. With the Republican governor George Voinovich advocating school vouchers, the *Cleveland Plain Dealer* reported, "House Republicans are giddy at the

---

19. Byrd-Bennett came in with strong mayoral support and a pledge to "step up the pace and increase the pressure" for school improvement. See "Message from Barbara Byrd-Bennett," *BEST News* 1(1999), pp. 1–2.

possibilities to remake primary and secondary education."[20] In January Councilwoman Lewis led a rally of 300 voucher supporters to the state capitol in Columbus. Given Cleveland's troubled racial history, vocal black support was crucial to the passage of a voucher bill that targeted the city. On the day of Lewis's rally, Governor Voinovich included a pilot voucher plan for 4,000 students when he announced his legislative budget proposal. The plan called for poor parents in selected school districts to receive a $2,500 voucher, which could be used at a private, parochial, or alternative public school of the family's choice. Students would be chosen by lottery, eligibility would be limited to students in grades K–3, and the tuition that participating schools could charge voucher families was capped at 10 percent above the voucher amount. Assembly Republicans soon rewrote the budget proposal to restrict the voucher program to Cleveland, while paring Voinovich's $12.5 million proposed appropriation down to $5 million. The bill also included language requiring that parents or unspecified sponsors cover 25 percent of tuition for each voucher student. The state's $5 million share of the voucher costs would be paid out of the state's Disadvantaged Pupil Impact Aid earmarked for the Cleveland district.

Voucher opponents, including the CTU, the Metro Cleveland Alliance of Black School Educators, the Ohio chapter of the American Civil Liberties Union, and the Interchurch Council of Greater Cleveland bitterly fought the proposed program.[21] The state Senate stripped the voucher program from its budget, but Assembly Republicans successfully fought to restore the program in conference.[22] Conferees rejected a proposed commission on school choice to oversee the voucher program, instead giving the state superintendent of public instruction oversight responsibility. On June 1, 1995, Governor Voinovich signed the two-year state budget; it included $5.2 million for the Cleveland voucher program.

---

20. Mary Beth Lane, "State Republican Majority Targets School Issues," *Cleveland Plain Dealer*, December 18, 1994, p. B14.

21. Democratic representative Ronald Gerberry's bid to strip the voucher program from the state budget was rejected by the Assembly on a forty-one-to-fifty-seven vote. On April 6 the Assembly passed the budget, with the voucher program intact, on a fifty-nine-to-thirty-nine vote. For a colorful account of the House action, see Thomas Suddes and Benjamin Marrison, "House Oks State Budget," *Cleveland Plain Dealer*, April 7, 1995, p. A1.

22. Thomas Suddes, "Governor Urges Cleveland Vouchers," *Cleveland Plain Dealer*, May 20, 1995, p. B6.

The Voucher Program

The voucher program, officially titled the Cleveland Scholarship and Tutoring Program (CSTP), was restricted to students who resided within the Cleveland city school district. The maximum state contribution was $2,250, with the scholarship amount depending on the recipient's family income. Vouchers were targeted to children in families with income of less than 200 percent of the poverty line; additional funds were available for families with income below the poverty line (in 1995 the poverty line for a family of four was $15,569).[23]

Private schools were allowed to charge no more than 10 percent of the voucher's value in additional fees or tuition. The money allocated for the program would provide approximately 2,000 students with vouchers. Any private school—including religious schools—that registered with the superintendent and agreed to certain restrictions was permitted to enroll voucher students. In the initial year of the program only students of grades K–3 were eligible. However, once they had received a voucher, scholarship recipients could continue to receive scholarship funds until they completed eighth grade. The legislation establishing the CSTP allowed up to half of the scholarships to be used by students already enrolled in private schools; that figure was later reduced by the Ohio Department of Education to 25 percent.

In short the voucher program was restricted in a number of important ways. It was limited to the city's poorest students, limited to certain grades, capped at a relatively low level of tuition, and limited in the number of available vouchers. In addition, students who accepted vouchers and left the public schools would continue to be counted in the enrollment of the CPS for state funding purposes, dramatically reducing the threat posed to the CPS by lost students. The maximum voucher was equal to less than a third of the $7,130 that the CPS spent on each student in 1994–95 and was only slightly more than half of the district's $4,017 per pupil instructional expenditures during that year.[24] These compromises were essential

23. The exact value of the voucher varied with family income. Students from families with income below 200 percent of the poverty line received vouchers worth up to 90 percent of their school's tuition (up to $2,250). Students from families whose incomes were equal to or higher than 200 percent of the poverty line were eligible for vouchers worth $1,875, or 75 percent of their school's tuition, whichever was less. For a good discussion of these figures and the mechanics of voucher distribution, see Greene, Howell, and Peterson (1998, pp. 359–60).

24. Cleveland City School District (1998, p. S15).

to the voucher program's legislative victory, but they curtailed the threat that vouchers posed to the CPS.[25]

The program launch was postponed in August, when Voinovich and the legislature decided to give education officials a year to set up the program. After the program did begin, it was largely drowned out by the noise of the state's takeover of the school system. The effort to fix the financial crisis and to build an accountability plan, and then the state's move to hand over control of the CPS to the mayor, attracted far more local attention than the voucher program. As one local education reporter observed, "In the midst of all of the noise involving the takeover, the voucher proposal got very little attention. . . . In a sense, people had so many problems of their own to deal with that this was more of a side-show out of Columbus."

The $5.25 million allocated for the program's first two years would be paid out of the state's general Disadvantaged Pupil Impact Aid budget. Under this arrangement, the CPS would keep up to 55 percent of state aid for each departing pupil as well as its entire local and federal allotment.[26] However, even three and four years after the passage of the voucher bill, union officials, CPS officials, and community respondents were unclear about how much money the CPS was losing due to vouchers and the mechanics of the program's funding. Union officials asserted that the funding was being taken directly from the CPS, though they admitted to some uncertainty about this claim and were less heated on the issue than were union officials in Milwaukee. In fact, it was impossible to trace, through either document searches or interviews, any discrete impacts on expenditures at the system level or in any particular school.

The Launching of the Cleveland Scholarship and Tutoring Program

When the CSTP office officially opened on November 1, 1995, Director Bert Holt's initial task was to inform potential recipients and to distribute applications. Given that 75 percent of parents or guardians did not subscribe to daily newspapers, Holt turned to Head Start centers, private

---

25. A brief but useful discussion of the constraints on the voucher program is provided by Greene, Howell, and Peterson (1998, pp. 358–60). They discuss the early evidence on why families chose to participate in the Cleveland program, satisfaction with voucher schools, and the performance of voucher students.

26. Rees (2000, p. 130).

schools, and welfare recipients—even pushing to have a message regarding the scholarships printed on welfare checks. Holt also turned to ministers of both large and small churches; the Interchurch Council did two mailings of application forms to churches throughout Cleveland.[27]

The CSTP received 6,244 applications and awarded 3,814 scholarships for the 1996–97 school year. Of these, 1,994 were utilized. About fifty schools were approved for participation in the program by January 1996. Between 1996 and 1998, fifty-nine schools participated in the voucher program, most of them religiously affiliated. Interviews suggest that private schools were frequently interested in voucher students as a means to offset declining enrollments. An administrator in the Blessed Sacrament School would report in 1999 that the school's enrollment had dropped in recent years from a high of 300 to the current 152 and that 73 of the current students were in the voucher program. The headmaster noted, "If we had not accepted voucher students we probably would not be here because of the financial burden on the parents."[28]

On January 10, 1996, however, just five days before the Ohio Department of Education was to award the first vouchers, the program was dealt a blow when a coalition of teachers' unions, public school administrators, and civil libertarians filed a lawsuit challenging its constitutionality. Voucher supporters mounted a vigorous defense. National voucher advocates, such as conservative Washington, D.C., lawyer Clint Bolick, the director of the Institute for Justice, announced their intention to assist in the program's defense. Governor Voinovich attacked the union's stance, arguing, "It is hypocritical for the union to oppose choice for parents applying for [the plan] when studies of 1990 census data indicate that 39.7 percent of Cleveland teachers . . . [are] sending their children to nonpublic schools."[29]

Plans for the voucher program continued to go forward despite the uncertainty. On January 23, 1996, administrators of the fifty-three par-

27. Holt provided this account in a 1999 memo.

28. The headmaster indicated that budget strictures prevented the school from doing much advertising but that the school did announce in the local newspaper that it would be accepting voucher students. Most applicants learned about the school through word of mouth or from the scholarship office, she said, adding, "We do not go out and solicit students." Tuition at Blessed Sacrament in 1998–99 was between $1,625 and $1,925 a year, several hundred dollars less than the maximum allowed under the voucher program. However, the school did not seek to raise tuition, because doing so would have required it to do so for both voucher and nonvoucher students.

29. Scott Stephens, "Educators, Others Sue over School Vouchers," *Cleveland Plain Dealer*, January 10, 1996, p. B1.

ticipating private schools held a school fair for prospective voucher parents at the Cleveland State Convention Center. Voucher applicants were required to submit the names of six schools, listed in order of preference, to the Cleveland Scholarship and Tutoring offices by February 15. As families submitted their choices, program administrators struggled to find sufficient spaces for the applicants.

Not only was the immediate availability of space a problem, but the lawsuit made it less likely that new schools would open or current schools would expand. One proposed new school faltered before it even got off the drawing board. Officials at several private schools made it clear that they were hesitant to participate in the voucher program, citing concerns about the academic preparation of CPS students, potential discipline problems, the effect that voucher students might have on their schools' identity, and the fact that the dollar amount of the vouchers would not cover per pupil costs. The private, mostly parochial, schools that did accept voucher students were either unwilling or unable to significantly expand available seating. Moreover, many of the private schools were housed in older buildings and had classrooms or facilities that could not physically accommodate more students.

Meanwhile, Bert Holt, the voucher program administrator, had been rebuffed by neighboring suburban districts when she sought to persuade them to open their schools to voucher students. No suburban districts chose to accept Cleveland voucher students, both because the voucher amount would not cover per pupil costs in those schools and because educators and officials in these communities had little desire to import children from inner-city neighborhoods or troubled schools. Explained one observer, "Suburban [school] boards and superintendents do not want to explain to their parents why they've decided to start bringing in black children from crappy schools in the 'hood."

As one voucher proponent announced in early 1996, "For the success of this program to occur, we are going to have to create new schools."[30] Akron industrialist and choice proponent David Brennan sought to address this need by creating a nonprofit group called Hope for Cleveland's Children, which would open Hope academies primarily to serve voucher students. At the start of the 1998–99 school year, Hope Tremont Academy and Hope Central Academy enrolled about 450 students. These

---

30. Desiree Hicks, "Opportunity Rings a School Bell," *Cleveland Plain Dealer*, February 20, 1996, p. B1.

schools limited class size to thirty, provided a teacher's aide in each class, and supplied six computers per classroom. The Hope academies, although ostensibly autonomous, were all administered by the White Hat Management Company, an organization created by Brennan that provided the start-up funds for Hope schools.

The Hope academies faced a number of serious obstacles. They not only had to recruit teachers, buy books and materials, and locate classroom and office space but also had to convince prospective parents to send their children to schools without a proven track record. The schools also had limited financial resources, which crimped their operations.[31] The per pupil voucher amount was less than a third of the total per pupil expenditures of the CPS, and voucher schools were not provided with public start-up funds.

The student population of the Hope academies also presented a serious challenge. Students were almost entirely voucher recipients, who by definition were from the poorest families in the city. Hope officials reported that voucher students often had a history of academic and behavioral problems. The Hope schools also shared the CPS's problem of high rates of student mobility—on average, 10 percent of Hope voucher students changed schools during the year. Moreover, one-third of the student population turned over from 1997–98 to 1998–99. The Hope schools did not utilize any substantial advertising, relying primarily on word of mouth.

Teacher turnover in the Hope schools was also high—in part because salaries, while slightly higher than at many local private schools, were significantly lower than those offered by the CPS. At Hope Central, for example, only two teachers from 1997–98 returned in 1998–99; turnover of assistant teachers was even more common. In an attempt to staunch their losses, Hope schools initially announced that their teachers would receive a 20 percent raise in 1999–2000.

The difficulties of the Hope schools illustrate the problems inherent in building private sector school capacity. Brennan blamed CPS opposition to vouchers and teachers' unions for his difficulty in starting up and oper-

---

31. The limited resources of the Hope schools were perhaps most visible in their physical plants. Hope Central was located in a run-down part of central Cleveland in an old Catholic school building. The school shared the building with a Head Start program. The gym was downstairs in a room that the church used Tuesday nights for bingo and that still reeked of smoke on Wednesday afternoon. The school employed thirteen teachers and thirteen assistants and had a 1998–99 budget of slightly less than $1 million, with about 80 percent of its revenue generated by tuition.

152 / *Cleveland, 1995–99*

ating the Hope academies. He also argued that the many constraints on the voucher program indicated that it "was designed . . . to fail." As a result of the continuing political and legal uncertainty surrounding the voucher program, in the summer of 1999 Brennan announced plans to close down the academies and reopen them as charter schools. This promised to shrink the political constituency supporting vouchers even as it undercut the capacity of the private school system.

A Rough Start for Vouchers

The CPS was rocked by a number of significant events in the years following the introduction of the voucher program in 1995. There was rapid and repeated turnover in the system's leadership, as Richard Boyd, Jim Penning, Lou Erste, and then Barbara Byrd-Bennett assumed control. In 1996 the district narrowly avoided a teachers' strike when the union postponed its initial strike date and Mayor White pressed the state to reach a settlement. Initially dissatisfied with the deal, which included no scheduled salary increases in the first two years, the union demanded and received substantial pay increases after the November 1996 passage of the court-ordered levy.

Union leaders remembered the frustration of the state's negotiator. Recalled one union official,

> His philosophy was, "Here's the amount of money we want from you in concessions. You can divvy it up any way you want to, but you have to give us that." . . . We looked at him and said, "Why do we have to do that?" His background was in the private sector, where he can threaten, "If you don't do this, we're moving the factory to Mexico." Well, we knew the school system wasn't moving to Mexico, so we just said, "No, we're not doing that."

CTU's influence limited the ability of state or district officials to pursue dramatic changes in school governance, teacher hiring or evaluation, and other basic practices.[32]

The ongoing legal battle over the constitutionality of the voucher program limited the program's effect by creating doubt about its permanence.

---

32. A CPS board member remarked, "Every significant reform idea we tried to put forward was killed by the union."

In July 1996, barely one month before the voucher program was scheduled to begin, Franklin County Court of Common Pleas judge Lisa Sadler ruled that the voucher program could go forward.[33] Two days later voucher opponents filed an appeal and requested an injunction from the Tenth District Ohio Court of Appeals. On August 12 the court denied the request for the injunction, permitting the voucher program to begin on schedule. On August 28 three of the newly created private voucher schools opened for business. The program began that fall with 1,607 voucher students, or roughly 2 percent of CPS enrollment. However, the actual effect on CPS enrollment was significantly less than even this figure suggests. Of the 1,607 voucher students, 376 had attended private schools in the previous year, and another 539 were entering kindergarten. Consequently, no more than 692 voucher students actually departed CPS schools.[34]

Political battles added to the uncertainty surrounding the voucher program generated by the court challenges, further clouding its future. Governor Voinovich submitted his biennial state budget on February 3, 1997, earmarking $5.8 million to expand the program by an additional 1,300 vouchers. Democrat John Bender responded by proposing an amendment to eliminate the program. Bender's amendment was tabled, but it served as a warning that the program could be eliminated if its opponents could recapture a legislative majority in Columbus. On May 2, 1997, as the Cleveland voucher program neared the end of its first year, the Tenth District Ohio Court of Appeals ruled three-to-zero that the program was unconstitutional because "it has the primary effect of advancing religion" and noted that about 80 percent of the fifty-three private schools participating in the program were religious in nature.[35] The district court postponed its ruling, however, to allow the voucher program to continue until the Ohio Supreme Court could rule on the matter. In May 1999 the Ohio Supreme Court reversed the lower court's ruling.

In 1997–98, the program's second year, it received 5,186 new applications and awarded 1,595 scholarships, of which 1,289 were used. Com-

---

33. For details, see Scott Stephens, "Plan Gets Day in Court," *Cleveland Plain Dealer*, June 25, 1996, p. B1. For good, brief overviews of the legal fight over the Ohio voucher law, see Viteritti (1999, pp. 174–76); Rees (2000, pp. 130–32).

34. For details and these figures, see Scott Stephens, "Experiment Begins," *Cleveland Plain Dealer*, August 29, 1999, p. A1. Note that reported figures on enrollment in the voucher program are not always in agreement.

35. For an account of the ruling, see Mary Beth Lane and Joe Hallett, "Court Rejects School Vouchers," *Cleveland Plain Dealer*, May 2, 1997, p. A1.

bined with the returning voucher students, that yielded a voucher population of 2,938. By 1998–99, this number grew to 3,744 students, roughly 5 percent of CPS enrollment. By 1998 thirty-three of the city's thirty-nine Catholic schools were participating in the program, many at or near capacity.[36] As Bert Holt, the CSTP administrator, noted, "We're reaching saturation real fast. As the program has expanded, existing private schools that are willing to take voucher students have filled all of their vacant seats. And they are unwilling to expand their facilities to accommodate more voucher students because of the legal uncertainty surrounding the program."

Private schools participating in the voucher program also reported logistical problems, such as difficulty obtaining students' records from the CPS. Said one private operator, "They just stall, or they forget, or they don't send us records that we have to have. It's just frustrating as hell."

The Petro Report

The voucher program came under serious criticism in April 1998 with the release of a critical report by the state auditor, Jim Petro.[37] The report claimed that the program lacked clear policies in some areas and failed to verify the eligibility of its participants; further, the program's six-member administrative staff failed to collect sufficient documentation from applicants about their residency and income level. Specifically, nonlocal driver's licenses, birth certificates, county identification cards, and a hunting license had been accepted as verification of residency.[38]

The Petro report stated that the biggest problems with the launching of the CSTP concerned transportation. The legislation establishing the CSTP gave the CPS responsibility for providing transportation for the scholar-

36. Warren Cohen, "Vouchers for Good and Ill," *U.S. News and World Report*, April 26, 1998, p. 46.

37. Petro (1998). The report exemplifies the kinds of logistical difficulty that can undercut participation in choice-based programs and the kinds of abuse that threaten to undermine political support. Both outcomes can reduce the competitive threat that programs pose, by reducing consumer participation and by calling into doubt the long-term viability of programs.

38. Although the voucher program was intended to serve low-income families, at least twenty-three children whose families made more than $50,000 a year received vouchers. The program also failed to establish a policy for verifying the guardianship status of parents; 29 percent of the 1997 fiscal year students and 38 percent of the 1998 students tested did not have the same last name as the individual who signed the application as the parent or legal guardian.

ship students to their new schools. However, rather than provide busing, the CPS opted to reimburse families at the end of the year for transportation expenses. In a late August meeting, just days before school was to start, the CPS transportation director told Bert Holt that the school system would not be able to transport voucher students. Holt remembered, "They thought they had us. They thought they had killed off this program by seeing to it that students couldn't get to school."[39] In the end, logistical difficulties forced the CSTP to transport students via taxicabs for several months. The bill for the taxis ultimately came to $3.5 million for the 1996–97 and 1997–98 school years, prompting the Ohio House to pass a bill requiring the public school system to pay the additional transportation expenses.[40] Ironically, while the CPS was largely to blame for the difficulties, it was the credibility and political prospects of the voucher program that took the blow.

The Petro report also revealed that the lottery drawing for scholarships was held before the eligibility of applicants had been determined and two weeks before the authorized date, thereby excluding three weeks' worth of applications. Ohio education officials responded by indicating that they would step up their scrutiny and guidance of the voucher program, and critics seized on the report as a reason to eliminate the program. Democratic senator C. J. Prentiss argued, "This pilot program appears to have been totally mismanaged. People have taken the money and done whatever they want with it without any kind of oversight."[41]

The Petro report gave rise to a 1998 amendment to the CSTP that required the CPS to provide voucher students with transportation. The results were dramatic. Although in 1997–98 just 565 of the 2,938 voucher students rode public school buses to school, while 1,084 were transported by taxi, in 1998–99, 1,853 of the 3,744 voucher students rode buses, while just 95 rode taxis.[42] Statutes and logistical support can make market choices more or less accessible, affecting transaction and switching costs and influencing the number of families able and willing to use choice programs. Policymakers and state officials can act either to forestall or to provoke

---

39. Buckeye Institute (1998a, p. 20).

40. The taxicab companies used to transport voucher students consistently and egregiously overbilled. Of the approximately $1,400,000 charged during fiscal 1997, almost 10 percent ($140,000) was fraudulent. Of the $2,100,000 charged in fiscal 1998, approximately $280,000 in overbilling was found.

41. Jeff Archer, "Policies of Cleveland Voucher Program Faulted," *Education Week on the Web*, January 20, 1999.

42. Blum Center (1998).

embarrassments that will influence the political prospects of choice-based reforms.

The Return of Local Control

On March 27, 1998, U.S. District Chief Judge George White declared that Cleveland had fulfilled its legal obligations to desegregate its public schools, declared the school system to be "unitary," and concluded that the state-appointed interim superintendent and district officials had done all that could be expected to remedy the harm created by past segregation.[43] On June 30, 1997, Governor Voinovich signed a biennial budget bill that included $4.9 billion in lump-sum school funding, to be divided up after the state devised its new funding formula.[44] The bill also renewed the voucher program for two years, added 1,000 new kindergarten vouchers, and allowed third grade graduates to continue using vouchers in the fourth grade. The changes meant that up to 3,000 children would be eligible for vouchers in the coming year.

In August 1997 Governor Voinovich signed House Bill 269, dissolving the powerless Cleveland school board, which had remained in office during the preceding three years of state control. The bill gave control of the CPS to the mayor, who appointed a new nine-member board and a new chief executive officer. The law giving control of the Cleveland schools to the mayor was initially challenged in court by the CTU and the NAACP, but their lawsuit was later dropped. The mayor's control of the CPS was slated to run from 1998 through 2002.

Bill 269 also made other significant changes, dictating that central administrators would henceforth serve at will and that building principals would no longer have to possess the traditional administrative certification. These changes held out the possibility that CPS officials might have substantially more ability to reshape and manage the system. The new superintendent seized upon these changes to push revisions to the accountability system, to modify the systemic push for decentralization, and to launch a major literacy effort in anticipation of a requirement that fourth graders would have to meet by 2002. The size, scope, and tumult of these changes, however, pushed the pilot voucher program into the background.

43. For a good account of the decision, see Caroline Hendrie, "Judge Ends Desegregation Case in Cleveland," *Education Week on the Web*, April 8, 1998.
44. Lynn Schnailberg, "Ohio Carves out Funding for Charter School Pilot Program," *Education Week on the Web*, July 9, 1997.

Byrd-Bennett enjoyed some modest success in reshaping the central administration under House Bill 269 provisions allowing her to terminate central office administrators and to use assessment as a new accountability instrument. But no local observers suggested her actions were in response to the introduction of market-based reforms.

The CPS's 1998 report highlighted a number of "major initiatives" under way, among them the decentralization of administrative authority from the central office to the schools, full-day kindergarten, annual targets for proficiency test performance and attendance, and the creation of "Academic Achievement Plans" and "Attributes of an Excellent School" surveys. Most significant was the effort to focus on accountability and measurable performance, largely to comply with the new high-stakes accountability regime mandated by the state. Several interviewees, both inside and outside the CPS, suggested that vouchers and charters were not a point of much concern for the public schools. "Forget about vouchers and charters. It's testing that's driving everything," said an outside observer. "That's why we're seeing the changes that the superintendent is pushing. . . . The state teacher conference was even moved from March to April so that teachers wouldn't have to miss school until testing was over. That's what everybody is focused on."

Program Size

In 1998–99 there were 3,744 voucher students enrolled in fifty-nine schools, more than 80 percent of which were religious. While the enrollment represented about 5 percent of CPS enrollment, respondents consistently tended to qualify that figure as "only" (or "just") 5 percent. Although the CPS program was not much smaller than the post-1995 MPS program, it was perceived as smaller, and that perception dictated the response of the CPS and the community.[45] Two factors contributed to the sense that the program was small: the number of voucher students who were already in private schools when they received vouchers and the limited capacity and

45. Even Bert Holt, the director of the CSTP, stated that "application returns might appear low for the 1999–2000 school year." See Holt (1999, p. 2). The reasons were unsurprising. Holt cited transportation difficulties, the decreased availability of seats, the hesitation of schools to change "the composition of their school community," and increased CPS efforts to "maintain parent/guardian loyalty."

slow growth of voucher and charter schools.[46] Of the students who received vouchers in 1998–99, 3,030 attended religious (primarily Catholic) schools. The number of voucher students enrolled in a given voucher school during the year varied from 1 to 174, with the typical participating school enrolling 50 to 100 students.

Unlike Milwaukee, Cleveland was the site of relatively little charter activity during 1995–99. Ohio did not pass its first charter school law until 1997. In 1998–99, only 2,543 students were enrolled in forty-eight charter schools throughout the state.[47] Charter schools were exceptionally small, with an average population of fifty-three, and Ohio charter schools primarily served at-risk students. While the effects of charter schooling were likely to evolve as school operators took advantage of the state's relatively "strong" charter law to open new charter schools, little such activity was evident in Cleveland through the end of 1999.

Interviews suggest that neither CPS educators nor non-CPS observers regarded the voucher program as a serious competitive threat to the CPS by late 1999. No interviewee could point to any specific changes in policy or behavior at the district, school, or classroom level that had been motivated by competition.[48] However, starting in January 1999, just months after the arrival of Byrd-Bennett, the district did launch a public relations periodical titled *BEST News: Building Excellence and Success Together.*

The one CPS action that several observers attributed to the voucher program was its decision to advertise its all-day kindergarten on city buses when the program was launched in fall 1997. This was about the time that the CPS learned that nearly 600 new voucher students were children about to enter kindergarten. The CPS funded the ads, first with money from the court-ordered levy and later with state aid. However, the formal

46. Although union officials generally appeared the most sensitive to vouchers and most likely to exaggerate their significance, one CTU official dismissed the dangers of the Cleveland voucher program, arguing that, "most of our kids in the voucher schools were already in private schools before this program came. They're not really taking kids away from [CPS]."

47. Rees (2000, p. 129).

48. A vignette illustrates the tepidness of the CPS response to competition. In the CPS administrative building, the public affairs office was located on the second floor. In spring 1998, three years after the voucher program was enacted, access to this office required that the building's solitary security guard manually call up to the office and receive permission to admit a visitor. On the second floor, CPS public relations were laid out on a cheap table along one wall in a dusty room. Downstairs, as of May 1998, the CPS "school selection" office was informing visitors that neither materials on the system's magnet schools nor school selection forms were yet available for the coming September.

record shows little evidence of a direct link between voucher enrollment and the advertising campaign, and observer opinion was mixed as to whether the campaign consituted a response to competition or simply a continuation of standard practice.[49]

A Cleveland Teachers Union official who urged a more proactive CPS response to vouchers reported that district officials were generally unresponsive. "When we asked [system officials] to start advertising, to get out there, they just nodded and then did nothing." Observers variously termed system officials "bureaucratically narrow" and lacking a "sense of self-promotion." Explained one veteran teacher, "The administration doesn't know how to handle teacher initiative or leadership. . . . There's an inability to see the value of someone who . . . has a transformative view of educational change and is aggressive or opinionated. . . . [The administrators] are kind of inept, and they're focused on 'safety first,' and they don't know what to do with teachers who are trying to make things happen."

The Response of the Teachers

To the degree that teachers responded at all to choice reforms, they complained about the voucher program as a political menace and expressed anger that money was being redirected from the public schools. Unlike their counterparts in Milwaukee and Edgewood, Cleveland voucher advocates did not even try very hard to claim that the existence of school choice had produced negative consequences. As one private headmaster said, the Cleveland school system was "so big that they don't really care about losing a few students. I never got the impression that they were worried about closing or anything. I don't think that's a realistic possibility." And an official at the independent Cleveland Initiative for Education echoed many when she said, "The district is always going to have plenty of students to teach. I mean, so what if they took 2,000 kids out. Now if you take 20,000 kids out, that's different. The voucher and charter initiatives didn't reduce our teaching force or touch teachers' pocketbooks. This stuff hasn't registered with principals either—it just is not high on their radar screen." Such comments were common even though CSTP participants amounted to nearly 5 percent of CPS enrollment by 1998 or 1999.

---

49. One district official said that the ads were just "an effort to tell parents about the program"; a community leader said, "I don't think anyone would tell you there was a connection between vouchers and the signs on the buses."

The lack of a perceived threat meant that the teachers never felt compelled to grant major contractual concessions. The severe shortage of teachers in Cleveland also enhanced the union's leverage. Between 1996 and 1999 the district was hiring 500 or more teachers a year—a turnover rate of 12 percent or more in a system with 4,100 teachers. Unable to find enough certified teachers by the start of the 1998–99 school year, the CPS had to fill about 100 slots with provisional teachers. This shortage meant that no teachers were in danger of being laid off due to a loss of enrollment. The CPS was also constrained by a lack of talented or entrepreneurial principals. During 1999 about a half dozen high-level CPS, CTU, and community observers estimated that only about 15 to 25 of the 118 CPS principals were autonomous or skilled enough to respond aggressively to the decentralization of school management.

Amid the ongoing commotion, school-level personnel evinced little real concern for or understanding of the voucher program. This apathy was more evident than in Milwaukee. In Cleveland teachers and principals were too preoccupied with their daily challenges, state testing, leadership turnover, and disciplinary problems to pay more than fleeting attention to choice-based reforms. "As far as the impact of vouchers," said one observer,

> there has not been a darn thing. There's so much other macro chaos that has hit the system. Since the [voucher] bill was passed, [three superintendents] have been in charge. . . . Principals and teachers have been busy trying to follow who is who. They are preoccupied with questions from "What is my latest evaluation instrument?" as a principal, to "Who do I call to get this purchase order through?" The idea that there's competition from Hope [schools] or the parochial schools has really not influenced them very much—it has not really been on the radar screen.[50]

Apathetic Elites

Even as the voucher program enrolled 3 percent, and then 5 percent of the school population, it drew apathetic responses from union officials and CPS administrators. In fact, in spring 1999 CTU officials expressed

---

50. As one union official noted, "Teaching is a difficult job—it takes a lot of energy, and our teachers in the classroom are struggling, trying to do the best that they can, and therefore they really don't worry about things like charters and vouchers."

more concern about prospective legislative battles over curricular reforms and class size than about efforts to reauthorize the voucher program. Explained one union official, "Right now class size, especially [for grades] K–3 is at the top of our state agenda. We're also concerned . . . about proficiency test scores, but the bigger concern is class size." Among six state and local union officials interviewed in 1998 and 1999, just one cited vouchers as one of their top two concerns.

Moreover, whereas Milwaukee school board members played a pivotal role in encouraging the MPS to respond to competition, the CPS board played no such role. In particular, the CPS board's appointed status and the loss of local control in the mid-1990s produced a sedate board whose members apparently felt little need to meet the concerns of constituents or to demand that the CPS take visible actions. The CTU's head of school board liaison observed in 1998,

> The appointed board doesn't really have a lot of power. The difference before was that the school board members were elected by the people . . . [who] could hold them accountable. Now . . . why should they worry? . . . Our executive members have the hardest time just getting the board members to call them back. If this was an elected board member, they'd be on that phone in a minute because they want to win their election.[51]

The CTU leadership responded to the voucher program by arguing that very few CPS kids were actually leaving the system to attend private schools under the voucher program and that most vouchers were issued to families that already used or intended to use private schools. The union leadership exhibited little fear of the voucher program and thus did not feel the need to respond to it by agreeing to substantive public school reforms. One board member noted that the teachers' unions effectively killed all of the board's reform initiatives: "Anything we try—if we try to move an inch—the union objects." Choice reforms had little effect, she said, because union obstruction remained the obstacle to significant improvement in the CPS.

This apparent lack of concern was even more evident at the school level. The principal of one public elementary school remarked that, while

---

51. A leader of a local, unaffiliated school reform group agreed, saying that a key difference between 1998 and the early 1990s was that the elected board felt it had to respond to constituent demands, while the appointed board did not.

there were Hope academies near his school, he did not see them as competition "at all," because their agenda was of a "religious nature" and because they had the benefit of selective admissions. In addition, the principal acknowledged that he had no idea how many of his school's former students were now enrolled in the voucher program, because the student turnover rate at his school was roughly 22 percent a year and because no one tried to track the students' reasons for leaving.

The primary education reporter at Cleveland's major daily newspaper observed during 1998–99 that the *Plain Dealer*, as well as other Cleveland media, had "not devoted much coverage" to the issue. In addition, despite the efforts of the CSTP office to build community awareness, observers felt that a large percentage of public school parents remained unaware of the program's existence.[52]

An Ambiguous Outcome

Lack of clarity regarding the performance of CSTP students confused parents and politicians, emboldened critics, and raised questions about the program's long-term political prospects. Studies of the program were conducted by Indiana University's Indiana Center for Evaluation and by a Harvard University team led by the same Paul Peterson who clashed with John Witte in evaluating the Milwaukee program. The Indiana Study reported mixed results. The Peterson team reported high rates of parental satisfaction with vouchers and found that voucher students significantly outperformed otherwise similar CPS students. Meanwhile, a study by the Ohio Department of Education attacked the findings of the Peterson team, questioning the validity of the test score analysis that showed voucher students outperforming their public peers.[53]

As with Milwaukee, the relevant issue here is not the relative merit of competing analyses. From the perspective of local voters and potential consumers, the mere fact that official-sounding reports issued by legitimate scholars differed on the effects of vouchers was more significant

52. As late as 1999 a Public Agenda study of parents in Cleveland and Milwaukee found that 60 percent knew "little or nothing" about vouchers. "It's hard to overstate how unfamiliar and confusing these proposals are to most citizens—parents included," commented one report author. See Scott Stephens, "Study Shows Parents Clueless on Vouchers," *Cleveland Plain Dealer*, November 17, 1999, p. B5.

53. Metcalf and others (1998a, 1998b); Metcalf (1999); Greene, Howell, and Peterson (1997, 1998); Ohio Department of Education (1997).

than the relative technical virtuosity of the competing reports. Doubts about the program's effects helped foster doubts about the value of voucher schools and about the long-term viability of the program.

A local education reporter noted the media's difficulty in gathering and disseminating accurate information on the voucher program to people in Cleveland:

> Think tanks are routinely coming out with reports about vouchers being good, about them being bad, conservative think tanks on one side, and the AFT on another side. . . . That kind of charged atmosphere doesn't exist when you are discussing going to a year-round school as opposed to a nine-month school or something else that you can maybe more rationally sit down and research and discuss. . . . The conflicting research is a handicap in trying to tell this story to parents and to taxpayers.[54]

The financial impact of the voucher program on the Cleveland public school system was also the source of much confusion, as public school defenders argued that the loss of the voucher funds would hurt the CPS. State officials, however, pointed out that the CPS was allowed to count voucher students in its enrollment numbers for funding purposes and that the funding formula for disadvantaged students was adjusted upward; so the district had not lost money as of 1999.

The Failure of the Hope Academies

The continuing legal ambiguity dampened the willingness of parochial schools and independent operators such as David Brennan to expand their capacity or to open new schools. In 1999 Brennan closed Hope Central and Hope Tremont and reopened them as charter schools, meaning they would no longer accept voucher students. The move, according to Brennan, was prompted by parents' concerns about the stability of the two schools, by the repeated legal challenges to CSTP, and by the much larger per pupil subsidy given to charter schools ($5,000 maximum, with $4,500 coming from state aid and $500 from federal Title I money) than to voucher schools. "The voucher system was totally inadequate to cover our costs," explained a Hope executive.

---

54. Peterson (1999, p. 14) would eventually observe, "In the end, firm conclusions cannot be drawn from the studies of the scholarship program in Cleveland."

The loss of the Hope schools created a serious capacity problem for the voucher program by fall 1999. The new head of the CSTP explained that the program was unable to place "a lot" of the new voucher students, given a lack of openings in participating private schools. This problem was exacerbated by the closing of two other private schools during the 1999–2000 school year due to financial difficulties, leaving the number of participating schools at fifty-six (only one more than when the program began in 1995–96).[55] The CSTP director indicated that future expansion was uncertain and in any event would not occur until the legal and financial uncertainties surrounding the program were resolved.

Doubts about the future of the voucher program were fed by other events during summer 1999. The state Senate passed a measure that would have prevented students in the program from using vouchers after the fifth grade, though the legislative budget that passed ultimately allowed current fifth-grade voucher students to continue into the sixth and seventh grades. A July investigation into voucher schools by the *Cleveland Plain Dealer* produced much negative publicity. The *Plain Dealer* found that some schools operated without a state charter or with unlicensed teachers (one school had hired a convicted murderer and drug dealer as a teacher) and that other schools had not administered required state proficiency exams. In addition, many facilities were reportedly in violation of health and safety codes. The publicity spurred the state to undertake immediate inspections and to try to remove three of the schools from the voucher program.[56] Such events continued to cast doubt on the political sustainability of the voucher program, undermining the threat it posed to the CPS.

Meanwhile, the program continued to struggle with legal challenges. On May 27, 1999, the Ohio Supreme Court upheld the program's constitutionality on church-state grounds but struck it down on the basis of having been improperly authorized in 1995 by a rider attached to an omnibus appropriations bill in violation of the Ohio constitution.[57] Subse-

---

55. Administrative difficulties also discouraged schools from participating in the program. In December 1999 the state was approximately $860,000 delinquent in tuition payments to voucher schools. Such logistical difficulties led some schools, including Marotta Montessori, to close some campuses. Mark Vosburgh, "School Cites Voucher Pay Delay in Closing West Side Campus," *Cleveland Plain Dealer*, November 10, 1999, p. B1.

56. Mark Vosburgh and Scott Stephens, "Three Schools May Lose Their State Vouchers," *Cleveland Plain Dealer*, July 9, 1999, p. A1.

57. Judge Paul Pfeifer created further confusion about the constitutionality of program expansion when he wrote in a footnote, "It is possible that a greatly expanded school

quent court cases first permitted the voucher program to continue and then held it unconstitutional. An adverse federal appeals court ruling in December 2000 finally left the program's fate in the hands of the U.S. Supreme Court.[58]

Conclusion

The small size, early difficulties, and bleak political and legal prospects of the CSTP, as well as the sparse capacity of the private school system, sharply limited the threat the program posed to the CPS during 1995–99. Ohio did not pass charter legislation until 1997, and charter schools enrolled fewer than 3,000 students statewide in 1998–99, so charter schooling did not contribute to the choice-based threat in Cleveland throughout the period.

The CPS underwent a number of dramatic changes during 1995–99, but there was little to link these to choice-induced competition. The competitive effects in Cleveland were overshadowed by the state takeover, frequent changes in leadership, system reforms, a state accountability push, and the mayor's new role. The lack of a significant provoucher political coalition meant that, whatever its absolute size, the Cleveland voucher program was consistently perceived as less threatening than the Milwaukee program. The muted impact of the voucher program was also due, however, to features common to many urban school systems, particularly the existence of strong unions, limited staff accountability due to rigid contract stipulations, teacher shortages, and student turnover.

The Cleveland private schools that accepted voucher students operated under a number of constraints that limited their effectiveness as competitors. The low level of program funding and the paltry resources of new voucher schools limited their attractiveness as an alternative to public schools. Participating parochial schools generally accepted only a few voucher students and made little effort to expand. The number of participating schools remained nearly flat over the program's first three years, increasing from fifty-five schools in 1996–97 to only fifty-nine in 1998–

---

voucher program or similar program could damage public education. Such a program could be subject to a renewed constitutional challenge." T. C. Brown and Sandy Theiss, "High Court Says Voucher Law Enacted Improperly," *Cleveland Plain Dealer*, May 28, 1999, p. A1.

58. For a discussion of the December ruling and a good overview of the related decisions, see Clowes (2001).

99. Meanwhile, voucher supporters viewed the Ohio Department of Education as an opponent seeking to drown the CSTP in red tape and bureaucracy. Said Bert Holt, "It was the worst mistake to put this program under the DOE. They didn't own it or want it. They threw bureaucracy at you, laying traps all the time. I was thwarted at every juncture."[59]

Public school administrators and union officials were aware that political opposition and limited private school capacity made vouchers a largely symbolic threat. They remarked often on both the small size and the limited future capacity of the program, especially when estimating its potential threat to CPS enrollment. Because CPS enrollment was steadily increasing during the period, there was little to prompt the system to mount an anticipatory response. A union official who attempted to spur CPS administrators to launch an outreach and advertising effort in response to the Hope schools found that "they just didn't want to bother, they didn't think it was necessary." CPS administrators were not in fact opposed to the departure of a small number of the most discontented families.

The lesson of Cleveland is not that competition cannot cause urban school systems to change. It is that the degree of such changes will be largely a product of the educational, political, and organizational context, issues considered in chapters 8 and 9. First, however, it is useful to examine the impact of private vouchers in Edgewood, Texas, where the program operated without the encumbrances of legal challenges or legislative constraints.

---

59. Buckeye Institute (1998a, pp. 20–21).

SEVEN

Edgewood, 1998–2000:
An Outside Invasion

THE HORIZON VOUCHER PROGRAM launched in the
Edgewood Independent School District (EISD) provides an opportunity
to examine competitive threat in a context substantially different from
that of Milwaukee and Cleveland. The EISD, located in San Antonio,
Texas, is a small, poor, heavily Hispanic district famous for its difficulties
with educational funding and performance. Whereas the Milwaukee and
Cleveland plans diverted public money to private schools, Edgewood's
program is privately funded, so no public money follows participants to
their new schools. When launched, the Children's Educational Opportunity (CEO) Horizon program was the forty-first privately funded voucher
program in the nation and by far the most ambitious and best funded.

Because public money does not follow voucher students in a privately
funded "tuition scholarship" program, the theoretical market threat to
the public school system is attenuated. However, it would be a mistake to
overstate this point, as proponents of competition note a number of reasons why districts ought to respond to privately funded programs. First,
state funding is based largely upon total district enrollment. Consequently,
even though district money does not follow students, the school district
still loses money when students depart. Second, the departure of students
may undermine community support for the public schools and create long-
term uncertainty for public educators. Third, educators may feel that their
legitimacy or contribution to the community is being challenged. Finally,
desirable students may be "creamed" off, a loss that may hurt public school
performance and also make teaching less rewarding. By offering vouchers

to all EISD students who qualified for the federal lunch program (95 percent of students), Horizon proponents hoped to provide a showcase for the systemic effects of vouchers.

The Edgewood Context

The Edgewood Independent School District is a 14.2-square-mile island of poverty just west of downtown San Antonio. The district, with twenty-seven schools, is one of fifteen independent school districts encompassed by the sprawling Bexar County school district, which stretches across metropolitan San Antonio. In 1998–99 the EISD had just over 13,300 students, of whom 97 percent were Hispanic and 96 percent were economically disadvantaged. The 1998 median family income was less than $16,000. Dominated by faded one-story houses and rundown businesses, Edgewood had the lowest property value of any urban district in the state.

The EISD is best known as the site of a famous 1968 lawsuit seeking a more equitable funding system for public schooling, an issue that continued to occupy local attention into the 1990s. In the landmark case of *Rodriguez* v. *San Antonio*, Edgewood parent Demetrio Rodriguez and several others charged that the Texas school funding system was unconstitutional because it provided unequal educational opportunity.[1] In 1973 the U.S. Supreme Court ruled against the plaintiffs and directed them to the state courts, launching a three-decade fight that eventually led, in the 1990s, to substantial state funding reform.[2] By 1998 the EISD had received a massive increase in state aid and was spending almost double what it spent ten years before. In 1998–99 Edgewood spent $6,060 per pupil, about $500 more than the state district average.[3]

Despite the infusion of new resources, fewer than half of the students who began ninth grade in the district's high schools graduated. A widely discussed 1998 *Houston Chronicle* profile described the EISD as "among the state's worst urban districts . . . a system of low expectations . . .

---

1. For an extensive history of the case and its aftermath, see Long (1996).

2. The ongoing efforts to redress inequities enabled advocates of school choice to propose vouchers as a potential remedy. See Parker and Weiss (1991).

3. For an extensive analysis of the condition of EISD and the problems the district faced, see Thaddeus Herrick, "Edgewood: After the Money," *Houston Chronicle*, November 22, 1998, p. A1.

divided by infighting and plagued by administrative bumbling."[4] The same piece offered this devastating assessment: "In some ways Edgewood is like a small Third World country, where scarce spoils are enjoyed by the party in power and intervention from the outside world is scorned. With its $85 million budget, the district represents a huge source of wealth in a desperately poor community."[5] The EISD was Edgewood's largest employer, employing roughly 10 percent of the community's working adults, and hired nonteaching staff (such as janitors and bus drivers) at a rate roughly 50 percent greater than the average Texas district. The district was also marked by political apathy, with turnout for school board elections rarely exceeding 5 percent. The unpaid school board typically met in full session once a month. Its seven members are elected to four-year terms in even years, with three members elected in one election and the other four in the next.

The school board served as base for the local political machine run by David Garza, a former state official, and Pablo Escamilla, a local attorney. The pair used their influence to win lucrative school district business for Escamilla's law practice (with a billing to the EISD of more than $400,000 during the 1997–98 school year), while they selected and funded most school board candidates and placed Garza's brother, Manuel Garza, in the board presidency.[6] Machine domination helped insulate the EISD board from public pressure provoked by the voucher program.[7]

4. In the late 1990s, the state's urban districts were being harshly critiqued. A 1999 study by the liberal Intercultural Development Research Association reported that student attrition in Texas's major urban districts (including the San Antonio area) had reached 51 percent in 1996–97. See Supik and Johnson (1999, p. 3).

5. Thaddeus Herrick, "Edgewood: After the Money," *Houston Chronicle,* November 22, 1998, p. A1. An EISD-commissioned survey conducted in 1998–99 found that employees had little faith in the district's leadership. Teachers and administrators gave poor performance ratings to the school board and the superintendent, even though more than half of 400 parents surveyed gave the leadership a grade of A or B. More than three-quarters of parents gave an A or B to EISD's teachers. See Anastasia Cisneros-Lunsford, "Teachers Give Low Marks to Edgewood Board, Boss," *San Antonio Express-News,* April 7, 1999, p. 1. Parents expressed great faith in public educators, while the teachers expressed little faith in the system leaders. Under such conditions, district leaders will have immense difficulty winning school-level cooperation but may be able to more readily rally community support.

6. As John Noriega, who served twelve years on the board before stepping down in 2000, explained, "Everyone that ever wants to come through Edgewood has to come through [Escamilla and Garza]. . . . You're only a friend as long as you do what they tell you to do." See also Cecilia Balli, "District Feels Like a Family Divided," *San Antonio Express-News,* May 28, 2000, p. 1B).

7. During 1997 personal conflicts led Garza and Escamilla to abandon most of the board members they formerly supported. In spring 1998 they ran new candidates against

A crucial difference between the Edgewood experience and that of Milwaukee and Cleveland is that Texas teachers do not have the right to bargain collectively. Texas teachers' associations do exist and do negotiate contracts at the state level, but teachers lack the leverage produced by the ability to strike. The lack of a formal bargaining agreement also prevents one union from speaking officially for local teachers. Consequently, Texas teachers lack the kind of institutionalized influence that the Milwaukee Teachers Education Association (MTEA) and the Cleveland Teachers Union (CTU) are accorded by their collective bargaining agreements and near-universal membership. Instead of one dominant union, Bexar County houses four teachers' associations, including one sponsored by the National Education Association (NEA), one by the American Federation of Teachers (AFT), and two strictly Texas organizations—the Association of Texas Professional Educators and the Texas Classroom Teachers Association. None includes a majority of Bexar County teachers.

Teacher turnover in Edgewood hovered at just under 15 percent between 1995 and 2000. Given that the district employed more than 900 teachers in 1998–99, this meant that Edgewood routinely had to hire more than 100 new teachers a year. In part this turnover was caused by a steady flow of teachers who left Edgewood for other, higher-paying Bexar County districts. In 1998–99 a new teacher in Edgewood earned $26,200, or less than a new teacher in seven of the other fourteen Bexar County districts. A thirty-year veteran with a master's degree earned $44,500 in Edgewood, less than peers in nine of the other fourteen districts.

Because it enrolls less than 10 percent of Bexar County students and does not serve children of the city's business or political leaders, Edgewood normally attracts little sustained attention from community leaders. A local leader explained, "We've got a lot of districts and, of course, they're just completely balkanized. That's why I just focus on one—San Antonio ISD." The much larger and higher profile San Antonio and Northside

the four incumbents. Their new slate swept to victory, handing Garza-Escamilla a five-to-two majority, on the basis of a platform that included the promise of salary hikes for EISD paraprofessionals and classified workers. The incumbents each spent $5,000 to $7,000 on the election. The figures for the challengers are unknown, as the official records disappeared after the election. Seated in May 1998, the new board sometimes met in secret or without notifying the two dissident members, in violation of state laws regarding open meetings and notification. Beset by conflict and accused of improprieties, Manuel Garza resigned as president of the board in June 1999, just before the trustees voted to change their rules so as to elect new officers a year early. The board then elected Magdalena Salas as the new president.

districts attract much of the community's attention. The local response to vouchers in the EISD was less intense than it might have been as teachers' association leaders, the local paper, and community leaders were distracted by turmoil in the San Antonio Independent School District and by growth and funding issues in other districts.

Since reaction to competition is often aimed at quelling angst among the civic leadership and the local media, the pressure on the EISD to act was muted. A reporter noted that the *Express-News* "has a hard time holding anyone's feet to the fire, because there are so many districts to cover that it becomes difficult for us to cover any one district in depth." Other observers noted that each district spends only a limited amount of time under scrutiny, reducing public pressure.[8]

What attention was paid to the EISD was negative. The district was held responsible for its low scores on the Texas Assessment of Academic Skills (TAAS) and for its high dropout rate, even though much of this performance could reasonably be attributed to the district's socioeconomic problems. Critics also berated the EISD for administrative bloat and inefficiency: between 1993–94 and 1997–98 the district's central administration grew 25 percent while some classroom jobs were eliminated. The school administration provided justifications—for instance, the high incidence of special education students—but the situation created at least the appearance of ineffective management. There were also allegations of theft and corruption regarding a 1992 $27 million bond issue.[9] And in 1998 the district was years behind on two major construction projects. Some critics worried that the district had cut its operating budget while building a costly performing arts campus that enrolled only about 150 of Edgewood's 14,000 students.

In 1992 the school board hired Dolores Muñoz as superintendent and charged her with reforming the system. Over the next several years Muñoz and sympathetic board members reportedly made incremental progress in reducing waste, changing some of EISD's controversial practices, and im-

8. Fuchs (1992) provides an illuminating analysis of how fragmentation plays out in local politics. Her point is somewhat different from that made here, as she shows how unified political control enables political leaders to emphasize the long-term benefits of fiscal discipline over the temptation to spend, but the key in both cases is the manner in which spatial fragmentation changes the incentives for public officials.

9. The bond issue was not an isolated incident, as the previous decade had seen board members convicted of crimes and federal money for free student lunches siphoned into a private slush fund. Meanwhile, the board president, Manuel Garza, was attacked for an unpaid $11,000 property tax bill.

proving school performance as measured by the TAAS. In 1997–98 three EISD schools were "recognized" based on the TAAS, while none was rated "low performing." After opening a small initial program at the new Edgewood Academy for Communications and Fine Arts, by fall 1998 the EISD could boast accelerated "academies" at its three high schools.[10]

Three Early Choice Programs

Three potentially competitive choice-based programs touched San Antonio in the early 1990s. None had any discernible impact on the public school systems of Bexar County in general or on Edgewood in particular. The three programs were the 1992 Children's Educational Opportunity San Antonio scholarship program, the Texas Public Education Grant (PEG) program, and charter schooling.

On April 15, 1992, three businessmen launched the CEO San Antonio program with an endowment of $1.6 million. Modeled on an Indianapolis program, it promised partial scholarships for roughly a thousand Bexar County students, paying 50 percent of private school tuition, up to $1,000 for elementary school students and $1,500 for high school students. Students eligible for the federal free or reduced-price lunch program could apply for scholarships. Approximately half of the program's students had been previously enrolled in private schools.

A significant portion of the initial funding for the program was contributed by the conservative activist James Leininger. By the end of 1998, Leininger had contributed $2.4 million to CEO San Antonio.[11] Leininger

---

10. The Fine Arts Academy, equipped with sophisticated performing arts facilities, was opened in 1996 after the district won significant external grant support to renovate the shuttered Edgewood High School and reopen it as the Edgewood Academy for Communications and Fine Arts.

11. Leininger would later promise to provide $45 million of the $50 million necessary to finance the CEO Horizon voucher program in Edgewood. Leininger, fifty-four years old in 1998, with a net worth estimated by the *San Antonio Express-News* at approximately $300 million, was ranked among the hundred richest Texans and among the five richest residents of San Antonio by *Texas Monthly* magazine. In the late 1980s, after taking his firm, Kinetic Concepts International, public (the firm specialized in producing high-tech hospital beds), Leininger supported the efforts of "tort reformers" in Texas to elect judges and legislators skeptical of personal injury lawsuits. In 1988 Leininger started a political action committee called Texans for Justice as part of the larger tort reform fight. Reportedly, more than 85 percent of the approximately $200,000 used to launch Texans for Justice was donated by Leininger. He and his family contributed about 20 percent of the $5 million raised by the Texas Public Policy Foundation between 1989 and 1998. He also

had first become interested in school choice in 1989, when he launched and funded the conservative Texas Public Policy Foundation (TPPF). Directed by Jeff Judson, a savvy conservative who had worked for U.S. Senator John Tower, the TPPF was active in local and statewide policy debates. Leininger also sponsored the Texas Justice Foundation (TJF), headed by Allan Parker, an attorney and former head of the Bexar County Christian Coalition. The TJF and the TPPF helped make the public case on behalf of CEO San Antonio in 1992 and CEO Horizon in 1998. As San Antonio residents, but not residents of the poor and heavily Hispanic Edgewood enclave, the CEO Foundation leadership and the allied voucher advocates would be depicted by community opponents as outsiders intent on advancing a hostile political agenda.

In 1993 Republican legislators in Austin pointed to CEO San Antonio as they made the first of several unsuccessful efforts to include vouchers in the state school finance bill. By the mid-1990s vouchers had become part of the state education discourse, although the idea remained an abstract threat to established Texas public schools.

An important ally in launching CEO San Antonio was the *Express-News*, San Antonio's leading newspaper, whose participation as a founding partner of the program helped frame the effort as a civic initiative. The newspaper cosponsored a luncheon to launch the program, announced the scholarship in a celebratory story that ran above a half-page advertisement promoting its role as a CEO San Antonio sponsor, and printed an application form in the same newspaper. The paper reportedly contributed $70,000 worth of free advertising and $50,000 in cash to CEO San Antonio between 1993 and 1995 and was cited by advocates for its "excellent coverage" and helpful "message control."[12]

A 1993 study found that families participating in the program's first year were generally very poor but were more educated and had higher educational expectations than families that did not participate. A subsequent study, conducted at the University of Texas–Austin, found that participating parents cited three concerns when rating the reasons they

---

gave to home schooling organizations, Christian state school board candidates, and organizations like the Christian Pro-Life Foundation and the Family Research Council. For a fascinating, if politically charged and critical, profile of the secretive Leininger, see Debbie Nathan, "God's Sugar Daddy," *San Antonio Current,* November 26 and December 2, 1998, p. 12 and p. 16, respectively.

12. For details, see Debbie Nathan, "Media Vouchers," *San Antonio Current,* November 26 to December 2, 1998, p. 15.

chose the school they did: educational quality, school discipline, and religious training.[13]

The program, which could provide scholarships to less than one-half of 1 percent of Bexar County's 200,000-plus K–12 students, was received calmly by local school districts and teachers' associations.[14] Several individuals prominent in local education were not even aware of the long-running program when interviewed during 1998–2000. Other observers agreed with the voucher advocate who said, "The 1992 CEO program really didn't have an effect on local school systems. The program was very small, and thousands of kids are dropping out every year in Bexar County anyway."[15]

In 1995, as part of an education reform law backed by Governor George W. Bush, Texas adopted the Public Education Grant, a measure intended to offer public school choice to students in low-performing public schools. Under the PEG program students attending any of Texas's more than 1,000 "low-performing" schools were permitted to transfer to a school in participating districts (until 1998 none of the school districts in Bexar County participated). Per pupil state funding, generally $4,000 to $5,000, followed each participating student. However, low parental and school district interest plagued the program, and only a handful of students participated. Further, participating schools often reported being overcrowded and unable to accept more students. Observers also reported that most schools exhibited little desire to attract eligible students, fearing that refugees from low-performing schools might prove an academic or disciplinary burden. There were also reports, in Bexar County and elsewhere, that superintendents had entered into gentleman's agreements not to poach upon one another's schools. Participation was also reduced by logistical and transportation challenges and by popular confusion about the program.

Texas authorized the state's first twenty charter schools in 1995, another hundred in 1997, and twenty-four more in 1998.[16] By fall 1998,

---

13. Dougherty and Becker (1995); Martinez, Godwin, and Kemerer (1995).

14. A CEO San Antonio official recalled, "The morning after the 1992 announcement, the media was calling superintendents trying to get critical quotes, and the worst they could find was the superintendent of San Antonio ISD saying that public educators should welcome the competition."

15. A union leader said that the program "had absolutely no impact on anyone. . . . It didn't worry anybody. If those people had a lot of money and they wanted to send kids to private school, God bless them."

16. For more detail on the history and evolution of charter schooling in Texas, see Fusarelli (1999, 2002).

Texas had authorized a total of 144 charter schools, sixty of which were open. However, in November 1998 the state board announced its intention to slow or halt the growth of charter schooling.[17] The announcement ensured that any potential threat was dampened. By the end of the 1999–2000 school year, there were only fourteen charter schools in greater San Antonio, enrolling about 2,500 students. Eleven of the schools enrolled fewer than 200 students, and most of the schools focused on serving at-risk populations.[18] Charters drew relatively little local notice through the spring of 2000, outside of the publicized difficulties of a few schools.[19]

The Horizon Program

The Children's Educational Opportunity Foundation posed a real competitive threat to the EISD when, on April 22, 1998, it announced that it would provide qualifying EISD students with scholarships to attend private schools. The Horizon program was to run for ten years, and $50 million in commitments ensured full funding for the life of the program. Jim Leininger committed 90 percent of the money; the remainder was contributed by the national CEO Foundation. Leininger's support in particular fueled outrage among local voucher opponents, who saw the program as a conservative attack on a community institution. By the end of the first week after the announcement, the CEO Foundation had received 402 scholarship applications.

The CEO San Antonio director, Robert Aguirre, recalled that the CEO Foundation selected Edgewood because it was small enough and poor enough that the CEO leadership thought the Horizon program could clearly illuminate the promise of school vouchers and demonstrate how the competitive effects of vouchers could compel a troubled school system to im-

17. For details, see Lucy Hood, "Board Tentatively OKs Request to Limit Charter Schools," *San Antonio Express-News,* November 12, 1998, online.

18. Charter School Resource Center of Texas (2000).

19. One union official said, "Not that many schools were granted licenses within Bexar County . . . and for the most part they have a very poor reputation. In some cases they are run by former public school teachers with a reputation for not really being able to do the job in the classroom, so how are they going to run a school? As a consequence, after the eyebrows were raised and a quick look was given, I don't think anyone saw this as anything really new." The point is not that a union official would bad-mouth charter schooling but that the perception that charter schools would be of low quality helped neutralize any threat they posed. For an extended discussion of this point, see Hess, Maranto, and Milliman (forthcoming b).

prove.[20] The decision to target Edgewood stirred intense conflict and prompted an outpouring of high-profile coverage in the local media, particularly the *Express-News*. Tensions would remain high for much of the next year. The CEO had not offered prior warning to the EISD or other local actors that it planned to launch the Horizon program. While the CEO did make outreach efforts to the EISD and made a point of sharing data on its participants, the lack of initial communication bruised some feelings, with one prominent local businessman terming it "rude" and saying that "it got the experiment off to a negative start."

All Edgewood families that qualified for the federal free or reduced-price lunch program were promised scholarships (in 1998–99, a family of four qualified if its income was less than $30,433). In 1998–99, the CEO received 2,202 applications and awarded 988 scholarships.[21] Families bore the responsibility for finding a school and gaining admission; the CEO would then pay all tuition up to the scholarship maximum—$3,600 for elementary and middle school students and $4,000 for high school students. For students who wished to attend schools outside of EISD's boundaries, the figures were $2,000 and $3,500, respectively. To spur the formation of new schools, the CEO would fund students attending new schools—whether or not the schools were located in Edgewood—as if they were attending school in the EISD.[22]

Some voucher critics claimed that scholarships were not sufficient to pay for tuition at most other local private schools, but this assertion was incorrect. The scholarships did cover full tuition at the vast majority of local parochial schools and at most local private schools.[23] However, the voucher did not cover associated fees (which ran as high as $670 a year in

20. For the official explanation of the decision to launch Horizon in the EISD, see CEO Foundation (2000, p. 7).

21. For detailed enrollment numbers and a full overview of the program, see CEO Foundation (1999).

22. Any school started after the launching of Horizon was to be perpetually regarded as a "new" school.

23. Average 1999–2000 tuition in inner-city San Antonio was $1,850 for grades K–8 and $2,350 for grades 9–12. See CEO Foundation (2000, p. 7). A sampling of tuition at local parochial high schools showed a figure slightly higher but generally consistent with these figures. For example, in 1998–99, Antonio High School charged $3,450 in tuition plus another $125 to $200 in fees; Incarnate Word High School charged $4,000 in tuition plus another $620 to $670 in fees; St. Gerard High School charged $2,650 in tuition plus another $485 in fees; Providence High School charged $3,500 in tuition plus another $600 in fees; and St. Francis Academy charged $2,070 in tuition plus another $350 in fees.

some local private schools), transportation, or uniforms.[24] Several private school principals explained that they could not afford to provide transportation and acknowledged that paying for uniforms might be difficult for some families.

In Horizon's first semester, fall 1998, it enrolled 837 children. Of those, 566 used the voucher to leave an EISD school and enroll in one of the fifty-four participating private schools. This group represented roughly 4 percent of EISD's 1997–98 enrollment. The remaining 271 recipients did not represent a direct loss to the Edgewood schools: 50 students had been enrolled in private school, 116 were starting kindergarten, and 105 lived in Edgewood but had previously lied about their residence in order to attend school in another district.[25] By spring 1999, 49 recipients had given up their scholarships and at least 21 had returned to the EISD.[26]

Interest in Horizon may have also been reduced by concerns regarding the stigma of a student being a "voucher kid" or by language barriers.[27] Because Edgewood is a primarily Spanish-speaking community, informing parents about the Horizon program was a challenge. Public awareness was reduced by the CEO's decisions to leave almost all advertising and outreach to the participating schools. The dampening effect on potential voucher participation weakened the threat Horizon posed to the EISD. The threat posed by competition is not simply a function of formal

24. As one Edgewood parent said, "I know several parents who took up the grants but are going to take their kids out of private schools. They found that the CEO money covered tuition but not all the extra costs: transportation across town, uniforms, and the weekly fund-raisers and demands for more money."

25. The 105 students who had been lying about their residence had been exercising "black market" choice, reflecting how badly some families wanted to avoid EISD schools. Without the voucher program, argued voucher proponents, EISD had no way of recognizing these individuals and therefore no incentive to address them. One proponent explained, "Lots of [families] are lying about where they live, because that's the poor man's choice. If you can't afford a home elsewhere, you lie about your residence. But school systems don't know about these people, they're invisible, they're below the radar screen. So one thing vouchers will do is that they will start to make these families visible and that may prompt district action."

26. For details, see CEO Foundation (1999). Also see Anastasia Cisneros-Lunsford, "Report Card Released on School Vouchers," *San Antonio Express-News,* February 9, 1999, p. 1A; Thaddeus Herrick, "Edgewood: After the Money," *Houston Chronicle,* November 24, 1998, p. A1.

27. One parent reported, "Some told me their kids were pointed out as the 'voucher kids.' Or they just felt uncomfortable being different. . . . All their friends, their teachers, everything they know are in this community." See David McLemore, "Voucher Program Tests Texas District," *Dallas Morning News,* October 18, 1998, p. 1A.

program design but also of marketing, logistical support, and cultural considerations.

EISD officials and educators feared that the district's more motivated or capable students would use vouchers to leave the system, hurting the district's performance on state testing, depriving schools of role models, and stripping EISD classrooms of their most enthusiastic students. Theirs was not the straightforward concern of losing market share but the fear that the schools would be less satisfying places to work and would lose public support. Regardless of whether skimming actually occurred, the point is that EISD personnel were worried about losing good students and that this concern helped spur the response that did emerge from the EISD. Demographically, voucher students looked like their public school counterparts but apparently performed at a marginally higher level. Harvard professor Paul E. Peterson (the same researcher who also conducted studies in Milwaukee and Cleveland) said that his team's research found no evidence that Horizon was "creaming" students but that there was some evidence of a modest selection effect. Critics such as Albert Cortez and colleagues disputed the Harvard team's claims.[28]

As in Milwaukee and Cleveland, the conflicting claims fostered public confusion about how to gauge the relative performance of the EISD and the private schools, rendering concrete EISD responses less fruitful and making symbolic or emotive appeals more likely.

Horizon and the Edgewood Independent School District

In 1998–99 official EISD enrollment was 13,336, a drop of 1,251 students (or 8.5 percent) from the previous year. About half of the loss was due to the voucher program (the other half was due primarily to housing renovation projects, which moved about 500 students out of Edgewood).[29]

28. According to the Peterson team, household incomes of Horizon students were similar to those of public school students. However, they also noted that the mothers of voucher students had completed, on average, twelve years of education, compared to eleven years for the mothers of public school students, and were somewhat more likely to be employed full time. Voucher students were slightly less likely to be in gifted programs and somewhat less likely to have learning disabilities than their public peers. Voucher students were slightly less likely to have limited proficiency in English (17 percent of voucher students, compared to 22 percent of EISD students) and on average outperformed their EISD peers on the TAAS. See Peterson, Myers, and Howell (1999); Cortez and others (1999).

29. Interestingly, elementary enrollment fell 9 percent while high school enrollment increased 8 percent. See Melissa Monroe, "Edgewood Considers Uniform Policy," *San Antonio Express-News*, March 10, 1999, p. 1H.

Because property-poor EISD relied heavily upon state aid and because state aid was based primarily upon enrollment, EISD officials feared the loss of substantial state funding.[30] In 1997–98 the EISD received about $4,900 per student from the state, or more than 80 percent of the $5,900 the district spent per student. Voucher critics pointed out that this meant that each departing student would reduce district revenue by about $4,900; voucher proponents countered that the district retained about $1,000 per departing student in other funding, while having one less student to teach. In 1997–98 the district received $67.9 million in state aid, so an 8 to 9 percent loss would cost the district roughly $6 million.

The significance of the losses depended on how the additional (or "marginal") cost of each EISD student was calculated. Neither the district nor its critics had reliable estimates of this figure. In claiming that the lost state aid would leave the EISD unharmed, voucher advocates pointed to a 1995 study by two University of Texas economists that argued that Texas districts would save 80 percent of the cost of a departing student.[31] Voucher critics disputed the study's assumptions and conclusions, though the opaqueness of EISD budgeting meant that interviewees were unable to provide precise figures for enrollment-driven costs or savings. In any event, Superintendent Muñoz opted not to cut personnel or services. Instead, the EISD used its $24 million reserve fund to cover shortfalls in 1998–99 and 1999–2000. By late 2000, this strategy had nearly eliminated the reserve. Meanwhile, the decline in district enrollment, combined with the absence of reductions in the teaching force, significantly improved the EISD student-teacher ratio.[32]

Horizon prompted little evidence of a substantive educational response from the EISD.[33] Instead, district officials and employees primarily reacted by lashing out at the program's advocates. While participating fami-

---

30. Texas school districts are funded on a weighted per pupil basis, with poor districts more reliant on state support than wealthier ones. Because the EISD was so poor, and because the Texas funding system (unlike that of Wisconsin) does not use multiyear average enrollment to allocate aid, the threat of substantial lost funding due to a drop in enrollment was a real and immediate concern.

31. Dougherty and Becker (1995).

32. One EISD administrator explained in fall 2000, "We're at 13,000 students . . . but we're staffed for 17,000."

33. Those seeking signs of competitive effects were forced to resort to reading tea leaves. The best example of this occurred after Muñoz stated in summer 1998 that the EISD would step up its efforts because officials were concerned that EISD exam scores would drop as high-scoring students entered Horizon. "I'm beginning to see very upset principals right

lies expressed immense enthusiasm for the program,[34] the EISD and its defenders were hurt and offended by what they perceived as a political assault by outsiders. Democratic state senator Gregory Luna of San Antonio charged, "This is another ruse to destroy public schools. The Edgewood ISD voucher program . . . declares war on public education."[35] A prominent voucher advocate characterized the district response as "one of anger and vituperation."

The EISD had long been regarded within San Antonio as isolated, due largely to its poverty, its lack of a local business community, its overwhelmingly Hispanic makeup, and the Garza-Escamilla dominance of school board affairs.[36] The split between EISD's local allies and the "outside" voucher advocates led the district, in the eyes of one observer, to "moat itself off." A prominent San Antonio Chamber of Commerce official recalled, "After the announcement I placed about a dozen calls to Muñoz and her people in order to talk to them about the CEO situation and to see what we could do, and they never gave me any response."[37]

---

now. We're going to have to redouble our efforts," she said. See Anastasia Cisneros-Lunsford, "Edgewood Loses 600 to Vouchers," *San Antonio Express-News*, August 14, 1998, p. 1A. Voucher proponents repeatedly pointed to such statements as evidence that competition was forcing the EISD to change, though they could offer no evidence beyond Muñoz's own claims. A similar 1999 story asserted that "district officials have been on the fast track to improve West Side schools and foster a more positive image," but presented no evidence or anecdotes to support the contention. See Anastasia Cisneros-Lunsford, "Report Card Released on School Vouchers," *San Antonio Express-News*, February 9, 1999, p. 1A. The irony is that those seizing on these statements were normally skeptical of EISD claims or promises.

34. See for example some of the quotations and profiles provided in CEO Foundation (1999, 2000) materials. For more extensive narratives, see McGroaty (2000, pp. 87–121).

35. David McLemore, "Voucher Program Tests Texas District," *Dallas Morning News*, October 18, 1998, p. 1A. One EISD parent bitterly commented, "I hope CEO can sleep with a clear conscience. How dare they stab us in the back, after how hard we've worked to finally get somewhere."

36. For instance, when the San Antonio Chamber of Commerce began hosting lunch meetings for superintendents, Edgewood superintendent Muñoz was the only superintendent to repeatedly skip the meetings. A local professor of education observed, "If I gave you a nickel for every time Dolores Muñoz said she would participate in something and then canceled at the last minute, you would be a rich man."

37. The district was often suspicious of reporters and outside researchers, refusing to cooperate with at least two sets of outside researchers and leading one local journalist to observe, "The district has really adopted a defensive posture." When Edgewood refused to participate in Horizon-related studies, one board member explained, "Edgewood has been used as a guinea pig too long." See Anastasia Cisneros-Lunsford, "Edgewood Voices Opposition to Study," *San Antonio Express-News*, November 18, 1998, p. 1B.

Shortly after the program was announced, more than 200 parents jammed an April school board meeting to demand more information on the program and decry its effects. On August 25 the EISD school board passed a resolution condemning vouchers and ran an ad in the *San Antonio Express-News* voicing the district's opposition to the Horizon program.[38] Muñoz initially responded in a more measured tone. In late April she welcomed the competition, praised the philanthropic bent of the program, and pledged that the district would "redouble" its efforts. She said the district was up to the challenge, saying, "Edgewood is known as a united community. Our parents see the schools as the best for not only their children, but for the entire community."[39] Some board members viewed this response as inadequate—they wanted a more combative tone—but it coincided with initial internal projections that the EISD would lose no more than 150 students in 1998–99. That estimate was based in part on the fact that three private schools in the area—St. John Bosco, St. John Berchmans, and Holy Cross High School—reported having only about 150 seats available for new students.[40] By early July, however, updated figures led Muñoz's staff to project voucher-related enrollment losses closer to 500.[41]

With extraordinary public scrutiny attending the high-profile launching of the Horizon program, the EISD reaction took three forms in 1998–99. First, the district began to accept students through the open-enrollment PEG program. Second, officials sought to reassure the Edgewood community and San Antonio influentials that they had matters under control. Most noticeably, EISD leaders worked with voucher opponents to rally community sentiment in opposition to Horizon, increasing local attention to schooling and fostering a sense of crisis.[42]

38. The resolution condemning Horizon read, in part, "The CEO scholarships targeting the Edgewood students are not ultimately focused on the welfare and education of all students, but are intended to make a political statement that could be used to lobby the Legislature to use public money for private education."

39. David McLemore, "$50 Million Vouchers Offer Splits San Antonio District," *Dallas Morning News*, May 1, 1998, p. 1A.

40. Anastasia Cisneros-Lunsford, "Six-Year-Old Receives CEO Scholarship," *San Antonio Express-News*, June 18, 1998, p. 3B .

41. The CEO leadership claimed that a survey it conducted before launching Horizon indicated that there were about 2,000 available seats in Bexar County. However, a CEO official explained, "That 2,000 is deceptive, due to struggles with transportation and the size of the county. . . . The practical capacity, considering location in this part of town, we figured to be more in the 800 to 1,000 range."

42. The program launch also provoked activity in the broader community that had the potential to magnify the threat posed. For instance, the soon-to-open Lago Vista Apart-

Participation in the Public Education Grant Program

The EISD adopted public school choice in August 1998, just before school began, becoming the first Bexar County school district to accept nondistrict students under the state PEG program. Muñoz credited the decision to the drop in enrollment driven by the voucher program. By participating in the program, the district broke what one local administrator termed an "unwritten code among Texas superintendents" that it was inappropriate to "try to take someone else's students." The EISD estimated that approximately 200 new students entered the district through the program, largely to take advantage of the district's high school specialty programs, especially the new Fine Arts magnet school.[43]

The district's PEG program produced one particularly interesting conflict. The TAAS accountability system encouraged principals to try to boost their school's test performance, but there was no such incentive to boost school enrollment. Since PEG students were from low-scoring schools, principals at schools that might receive these students worried that the new students would drag down their schools' test scores. An EISD administrator explained, "Some of our principals are so hung up on student performance that, if they lose a [low-performing] student here or there, it doesn't bother them."

Reassuring the Public

The clearest sign of a coherent organizational response to Horizon was the EISD's efforts to enhance its community public relations. In fall 1998, the EISD made available a "parent training" document touting EISD services and accomplishments. One side of the document, entitled "Edgewood Accomplishments," offered parents the "Top 10 reasons to be proud about your schools." The other side, a more explicit response to the Horizon challenge, was entitled "Reasons to Choose Edgewood." The ten top reasons included "Buses take students to and from school everyday, at no cost to parents . . . [whereas] private schools do not provide free transportation" and "Students receive their required books at no additional cost. . . . Parents are included on an annual textbook committee that selects

---

ments advertised that their residents would be Edgewood residents and would therefore be eligible for CEO Horizon scholarships.

43. Observers also suggested that at least a few students enrolled in the EISD to avoid the San Antonio ISD dress code.

and approves books . . . [whereas] private schools charge for books and other materials and parents may have no input on the selection."[44]

In 1998–99 the district's newsletter, the *Edgewood News,* introduced a new page-two feature entitled "Why I'm Staying in Edgewood." In these short four- or five-paragraph discussions, EISD students explained why they preferred Edgewood schools to private alternatives. The entries were part of the district's persistent, if small-scale, effort to make its case using parents, teachers, and students.

Rallying the Community

The district leadership also took steps to reassure the local community, including hiring a management consultant, adopting school uniforms for elementary school students, and promising to keep the new Fine Arts Academy specialty school intact.

The district's decision to hire a consultant was cited by some as a response to Horizon, but an anti-Garza board member pointed out that Garza had proposed such a move during the 1998 school board campaign and a Muñoz confidant said there were plans to hire the consultant before the launching of Horizon. Two other sources suggested that the consultant was a pretext for forcing Muñoz out and was unrelated to Horizon. Board minutes shed no light on this question, and observers' accounts may be colored by political motives, so the truth is hard to establish.

In spring 1999 the board adopted white, khaki, and navy blue uniforms, effective for the 1999–2000 school year. Several observers reported that this decision had been under discussion for a while and that uniforms were being adopted by a number of districts across Bexar County.[45] "I think you'd have a real hard time drawing a connection between our allowing schools to adopt a uniform policy and the voucher program," commented one EISD official.

---

44. Other reasons for chosing Edgewood included "Edgewood has nationally recognized special education programs . . . [whereas] private schools rarely provide adequate special need programs," that "Edgewood schools . . . are required to administer the Texas Academic Assessment Skills tests . . . [whereas] private schools are not required to provide standard Texas tests—no accountability," and similar points relating to teacher certification, parental involvement, extracurriculars and summer school, school lunch programs, and so on.

45. Cecilia Balli, "Millennium's End Sees Changes," *San Antonio Express-News,* July 18, 1999, online.

Some argued that the publicity brought by the voucher program forced the board to move forward with the Fine Arts Academy, in spite of Manuel Garza's suggestion that it be converted back to a traditional neighborhood school. The glare of Horizon-induced publicity might have made board members leery of seeming to back away from educational quality. Other observers, however, said Horizon-induced pressure played a negligible role. A reporter said, "This was the crown jewel of their system. There was just no way that they weren't going ahead with it, vouchers or no vouchers. It would've been too embarrassing."

In the case of the Fine Arts Academy, as with the consultant study and school uniforms, it is impossible to determine with any certainty the degree to which it was a response to the Horizon program.

Political Developments

The most visible reaction to competition was political, as the introduction of Horizon created a sense of violation among Edgewood residents and left many eager to attack the program and its sponsors. Teachers' associations, civil rights leaders, community activists, and EISD officials led the opposition to Horizon. These groups, as well as the Edgewood public school community, did not view vouchers as an impersonal challenge but as a moral summons and an assault on a sacred trust.[46]

The reaction was in part a response to the manner in which the voucher program was launched and pursued by the CEO and its advocates. The fact that Horizon proponents were generally Anglo and did not live in Edgewood, while most EISD defenders worked or lived in Edgewood, fed a sense of grievance and a sense of being "picked on, again."[47] This is not

46. Feelings ran high among EISD employees and active district parents. Parents of voucher students publicly praised the program, but some community members considered it an assault on Edgewood. One EISD parent charged, "They're just trying to destroy the public education system, and they are making it by saying they are helping the poor. . . . Many jobs could be lost. People would be displaced. The neighborhood would go down." Another parent said, "It just makes my blood boil. How dare them. I'll do whatever it takes to help Edgewood, to speak against vouchers." An EISD employee raged, "I want to know where these men, these CEOs, get off. . . . When I first saw Walton's name on the list of the directors, I said, 'To hell with this man. I'm not going to go to Wal-Mart any more.'"

47. A twenty-five-year veteran of the EISD gave voice to the widespread sentiment of district personnel. After arguing that painful battles to reform financing and schooling were finally paying off, the teacher lamented, "I am dismayed to find a new antagonist contending with us. Wrapped in the deceptive cloak of parental choice . . . CEO attempts to siphon away Edgewood students to a 'better' education. . . . I was angered at the com-

to suggest that the Horizon program was without Edgewood-based or Hispanic supporters or that the opposition was not aided heavily by national unions and noncommunity allies, only that the public image of the political conflict was significant in shaping the EISD response. Because most of the Edgewood community rallied to the defense of the public schools, while the most vocal and organized advocates of Horizon lived outside the district, and given the Garza-Escamilla dominance of the school board, there was no local group around which Horizon advocates might organize.

The provoucher alliance included, among others, dissident leaders of the League of United Latin American Citizens, as well as leaders from the CEO, the TJF, the TPPF, and a few officials from local private schools.[48] However, lacking a coherent political infrastructure or visible leadership in the Edgewood district, this effort had largely petered out by early 2000. By late 2000 however, there were a few tentative signs that a more native pro-Horizon network was emerging in the EISD, with the encouragement of the CEO.

Teachers' unions led the opposition to Horizon. In November the NEA formally announced its intention to help the EISD market its schools, improve district performance, and fight voucher proposals. On December 11 the NEA held a closed rally for teachers, EISD personnel, and other supporters. The substantive role of the union was limited, however, by the lack of a collective bargaining agreement and the absence of a dominant local union.[49]

---

ments that heralded a 'new day' for 90 percent of our Edgewood students. I was personally offended in August when further opinions, masquerading as fact, denigrated the efforts of my colleagues and me. . . . I will not allow the improvements we make as a district, many of which have been planned for years, to be directly attributed to CEO competition." Voicing the distrust of private schooling and emotional attachment to public education shared by many colleagues, the teacher concluded, "I question the exclusive nature of private schools and wonder which of my students may be excluded. I, and other teachers in Edgewood, intend to teach all children."

48. In the first year or so after the launch of the Horizon program, about twenty-five members of the local coalition met every Friday morning, primarily to coordinate support for a state-level voucher initiative.

49. Some observers suggested that there were some signs of a substantive union response. A business community leader recalled a spring 1999 meeting at which Shelley Potter, the head of the local AFT chapter, raised issues of teacher quality and accountability. "I . . . said, 'Shelley, I have never heard a union official say anything like that. Why are you saying it now?' She said, 'If we don't improve the educational process, something like a voucher program is going to come in and take over, and just take it away from us.' So," the observer concluded, "there is evidence that the union is thinking differently."

In the fall Muñoz adopted an increasingly strident tone in response to the Horizon program. While her feelings were mixed, especially since the EISD would have to coexist with the voucher program, she was pressed by board members and community leaders to publicly oppose the program and its sponsors. By October 2 Muñoz was declaring—at a "pro–public school community forum" held at Gus Garcia Junior High School—"There are 13,300 students who are choosing Edgewood today and let me tell you something, those 700 [Horizon students] will be coming back."[50] On February 3 several organizations, including the Edgewood Classroom Teachers Association, the Texas State Teachers Association, and the NEA, sent more than a hundred Edgewood parents and community members to Austin to lobby against vouchers. On March 6 the Coalition for Equity and Excellence in Public Education hosted an antivoucher press conference at Fox Tech High School in the San Antonio ISD that included Muñoz and other local leaders. More than 250 attended, cheering a Democratic state representative who attacked vouchers as an "insult" to public schools. Such efforts invariably received prominent and favorable mention in *Newsline*, the monthly EISD employee newsletter, and in the EISD's *Edgewood News*.

Edgewood voucher opponents enjoyed some significant successes. They helped to stop the state legislature from adopting pilot voucher legislation in 1999 and created enough concern that a few influential local corporations, including the *San Antonio Express-News*, chose to stop sponsoring the CEO in early 1999.

Officials at schools participating in Horizon uniformly reported that none of this turmoil affected their relationships with the EISD. A private school official remarked,

> We have to work together with the public districts on a number of things, primarily the federal programs. We're constantly calling or communicating or meeting with them, and we never have problems. . . . The CEO program hasn't affected any of this. For instance, we're next to a couple of Edgewood schools. Sometimes we share parking lots, they share our playground and our field for physical education. . . . There have been no problems.

50. The assigned *San Antonio Express-News* reporter was barred from the rally, illustrating the distrust of outsiders that came to characterize the district response. See Anastasia Cisneros-Lunsford, "Edgewood the Focus of Public Forum," *San Antonio Express-News,* October 3, 1998, p. 1B.

Horizon and Systemic Change

EISD losses ranged widely among schools, from fewer than 1 percent of students at the 1,600-student Kennedy High School to 11.8 percent of the 95 students at the K–12 Jose A. Cardenas Center and 7.9 percent of the 458 students at Gonzales Elementary.[51] While the careful records shared with the EISD by the CEO made it possible for Edgewood to identify the schools losing students, both EISD officials and observers reported that there was no variation in response among the Edgewood schools due to lost enrollment.[52] In fact, in fall 2000, three years after the launch of the Horizon program, the new EISD superintendent said of his schools' principals, "It's a real challenge. . . . For the most part, even with vouchers here the last few years, principals haven't paid attention to the customer service dimension. . . . I don't think they really know how many kids leave their schools due to vouchers [as opposed to] leaving due to family situations or whatnot. So they haven't worried about vouchers here the last few years."

First-hand observers brushed off any suggestion of classroom-level changes attributable to competition. A reporter who covered the EISD extensively in 1998–99 explained, "They had enough troubles just making do and trying to get TAAS scores up. The only reaction I could find was in the PR and the rallies and the union statements." No principal had developed a schoolwide response or plan of action. "They haven't really thought about how to deal with the coming changes," she said. An elementary school principal observed that the voucher program "hasn't affected us much. We're trying to help the kids who are here. There's nothing we can do about [the program] or about the kids who leave, so we're just focusing on the kids we do have." The vice principal nodded in agreement, adding that several voucher students had returned to the school since the start of the school year.[53]

---

51. For the specific school-by-school figures, see Cortez and others (1999, pp. 16–18).

52. Only the CEO kept records on school-by-school losses. The EISD, like the MPS and the CPS, did not have a student-tracking apparatus in place to generate such figures on its own.

53. A local education professor who frequently worked with EISD personnel observed, "The thing is that the voucher program just doesn't seem to be a major concern for the Edgewood people. They have other priorities and other problems that absorb their attention." Said one EISD board member, "The teachers and administrators are already doing what they can. They were giving it their best before [Horizon]. . . . If anything, the time we've spent worrying about CEO . . . may have distracted . . . [us] from instruction."

A senior administrator indicated that only about one-fourth of EISD principals had increased community outreach and contact with parent groups. "These weren't the schools that are losing kids," the administrator observed. "These were the schools that were doing well anyway, but [the principals] saw the CEO program as a way to do new things and get their staffs to [cooperate]. The losses are coming from the other schools . . . where principals don't give a hoot, where they don't think [treating parents as customers] is their job."

Despite sporadic activity on the part of EISD administrators, there is little evidence that they were tackling EISD's systemic problems. For instance, a community outreach executive for a major corporation recalled approaching the EISD in September 1998 "to ask if we could help the district in any way, by raising funds or providing other assistance. . . . The superintendent [Muñoz] was very appreciative and mentioned [a multi-million-dollar grant proposal]. We said we'd be happy to help with it, and she said it was a priority and that they'd move on it promptly. . . . Finally, more than three months later, just before Christmas, they got us a proposal that was hard to follow and needed work. We asked them to revise it and present it again, but by the spring [of 1999] we still hadn't heard from them. I know they're wrestling with a lot, and I don't know the full story, but around here that just wouldn't be tolerated."

Similarly, in March 1999 the district received the $120,000 management study prepared by the Austin-based consultant MGT of America, Inc. The report was kept confidential for nearly a month. Recommendations included closing three elementary schools, reshuffling administrative responsibilities, eliminating three top administrative positions, and eliminating several custodial and bus driver positions. Savings from all proposals were projected at $3 million a year starting in 1999–2000. Muñoz quickly moved to dispel fears that any significant steps would be taken, promising that no one would be terminated and that no schools would be closed before 2000–01, at the earliest.[54] In the end, few of the MGT recommendations were ever adopted.

54. For details, see Anastasia Cisneros-Lunsford, "Three Edgewood Closures Suggested," *San Antonio Express-News*, April 20, 1999, p. 1B; Anastasia Cisneros-Lunsford, "School Officials Quell Concerns on Closing Edgewood Campuses," *San Antonio Express-News*, May 19, 1999, p. 3B.

Horizon and Supply Side Development

Edgewood provided an opportunity to see how a largely unregulated voucher program affected the development of private school capacity. The Horizon program did not depend on continued legislative support, it was not subject to judicial intervention, and its initial funding ensured that it would be in place for at least ten years. Moreover, the program did not require participating schools to accept all takers, to abide by state regulations, or to fill out extensive paperwork.

Prior to Horizon, private school capacity in San Antonio had been relatively stable for an urban area. The number of private schools listed in the San Antonio yellow pages rose steadily, from 69 in 1978 to 101 in 1986. Between 1986 and the mid-1990s the number hovered around 100, and in 1998 Bexar County had about 110 accredited private schools.[55] The CEO leadership looked particularly to Catholic schools. In 1998–99, the Archdiocese of San Antonio listed 40 schools inside San Antonio and another 9 outside the city. The 8 high schools in the city had an enrollment of about 3,300, while the 32 elementary schools enrolled approximately 10,200.[56] The 3 Catholic schools in Edgewood had about 150 seats available entering fall 1998, while the entire parochial school system reported about 1,000 available seats citywide.[57] A parochial official said, "We just don't have very much room, and I think just about all of that would be at the elementary level."

The superintendent for the San Antonio Archdiocese expressed support for the voucher program, even announcing, "If the demand is there, we're ready to expand existing facilities." At the same time, he cautioned, "But there are no plans to build new schools."[58] By spring 1999 a prominent parochial official reported that he was unaware of any of the parish's schools seeking to expand or to open new facilities. A private high school principal said, "We don't really have any interest in opening up a branch

55. Dougherty and Becker (1995, p. 22).

56. Figures reported in the "Catholic Schools Office, General Directory, 1998–1999," produced by the Archdiocese of San Antonio.

57. The figure reflected schools somewhat fuller than was typical of private schools across Texas. A 1995 statewide survey of eighty-six private schools found that they were at about 86 percent of capacity. See Dougherty and Becker (1995).

58. David McLemore, "$50 Million Vouchers Offer Splits San Antonio District," *Dallas Morning News*, May 1, 1998, p. 1A.

school. If you do, you have to have a whole new administration, really a second administration, a second this and a second that. It would not be practical or desirable." Of all voucher students, 53 percent attended Catholic schools, 38 percent attended nondenominational Christian schools, and the remainder attended a variety of Baptist, nonreligious, and even public schools.[59]

A leading San Antonio bank officer explained why expanding private capacity was so difficult.

> There's just not a local source of foundation or corporate money for expanding or opening schools. Really, the only place these schools can get the money is from their constituents. . . . The private schools I've worked with are better off without any debt. If you're trying to start a private school with debt, you're going to have a hard time unless you have a very strong sponsor, like a parish . . . and most parishes are pretty leery now of supporting parochial schools. They've all been burned on that.[60]

Initially, five schools announced an intention to open in fall 1998 in order to take advantage of the CEO program. In fall 1998 three of the five actually opened, enrolling 160 voucher students. By far the largest of the three new schools was El Sendero Christian Academy, located next to its parent 960-member church, El Sendero Assembly of God. Responding to parental concerns about local education, the church leadership decided in the late 1990s to open a small school. In spring 1998 the church moved into a new building, partly to provide space for the school. Although not located in Edgewood, the school is very close, and its officials made a point of informing Edgewood residents that their children were welcome and that tuition was set at the amount provided by the Horizon vouch-

59. CEO Foundation (1999, p. 10).

60. For instance, Holy Cross High School was well acquainted with that challenge. The school, which charged $3,300 for high school students and $2,530 for junior high students in 1998, increased its capacity to 542 in 1998–99 by adding a trailer, at a cost of $50,000. The school added 80 students in 1998–99, 37 of them voucher students. Holy Cross had recently added nine acres of land to its campus and was planning to build a coeducational facility to serve 1,100 students, but raising the necessary funding was proving difficult. In 1999 the facility was projected to cost $10 million to $12 million; that figure grew to more than $20 million by late 2000.

ers.[61] In fall 1998 the school's 300-member student body included 150 voucher students.[62]

The church subsidized the opening of the school, including the acquisition of items like furniture and two school buses, at a cost of about $100,000. In 1998–99, the church renovated the school to accommodate a larger student population in fall 1999 and even considered building a second school. The church drew on its established line of credit to finance expansion. "We've been here for forty-eight years, we've got credibility," explained one official, who said that the church's interest in expansion was rooted in its desire to offer as many children as possible an appreciation for Christ and his works. Another official added, "We're here for ministry."

The school featured strong discipline, with strictures that would not be possible in a public school. "We have no cussing, no fighting, no drinking; if they use drugs or liquor, they're expelled immediately. We don't tolerate anything," explained one school official. "We want to change kids. But if they have real bad records, we don't want them ruining the other kids. Most of the kids we accept change; if not, we expel them."[63] The contrast between the mission voiced by these educators—the need to build character and reclaim children's lives but also the belief that some children were "bad seeds" and might stand in the way of others—and the all-inclusive philosophy voiced by public school administrators was quite stark.

The two other new schools were much smaller, enrolling no more than about forty students between them. Both El Shadai New Hope Christian Academy and Family Faith Academy shared with El Sendero a missionary purpose. El Shadai, wedged into a run-down strip mall alongside Simply the Best Pro-Cuts, the closed-down Joe's Thrift Store, and the Arizona

61. Anastasia Cisneros-Lunsford, "Christian School Seeking Vouchers," *San Antonio Express-News*, May 1, 1998, p. 9B.

62. School officials estimated that the school accepted about 85–90 percent of applicants in its first year, a figure typical among the area's parochial and religious schools, and that it expelled fifteen students during the course of the year. The school was able to hire the necessary teachers due to the contemporaneous closing of two nearby schools. In 1998–99, teachers earned $22,000 to $32,000. Five of the school's eighteen teachers had taught previously in public or private schools.

63. Another official recalled some of the changes in student behavior and the parental appreciation it had garnered. "We teach them to respect their parents, authority, police— we get parents calling after a month or two to tell us how much their child's behavior has improved and how thankful they are."

Café, opened in fall 1998 with about fifteen students.[64] Family Faith Academy, a tiny school that started with only about twenty students, was in a building that had previously housed Chino's Ice House. Modeled along the lines of a Sylvan Learning Center, with students seated in cubicles, the school emphasized workbook instruction, allowing students to operate at their own pace.[65]

Public school advocates were highly critical of these kinds of schools.[66] There was some reason for skepticism. Both El Shadai and Family Faith Academy encountered significant problems and faced an uncertain future. Family Faith lost all but five of its students by spring 1999 and was taken over by a new administrator, who implemented the evangelical "School of Tomorrow" curriculum. El Sendero made changes in its school in the second year of operation amid concerns regarding teaching and academic performance.

Horizon provides three clear lessons regarding the development of market capacity. First, given the financial uncertainties and difficulties of opening a school, it is those with missionary zeal and sufficient resources that are most likely to make the effort. Consequently, the greatest potential source for choice entrepreneurs is among those either operating out of religious obligation or a desire to reap a profit. Second, the limited capacity and uneven quality of new schools may limit the competitive threat they pose. Third, given that the appeal of new schools may be based upon values or discipline rather than educational quality, it is not clear how strong the incentive will be for the public system to compete on the basis of academic instruction.

Horizon's Third Year

Since 1998–99 was Horizon's first year, it is useful to briefly trace a few key developments up through fall 2000. The visibility of the EISD and

64. The Horizon scholarships were essential to the creation of these two smaller schools. As one cofounder of El Shadai, who gave up a law practice to help start the school, acknowledged, "Did we go after the money? Absolutely. We couldn't have opened the doors without it. We started a few weeks ago with seven students and a vision. . . . Without the CEO grants, we couldn't do that." See David McLemore, "Voucher Program Tests Texas District," *Dallas Morning News,* October 18, 1998, p. 1A .

65. For a good description of the school, see Thaddeus Herrick, "Edgewood: After the Money," *Houston Chronicle,* November 24, 1998, p. A1.

66. Samantha Smoot, director of the Texas Freedom Network, a public school advocacy group, argued, "You can rent a room, hang out a shingle and call yourself a school in

Horizon fell considerably by fall 2000, as the media and the business community had other challenges and other school districts demanding their attention. Meanwhile, charter schools remained a local nonissue. None operated in Edgewood, and the handful in Bexar County—even the one operated by the former San Antonio Spurs' great George Gervin—attracted little attention.

In September 1999, after nine years as superintendent, Muñoz resigned.[67] Her move was widely viewed as a reaction to the new board majority, which earlier in the year had twice tried to reprimand her. There is no evidence that the voucher program played a role in her departure. In May 2000 the board replaced Muñoz with the thirty-eight-year-old Brownsville administrator Noe Sauceda, who was hired only after the board made certain he was willing to forcefully oppose vouchers, signaling that the board saw the leadership change as a chance to strengthen its resistance to the Horizon program.[68]

Also in September 1999 two EISD schools were rated as "exemplary" and four as "recognized" in the state's annual TAAS accountability ratings report.[69] The two exemplary schools—Hoelscher Elementary and Perales Elementary—were the first EISD schools to attain that status since Texas introduced its accountability system. The announcement triggered a dispute between voucher advocates and the EISD, with Horizon proponents claiming that competitive pressure generated by the voucher program played a role in the evident improvement, both by removing some low-performing students and by providing an impetus for change. A prominent voucher advocate said, "Even if someone disputes that the voucher program has caused Edgewood to improve, it is undeniably clear that the voucher program did not destroy public education in the Edgewood district. The program did not hurt the district in any way whatsoever." EISD

Texas. . . . Dangling $50 million out there makes the potential for fly-by-night operations great." See David McLemore, "Voucher Program Tests Texas District," *Dallas Morning News,* October 18, 1998, p. 1A.

67. For details, see Anastasia Cisneros-Lunsford, "Munoz Leaving District," *San Antonio Express-News,* September 10, 1999, p. 1B.

68. For a summary of the convoluted process by which the EISD hired Sauceda, see Cecilia Balli, "Edgewood Search Took Odd Twists," *San Antonio Express-News,* May 6, 2000, online. An individual who witnessed the board's initial interview with Sauceda recalled, "When the board asked about vouchers, [Sauceda] said that they weren't necessarily a bad idea, that there could be some merit there. It wasn't until . . . [Sauceda] indicated he was open to a harder line that it all worked out."

69. The TAAS has four ratings: exemplary, recognized, acceptable, and low performing.

supporters, however, scoffed at such assertions, credited the results to ongoing efforts, and pointed to the fact that the EISD had to cover budgetary shortfalls by drawing down its emergency reserve, meaning that it would soon have to cut staffing and services.[70]

In spring 2000 the Escamilla-Garza machine lost its control of the school board when its ticket was swept out of power by the Family Alliance, a group associated with the EISD attorney. The four new board members, who had received campaign assistance from the three hold-over trustees, won their races by margins ranging from 6 to 22 percent.[71] The voucher conflict played a relatively small role in this contest, with both sides expressing heated opposition to the outsider incursion represented by vouchers. However, some observers thought the added attention that the Horizon program brought to the EISD helped the Family Alliance slate to make the case that the board was plagued by inefficiency and corruption.

In 2000–01 Horizon enjoyed a dramatic expansion in enrollment. After plateauing in its second year, enrollment grew to over 1,300 in the program's third year, due in part to approximately 100 prekindergarten students, who enrolled when the CEO extended the scholarships to this group, and to a sizable increase in K–12 enrollment.[72] Despite the defections to Horizon, however, total EISD enrollment at the beginning of 2000–01 was up more than 1,000 students from fall 1999.

In fall 2000 there was one significant addition to private schooling, the Christian Academy of San Antonio (CASA), which enrolled more than 200 students (with a projected capacity of 600). Its principal, Yolanda Molina, a former Northside ISD principal, was variously described as "exciting," "charismatic," and "highly motivated" by educators, observers, and reporters. The school boasted resources beyond those of most private schools, including a staff of fully certified teachers and multiple sports

70. A senior EISD administrator privately termed the CEO claims "absurd," and EISD administrators argued that school changes had begun several years previously. For instance, at Perales Elementary, Sharon Dougherty had been named principal several years before and had reportedly made a sustained effort to transform the school. See Lucy Hood, "Voucher Program Boasted," San Antonio Express-News, August 28, 2000, p. 1A.

71. Cecilia Balli, "Family Alliance Sweeps Remaining Board Seats," San Antonio Express-News, May 7, 2000, p. 18A.

72. Enrollment growth was largely driven by word of mouth. Media attention to the program was down from 1999–2000 and the CEO consciously chose not to take responsibility for advertising the program. The CEO leadership left advertising to the participating schools, which reported lacking the resources to mount an aggressive advertising campaign.

facilities. The new school could afford these due to backing from supporters affiliated with Jim Leininger.[73]

Meanwhile in the public schools, budget restraints heralded changes.
A top EISD administrator explained that in the next year or two the
district's eroding financial position would force it to scale back or eliminate the cost-intensive academies and to begin implementing some of the
school closings and cost-cutting measures recommended by the MGT
analysis. "Look," he said, "it's hard to close a school or cut a program.
That's not what [we do] . . . until the money is gone, or until we have no
choice."

Conclusion

Five significant lessons can be derived from the Edgewood experience.
First, a public school system does not necessarily react to the financial
pressure of choice schools by reducing services, laying off personnel, or
closing schools. Edgewood opted instead to make up any shortfalls out of
its reserve fund and to simply push back the eventual day of reckoning.

Second, competitive capacity is only partially a function of program
design. It also depends upon the capacity of local private schools and
upon their ability to expand capacity. In Edgewood most new private
schools were sponsored by organizations with either a religious or a
profit-seeking motive. The organizational difficulties of starting or expanding a school—not the least of which is financing—suggest that only
bodies like churches, community organizations, and private firms are
likely to be inclined to launch schools of any size. Further, the headaches and challenge of starting a school may dissuade potential entrepreneurs unless they are motivated by goals that transcend the simple

---

73. The school building and close to eleven acres of surrounding land were purchased
for $690,000 in June 1999 by the Vineyard Foundation, a nonprofit real estate holding
group that was hastily formed in 1998 to protect a private school when its land was put up
for sale. Although Leininger did not serve on the Vineyard Foundation's board of directors, he was reported to be a prominent contributor. Several individuals who sat on the
boards of Leininger-backed organizations served on the foundation's board. The Vineyard
Foundation was created to buy properties, fix them, and then lease them to charter or
private school operators. For more discussion of Vineyard and its involvement with CASA,
see Cecilia Balli, "Neighborhood Pins Hopes on New School," *San Antonio Express-News*,
July 10, 2000, p. 1A.

provision of instruction—such as the satisfaction of having accomplished God's work or the possibility of reaping sustained profits.[74]

Third, given the tools at the disposal of school board members and school system leaders and given their need to respond rapidly and visibly to political pressure, much of the competitive response is likely to take the form of political protest and mobilization directed at proponents of school choice. This will be particularly true in a context such as Edgewood's, where the school system is central to the community and where choice-based reform is seen as being promoted by outsiders with partisan or ideological agendas. The steps that the administration did take tended to be self-executing board directives, to have symbolic import, and to be targeted at producing quick increases in enrollment.

Fourth, a school board isolated by political machinery, unthreatened by a community provoucher coalition, and composed of unpaid board members will be less inclined to respond to competitive threat.

Finally, choice-induced competition can refocus attention on the performance of the public schools and the local educational agenda. The voucher dispute in Edgewood helped clarify public school goals and had the potential to provide political cover for difficult management decisions. Much as in Milwaukee, debates triggered by the program raised the profile of school quality and helped to focus local attention on measured classroom performance. This focus was fostered by the presence of the TAAS testing regime, which offered a clear and easily grasped (if hotly debated) scorecard for district performance. As one high-ranking EISD administrator wryly noted in late 2000, "The voucher program makes it easier to rally support for what we have to do; we can blame them when we have to make hard choices."

In the chapters that follow, I attempt to put the lessons of Milwaukee, Cleveland, and Edgewood in comparative perspective, and then see what policy lessons one might draw from these experiences.

---

74. An Edgewood observer recalled a 1999 meeting in which a few dozen veteran teachers were told that the Horizon program meant they now could launch a school of their own. Nearly all the teachers reportedly greeted this invitation with sighs and rolling eyes. As the observer recalled, "They focused on all the impediments, from finding a facility, to getting financing, to hiring a staff, to recruiting students." Only the most driven or messianic of educators are likely to desire to build a school from scratch for little or no personal gain, with no institutional support from a school system, and with little security or support.

EIGHT   *A Political*
Market

COMPETITION IS OFTEN IMAGINED as a mighty bull-
dozer, flattening ineffective firms and compelling others to become more
efficient and effective. In the cases of the Milwaukee, Cleveland, and
Edgewood public school systems, however, there was little evidence of
such change. The effect was more muted and more oriented to public
opinion than the market metaphor might anticipate.

One must be cautious about interpreting the limp response evident in
these three school systems. Choice proponents, in particular, might con-
clude that the limited reach and scope of these early choice-based programs
prevented market pressure from emerging. However, scrutiny of the most
significant responses may uncover the faint outlines of the responses that a
more ambitious choice program would be likely to produce.

This chapter summarizes the themes that emerged from the cases presented in chapters 4 through 7. Most change was driven by politically
motivated officials wrestling with balky systems. Seeking to offer some
response to a public challenge but unwilling to frontally challenge the
status quo, elected officials and school system administrators sometimes
resorted to empowering intrinsically motivated entrepreneurs to exploit
new opportunities within the school systems. There was no evidence that
competition bulldozed away inefficiencies or forced systemic efforts to
reform policy or improve practice, as officials had neither the incentive
nor the ability to mount aggressive assaults on organizational culture or
procedure. However, under sufficient duress, the leadership of the Milwaukee Public Schools (MPS) chipped small holes in the system's bureau-

197

cratic facade, and through those holes sprang a handful of entrepreneurial educators.

The effects evident in Milwaukee, and to a lesser extent in Edgewood, were not the substantive changes anticipated by claims that competition makes public systems "better." Unlike the radio industry in the 1920s, the electronics industry in the 1960s, the airline industry in the 1980s, or the financial services and telecommunications industries in the 1990s, these organizations did not react quickly or aggressively to competition. There is, however, evidence that competition can provoke significant change in public school systems.

The response of public school systems to competition is politically determined, while the extent and nature of this response is restricted by institutional and organizational limitations. When seeking to promote more radical, visible changes, system officials had incentives to abandon efforts to compel cooperation and to instead rely upon the self-directed efforts of hard-charging subordinates. Consequently, it is crucial to consider the role of intrinsic motivation in shaping the school systems' responses to competition and in determining the growth of competitive capacity.

Common Themes

The threat posed by choice-based competition in the three school systems tended to be future oriented and vague, making it anticipatory rather than immediate. Competition did produce changes in both the political environment and school system behaviors, but competition did not force the Milwaukee Public Schools, the Cleveland Public Schools (CPS), or the Edgewood Independent School District (EISD) to substantially alter system governance, management, or operations. As one nonpartisan Milwaukee observer summed up the situation in 1999, "If you're asking, in terms of the whole period since 1990 . . . 'Do vouchers affect what happens in 38th Street Elementary School or Maryland Avenue School?' then no. Those teachers have thirty kids in their classroom just like they did last year, just like they did ten years ago. They still teach the same way. [Vouchers] haven't affected what they do."

There was little evidence of system administrators attempting to increase organizational productivity or efficiency. Only when they believe that outcomes will be accurately assessed, can be readily controlled, and will be used to evaluate their performance do these leaders have incentives to disregard politically inspired compromises and organizational angst and to endure the risks associated with a ruthless emphasis on performance. These conditions rarely hold in urban systems, and introducing choice-based competition does not change that fact.

The three school systems did exhibit a tendency to launch popular programs, advertise themselves and their services, and lash out at their competitors. In Milwaukee and Edgewood a political counterweight to the teachers' union emerged. When caught in the glare of public frustration, Milwaukee's union demonstrated some willingness to relax procedures. Under duress, MPS officials sought to enhance public relations and offer more appealing services; MPS defenders also attacked system critics in an effort to undermine their legitimacy. In Edgewood the attack on the system's critics was far more evident than were efforts to enhance customer satisfaction.

Individual educators tended to be confused about the differences between vouchers and charters, about the specifics of the plans, and about the way they impacted the public school system. In all three school systems, educators generally explained that they were too busy with their daily tasks to pay attention to school choice or to change their practice in response, while expressing anger that choice advocates would dare to attack the community's public schools. Market proponents suggest that these responses are irrelevant, because educators will be forced to respond—busy or not. Such an analysis fails to account for the underlying context in which competition plays out.

Because competition depends largely on producers reacting to anticipated—not just existent—threat, insulation from sanctions may leave educators able and willing to ignore pressure. Educators have at times exhibited a lethargic response to other incentive-driven reforms, such as merit pay and career ladders. In each case, a lack of teacher enthusiasm and the inability of officials to sanction noncooperation has blunted the effectiveness of such programs.[1] Selective incentives are effective only if employees are willing to work for the incentives or are afraid to forgo them.

Educators' hostility to choice-based reform is significant because public educators have substantial resources of legitimacy and goodwill upon which to draw. If they answer competition by marshaling public opinion or mounting legal challenges, they may win statutory or judicial protections that lessen the threat posed by choice programs. This type of politi-

---

1. For instance, Brandt (1990, p. 160) notes that when teachers were asked to explain their disinterest in career ladder programs, many said, "I'm already too busy."

cal response is disconcerting to those who see markets as irresistible and as a means to bypass the frustrations of education politics.

In the three districts, organizational protections and routines insulated system officials and educators from competition. An antivoucher MPS board member explained, "The bureaucrats who come out of the schools of education don't intend to be affected by competition. They are going to concede 5,000 students, or even 25,000 students, simply because they are insulated within the walls of a bureaucracy that need not respond to competition." The claim is not outrageous. Given the rules, regulations, contracts, and statutes governing competition, educators had the luxury of "refusing" to respond.

In Milwaukee and Edgewood market pressure prompted the emergence of political coalitions that enhanced a sense of education crisis and spurred efforts to respond appropriately. Edgewood's political insulation and the absence of a local reform coalition limited the substantive consequences of this pressure. In Milwaukee the pressure led to school system and union decisions that eased the way for entrepreneurs to provide new schools, new services, and—ultimately—potentially radical leadership within the MPS. These political developments also clarified the education debate, nurtured a coalition committed to radical reform, and fostered clear partisan divisions that enabled the community to more readily hold board members accountable for proposals and their effects.

Marketplace Constraints

The effects of competition appear both weak and surprisingly political. This is due both to the nature of education as a market good and to the very limited threat confronting the school systems studied. Conventionally, producers respond to competition by more effectively identifying and servicing distinctive market niches. School systems can do this by offering programs and services tailored to particular tastes and needs. The problem for school systems is threefold. First, their inability to charge more money limits their ability to offer designer programs. Second, it is difficult to design and faithfully implement appropriate efforts in the face of bureaucratic and organizational constraints. Third, differentiating services can trouble those committed to a vision of common public schools.

When school administrators seek other, nondivisible responses more consistent with the provision of a uniform service, they find it difficult to satisfy communitywide preferences. In the short term, it is very difficult for urban officials to significantly improve systemwide outcomes on measures like reading scores and graduation rates.[2] Outside of such measures, however, it is not always clear what the public considers evidence of improvement. Even if a particular outcome improves, observers may discount the results if other measures do not show similar improvement. Meanwhile, proposals that seek to boost efficiency or performance by closing schools or cutting services generate heated opposition and attract little or no support.

More generally, schools have multiple missions—from serving special-needs children to preparing students for college to providing vocational training—and officials are often uncertain how to balance these obligations. Leadership turnover and public impatience for improvement discourage long-range approaches and may induce officials to focus on visible, proactive measures.

School system officials are concerned not only with retaining customers but also with satisfying the broader political community. Caring about the satisfaction of both consumers and nonconsumers, officials find media coverage highly salient. While families care primarily about the performance of individual schools, the community gauges the relative performance of the entire system. If the system appears reasonably effective, or if choice-based alternatives appear ineffective, community support can safeguard district funding and blunt efforts to expand the choice threat. In Milwaukee, Cleveland, and Edgewood reporters, influential community leaders, and public officials were unable to sort through or assess competing scholarly claims about the merits of choice schooling.[3] As a result, proponents were unable to marshal clear evidence that choice schools outperformed public schools, muddying the program's prospects and blunting the pressure on public schools to react.

Several elements of the 1990s urban school context weakened the threats that administrators could wield to compel cooperation in the schools. With school systems facing high rates of teacher turnover and a possible teacher shortage, there was little danger that lost enrollment would lead to the firing of teachers. Moreover, steady enrollment growth and problems with

---

2. See Hess (1999, pp. 30–58).

3. A reporter explained, "You academics have these tiers of journals, these debates over who has the better sample or model, or whose papers are more legitimate. . . . And you make all of these subtle distinctions based on all of this. Well, I'll tell you what, when I'm writing a story I don't have the time or training to sort through all of this. So there's really no way for me to make clear which side has a stronger case."

aging and cramped facilities meant that these systems were amenable to seeing some number of students enroll elsewhere.[4] In communities with declining enrollment, those without facilities concerns, or those with low rates of teacher turnover, the enrollment threat will weigh more heavily.

Moreover, by design, the choice programs launched in Milwaukee and Cleveland were constrained in a number of significant ways. The programs capped the number of vouchers granted, set restrictions on private schools that wished to participate in the program, and operated in school systems experiencing enrollment growth and a facilities shortage. For much of their history these choice programs were in legal peril. The incentive for private schools to participate in the Cleveland program was limited by Ohio's decision to fund the voucher at a very low level. Legislative and judicial decisions kept religious schools out of the Milwaukee program until 1998, and charter schooling was largely insignificant in Milwaukee until 1997. Consequently, neither the CPS nor the MPS faced a significant monetary threat before 1998. Moreover, in 1999 the Wisconsin legislature amended state financing in a manner that weakened the threat choice programs posed to the MPS.

The growth of the Milwaukee and Cleveland programs was also slowed by logistical obstacles and by opposition from the education establishment. For instance, private school operators in Cleveland reported that CPS's foot-dragging on transportation and on sharing student records created major problems.[5] Similar concerns were voiced regarding the role of the Wisconsin Department of Public Instruction in Milwaukee.

Edgewood faced an uncapped, private, and richly funded voucher program. Combined with EISD's reliance on state aid, the program posed a significant potential threat. In practice, a number of factors limited the actual threat. Informing Edgewood's poor, largely Spanish-speaking popu-

---

4. In large part, this was due to the fact that the 1990s happened to mark the high tide of the "baby boomlet," the period during which children of the baby boom generation (born 1946–64) reached school age.

5. In some locales (although relatively uncommon in the school systems examined here) reported practices have included harassing charter school employees, spreading malicious rumors about charter schools, and denying facilities to charter school operators. Public schools have occasionally refused to accept transcripts from charter schools, and charter school teachers have reported being excluded from their professional networks by their public school colleagues. Public school systems have sometimes blamed cuts in popular services, such as art and music classes, on fiscal pressure brought on by competition. For anecdotal evidence, see Hassel (1999); Hess, Maranto, and Milliman (forthcoming b); Loveless and Jasin (1998).

lation of the voucher program was no easy task. Officials of Children's Educational Opportunity (CEO) chose not to mount an explicit advertising campaign on behalf of the Horizon program, leaving that task to the private schools, even though these schools lacked the resources for an aggressive effort. Substantial economic and cultural attachment to the EISD meant that many district residents supported the school district without regard to measurable educational outcomes. Logistical problems ranging from transportation limitations to school fees also limited the number of EISD parents able or willing to use vouchers. Finally, there was limited private capacity in the Edgewood area. Potential entrepreneurs were intimidated by the resource and managerial challenges. In the end, religious organizations and educators provided the main source of interest in developing capacity.

Political Developments

Political conflict is endemic in urban school systems. While Progressive Era efforts to depoliticize schooling by centralizing and bureaucratizing urban school systems left them largely free from conventional partisan elections and debate, conflict over resources, positions, and influence is not so easily whisked away.[6] Without the organizing influence of partisan conflict, active, organized interests rarely face coherent opposition. Most prominent among these interests are employee unions, which have concrete and enduring interest in school system governance. Moreover, in the thirty-some states with collective bargaining, union influence is codified in often stringent contracts.

In Milwaukee and Edgewood, voucher-induced conflict raised the profile of education and intensified the existing sense of urgency. Concerns about low achievement, dropouts, and so on can become routine when school systems are in an ongoing crisis. Voucher proposals posed a radical, fundamental challenge to the status quo, reframing the debate and mobilizing public sentiment. Voucher proposals took the question of school reform from the technical domain of whether certain reforms work to the more visceral question of whether the public schools could be saved.

The political and emotional dimensions of the debate over public schooling proved central. Most urban school boards are formless collections of

6. For the classic account of the creation of contemporary urban school systems, see Tyack (1974).

amateur and nonpartisan members, over which a few concentrated and attentive constituencies—primarily employee unions—exert great influence. Factions tend to be personal and their agendas informal, making it difficult for the community to hold board members accountable for their actions or to empower a coherent board majority.[7] By offering a rallying point for critics of the MPS and the EISD, vouchers helped birth a countervailing force to employee unions. In Milwaukee, where open school board seats, a broad and stable coalition, and financial and organizational resources created favorable conditions for the provoucher alliance, system politics were fundamentally altered. In the EISD, where the board was insulated by political machinery, where the provoucher coalition relied on non-Edgewood support, and where the political resources evident in Milwaukee were lacking, the impact was much less direct.

The Politics of Grievance

Once choice programs were seen as threatening, school system personnel lashed out at choice advocates, challenging the legitimacy of choice programs and the motivations of supporters. Political complaints and emotive appeals are not what one thinks of as typical market responses. In most private sector activities, such efforts offer little of value, except when firms jockey for legislative or judicial protections or when small businesses try to tap into community sentiment as a strategy to combat large new competitors.[8]

Public school systems, however, are able to draw upon the public school ethos that links communities and their public schools in something approximating a civic religion. While taking steps to reassure the community that school improvement efforts are under way, district officials have incentives to rally public sympathy by representing choice advocates as enemies of democratic schooling. The public's commitment to community schooling in principle becomes a commitment to the school system in particular.

One advantage enjoyed by public good providers in rallying sentiment is that supporters need not use the product to join the crusade. Although

---

7. For an extended discussion of how the absence of established parties makes political accountability more difficult, see Key (1949).

8. For instance, small retailers often compete against new, lower-priced superstores (such as Wal-Mart or Home Depot) by appealing to customers on the basis of community ties and sentiment.

consumers of divisible goods must buy the product to support the producer—even if it means paying more to shop at the neighborhood grocery than at the new superstore—community members can support a collective provider without using the service. They can instead supply support through protest, agitation, and voting. In the case of schooling, voters can express support even if they are childless or enroll their children in private schools.

Traditional civil rights community leaders in both Edgewood and Milwaukee described voucher advocates as racist and rapacious ideologues. In Milwaukee, teachers threatened not to work with employees at the University of Wisconsin–Milwaukee when that university announced that it would start to authorize charter schools. However, such attacks were more difficult to pursue in Milwaukee, where school system travails received sustained publicity and where the provoucher coalition was community based and included prominent black leaders, a Democratic mayor, left-leaning school board members, and the established business community. In Edgewood, where the most prominent voucher advocates were Anglo American and conservative and did not live in Edgewood, voucher opponents found the vilification strategy more effective. In the EISD, more limited media attention and the isolated nature of the district reduced the intensity of the spotlight and permitted the established business community to sit out the dispute, depriving voucher proponents of a crucial political ally.

In Cleveland the surfeit of other activity, the state takeover that left public officials free to disregard community opinion, the limited nature of the voucher program, and the lack of a coherent provoucher coalition meant that the defenders of the CPS never needed to adopt a mobilization strategy similar to that of their counterparts in Milwaukee and Edgewood. Moreover, the legal challenges to vouchers in Cleveland—as in Milwaukee—dampened the concerns of public school defenders and reduced their incentive to mobilize supporters.

The Paradox of Strong Unions

The voucher threat, and the political activity it unleashed, spurred employee unions and civil rights groups to mount a vigorous defense of the public system and the status quo. These groups sought to defend the hard-won protections and policies they held dear. In making their case, employee unions in particular were forced to defend their commitment to effective schools. The central purpose of any union is to advance the interests of its members, whatever the effects on organizational performance. Union leaders who drift from this purpose soon find themselves replaced.[9] However, it is not in members' interests that the unions go so far that they undermine or destroy an employer. Consequently, unions have an incentive to moderate their demands when doing so is essential to an employer's long-term prospects. Traditionally, in education, advancing the interests of union members has meant battling for interests common to all teachers, such as enhanced security, procedural protections, heightened autonomy, and higher pay. These protections insulate educators, regardless of their performance, and leave school systems less agile and more bureaucratic. Strong unions are then blamed for leaving producers inflexible, inefficient, and rule bound.

In Milwaukee, the emergence of vouchers changed the definition of what was in the interest of Milwaukee Teachers Education Association (MTEA) members. The collective interest of union members depends on preserving the legitimacy of the employer and the political fortunes of the union. When the public school system and its teachers come under scrutiny, it is in the teachers' interest that the union appear responsible. If the union does so, it can bolster members' long-term welfare by strengthening its own position and enhancing the system's legitimacy. In the absence of a strong union, no individual teacher has any incentive to sacrifice protections in the name of the collective work force. Not only would individuals be making sacrifices that would far outweigh their small share of the collective benefit, but the ability of a few individual teachers to affect public attitudes toward the entire work force is limited. Weak or fragmented unions will have difficulty overcoming the collective action problem and may be unable to take symbolically potent actions.

A strong union resolves these collective action problems by spreading the burden of concessions among its members. It can attract significant publicity, which it can wield in the court of public opinion. An established union with a recognizable public visage can readily claim credit for any sacrifices it makes and can count on trading on that in the future. The

9. This does not mean that union leaders are unconcerned with children but that their job is not primarily to protect the interests of students. Just as the head of the United Auto Workers is concerned with protecting the interests of workers who manufacture cars, rather than those of the people who buy cars, the head of a teachers' union is employed to advance the interests of the membership and not of the children who receive the service that union members provide.

result is that strong unions have incentives to offer concessions on particular material or procedural concerns when they think that the improvement in the reputation of either the school system or the union will advance the broader interests of their members.[10] This is the calculation that explains the MTEA's concessions on issues ranging from school staffing to contract school relationships. The lack of intense public pressure in Cleveland meant that the union had no need to make similar concessions.

The case of Edgewood highlights the paradox of strong unions. The absence of collective bargaining in Texas, the fact that no one union dominated the public stage, and the general weakness of the teachers' associations meant that no one organization had the ability or incentive to grant visible concessions to the EISD. Of course, the EISD was subject to less pressure than was the MPS for other reasons, so it would be a mistake to attribute too much of the difference between the Edgewood and Milwaukee cases to the union's role. The point is that, *other things equal,* strong unions have the incentive and the ability to partner with school system officials when the system's legitimacy is at stake. Paradoxically, the competitive pickax is likely to prove more effective at knocking down procedural and contractual constraints in systems with strong unions.

The Administrative Response

In response to vouchers, school system administrators increased, to a greater or lesser degree, their public relations efforts. While this response looks similar to the advertising engaged in by traditional private sector firms, the difference is that—except in the case of firms fearful of government intervention and therefore desirous of cultivating public opinion (as with producers of pharmaceuticals or alcohol)—private sector advertising is focused on attracting customers. School system outreach generally seeks to assuage the public—including both customers and noncustomers—and to cultivate political support. For private sector firms, advertising is part of a larger effort to maximize profitability, while for public organizations it is a tool to preserve community and legislative support.

A variety of outreach and public relations efforts were evident in Milwaukee and Edgewood, and hints of such efforts emerged in Cleveland.

---

10. The observation that significant changes in collective bargaining occur as the result of such deals is a familiar one. King (1993, p. 61) notes, "Most breakthroughs in labor relations are the products of a 'deal made at the top,' in which the union president and the superintendent agree."

Measures included using flyers or radio to advertise their services or performance, trumpeting toughened standards, adopting new slogans, and increasing efforts to publicize the choices available within the public system. The MPS adopted the motto "High Standards Start Here" and emblazoned it on large banners hung on every MPS building. Administrators at some MPS schools distributed t-shirts and flyers, a few high school principals made more of an effort to visit junior high schools to recruit students, and a handful of MPS schools turned to radio or newspaper advertising. A former Milwaukee superintendent observed, "Our student services divisions are trying to become more customer friendly," with "longer and more convenient hours" and simplified forms and registration. "They're trying to accommodate the public's needs, their requests, but still within board policy."

Such outreach efforts were limited, for a number of reasons. First, all school system officials were not convinced that seeking to retain or recapture enrollment should be a central concern. A Cleveland administrator said, "I believe our job, our only job, is serving the students in our schools. It is wrong for us to shortchange the children in the schools because we're busy trying to win over families that choose to send their child elsewhere." Second, school officials did not know where they were losing students, why students were departing, or what would prompt them to stay. In Milwaukee, for instance, system insiders estimated that perhaps 5,000 students moved per month and that one-third of the student body in a typical school turned over in the course of a school year due to poverty and unstable home situations. This natural turnover diffused the impact of choice-based exit. Only in Edgewood, where the CEO shared its records with the EISD, did public educators know exactly which schools were losing students to a choice program. Finally, even if officials knew what steps to take, unlike their private sector counterparts, they had little incentive to act and few tools with which to operate. Administrators did not fear losing their jobs due to lost enrollment; they were far more concerned about managing the staffing and ongoing practices at dozens of district schools.

School officials did fear the loss of community support and the wrath of the state legislature. When school choice prompted renewed attention to the public schools, as in Milwaukee in 1995 and 1998–99 and in Edgewood in 1999, officials took steps to reassure the community and quell criticism. The most popular public system responses were added programs, new schools, and new opportunities for entrepreneurial teachers and principals. For instance, when dramatic expansion of the Milwaukee voucher program was before the Wisconsin legislature in 1995, the MPS board rapidly approved the launching of several themed, innovative schools, which were freed from many regulations. Such behavior was less evident in Edgewood and Cleveland, where the competitive threat was relatively mild, but has been widely reported in previous research.

Some measures offered school officials a simple way to add enrollment and forestall the erosion of the public school system's position. In Milwaukee the MPS got into a bidding war with the city over a contract school to ensure that its 500-odd students would count toward district enrollment; and in Edgewood, after the Horizon program was launched, the EISD started accepting open-enrollment students, a largely symbolic step but one that sent the message that the system was not cavalier about competition. These reactive steps suggest that school officials were concerned with the loss of potential funding and would take steps to combat a clear and immediate threat. Such steps were simple, visible, and aimed at avoiding large and noticeable declines in enrollment. Perhaps most significantly, they did not force administrators to change practice in the city's schools or classrooms.

In Milwaukee, where school system efforts were spearheaded by a reform board faction and were met with cooperation by a strong union that stood to make political hay for its concessions, they proved significant. Similar efforts were milder in Edgewood, while they were little in evidence in Cleveland.

The publicity and political coalescence produced by the Milwaukee voucher plan led school officials to relax some statutory and cultural norms, affording entrepreneurial personalities new opportunities. Officials won union cooperation on changes that relaxed staffing procedures, making it easier and more inviting for principals and teachers to launch new programs. This avoided the need to compel behavior while ensuring that crowd-pleasing schools and services would emerge. A handful of entrepreneurial school-level leaders who had previously struggled with the bureaucracy seized this opportunity, using the leverage generated by choice to obtain new resources and operational freedom. Only a few educators fit this mold; most who did had been previously regarded as oddballs and marked as suspect for their entrepreneurial streak. Crucially, these entrepreneurs were not spurred to action by the promise of personal rewards. Rather, they continued to do what they had always done but now found opportunities where they had previously encountered obstacles.

To Catch a Thief

Why would system leaders suddenly embrace employees they had long disregarded? Because they are neither equipped nor inclined to compel reluctant employees to take action, self-interest impels them to capitalize on the efforts of intrinsically motivated employees when they need to deliver evidence of school-level change. Rather than forcing ranks of resistant subordinates to change, system leaders can co-opt educators who wish to do more. Much as an unconventional lawman may suddenly seem useful when authorities are charged with apprehending an unconventional criminal (thus the expression "it takes a thief to catch a thief"), so do administrators enlist the efforts of unorthodox educators who were previously marginalized for being "difficult." When the MPS administration found itself vulnerable, it turned to the spirits who had bridled under the system's conventions and promoted change by permitting the most strident to become champions of the public schools.

Markets typically encourage entrepreneurs to invest time, energy, labor, and creativity through the promise of material rewards. While inventors, founders, and builders may derive great psychic rewards from their efforts, the market presumption is that these intrinsic rewards alone do not drive entrepreneurial activity. For instance, a programmer who enjoys tinkering with computer code will not necessarily immerse herself in an effort to design or refine software for others, even after she had designed a useful application. There is no reason to believe that the inventor would selflessly focus on providing what potential customers will find appealing, hire others to work on the product, build a production and distribution apparatus, or market and continually improve her product. Even if she enjoyed creating the product, it may take the promise of selective rewards to prompt the programmer to undertake the less appealing tasks necessary to make her creation useful and publicly available.

Imagine the committed educator who finds his work a labor of love and who throws heart and soul into teaching and planning. His professional freedom is limited by statute, system procedures, and school organization. Official policies may prevent him from acquiring nonstandard teaching materials, from using preferred pedagogical approaches, or from exercising a specific brand of discipline. Traditional school management prohibits him from modifying the length of class periods, adopting a mixed-age grouping, teaching only students who respond to his methods, or ensuring coordination across courses. These restrictions limit the educator's ability to operate in the fashion he thinks appropriate, rendering the job less rewarding. When this educator seizes the opportunities offered by newly relaxed system rules or procedures, it is typically to escape such burdens, not to reap material benefits.[11]

So it is for those who found innovative or charter schools. Their intrinsic rewards are the ability to run a school as they see fit, to assemble a staff of like-minded teachers, to focus on a shared mission, and to attract like-minded students and families. Education entrepreneurs generally earn no extra money and receive no selective perks, nor are there material rewards for attracting a large number of students or running a highly regarded school. Meanwhile, these enrepreneurs invite additional work and new uncertainties.

Markets characterized by bulldozer competition do not just permit entrepreneurial activity but also use selective rewards to encourage it. In the public sector, however, introducing competition loosens the barriers to innovation but does not necessarily reward or encourage entrepreneurs. In general, observers and administrators in the case cities estimated that no more than 20 percent of administrators were comfortable operating with heightened autonomy. If that figure is taken as an upper bound on the number of current principals likely to found new schools, then the challenge posed by a reliance on intrinsic motivation becomes clear. Teachers as well as principals may serve as entrepreneurs, but their numbers are limited and they lack the managerial experience that principals possess.

The elimination of barriers created new opportunities for entrepreneurs to take action and made the job more rewarding for them. However, reducing barriers does not provide systemic rewards to entrepreneurs, encourage other individuals to engage in entrepreneurial behavior, or actively recruit entrepreneurial talent into the profession.

Education Entrepreneurs

Absent extrinsic incentives, why do people become education entrepreneurs?[12] Those motivated by the traditional rewards—money, prestige, or

11. For an analysis of entrepreneurship in the public sector, see Schneider, Teske, and Mintrom (1995), especially the discussions of "the psychology of the entrepreneur," pp. 71–74, and of "bureaucratic entrepreneurs," pp. 147–152. For an overview of entrepreneurship and the skills it requires, see Mintrom (2000a, pp. 70–112).

12. The question of why individuals choose to become education entrepreneurs is analogous to the question that confronted Mintrom (2000a) in his study of policy entrepreneurs.

perks—have little incentive to become educators in the first place. For those who do become educators, most public systems currently offer little to stir their entrepreneurial inclinations. The result is that education entrepreneurs are generally impelled by intrinsic incentives. This has significant implications for how school systems respond to competition.

In the course of this research it became evident that intrinsic motivation is a crucial part of the story and that it takes the form of three distinct impulses among educators: *work embracing, mountain climbing,* and *missionary.* Two key questions emerge for policymakers. First, what percentage of today's educators are entrepreneurial or might be induced to become education entrepreneurs? Second, among these entrepreneurs, what is the relative prevalence of the three impulses? These questions, to which research has only the most imprecise answers, will prove crucial going forward.[13]

Mintrom noted that there are many possible sources of such motivation but did not pursue the issue further. The discussion here provides one approach to the question of motivation.

13. The three impulses are not unique to education but may characterize public service entrepreneurs more broadly. The following example, far removed from the classroom, is drawn from Peter Perl, "Building Inspector with a Bulletproof Vest," *Washington Post Magazine,* June 27, 1999, pp. 8–30. James Delgado, one of thirty-two building inspectors in Washington, D.C., had expanded his nominal job of ensuring that buildings meet the city code into a license to take on corner stores selling drug paraphernalia, chop shop garages, prostitution operations, and after-hours nightclubs. A City Council member remarked, "If you just turned Delgado loose in your neighborhood for a month, you could clean it up."

Despite his impressive record—or because of it—Delgado's personnel folder, although bulging with commendations from government agencies and civic groups, was bereft of promotions, honors, awards, bonuses, or merit raises from his employer, the Department of Consumer and Regulatory Affairs (DCRA). Like the public school system, the DCRA is a public agency charged with multiple missions and is vulnerable to influential political constituencies. DCRA officials prefer employees who follow procedure to those who risk conflict in their pursuit of results. Some supervisors viewed Delgado as a reckless "cowboy." Even after Delgado had several run-ins with armed felons, the DCRA refused to issue him a bulletproof vest, because to do so would have violated policy.

Nonetheless, even after being assaulted five times, threatened with violence, and the subject of more complaints than any colleague, Delgado kept kicking in doors. Why did Delgado make these extraordinary efforts on behalf of employers that ignored and belittled him? Why did he struggle against a tide of dealers and absentee landlords, when new ones only sprang up? He made these extraordinary efforts not for his employers, or even because he thought he could solve these problems, but because he believed in the sanctity of his task. He said, "I truly believe God has granted me this mission." He loved the work and embraced "with messianic fervor" the task of bringing "hope to neighborhoods."

However, Delgado planned to take early retirement in 2000. "The only reason I would stay is if they cared enough about this city to say, 'This is really a viable solution for poor

The Work-Embracing Impulse

The work-embracing educator is motivated by the rewards that inhere in professional practice. Such educators are compensated for their efforts in the currency of enjoyment.[14] These educators love their work but often feel stifled by the public bureaucracy and will seize opportunities to create environments that permit them to enjoy their work more fully. Many charter schools are born of this impulse, as were most of the innovative schools launched in Milwaukee.

The work-embracing impulse is unconcerned with profits, reaching large numbers of students, or gaining renown. Work embracers seek a school community in which teachers can interact with children as they see fit, count on parental support, work with colleagues with common values and beliefs, and teach in their own way. When routine bureaucratic and administrative burdens weigh too heavily, these educators may decide that the trouble of starting a new school or program is well worth the opportunity. The schools and programs they launch are generally small and are generally started by like-minded teachers. The founders and faculties have no interest in expansion or franchising, because the goal is to develop a small and committed learning community. Thus work embracers are unlikely to generate significant new competitive capacity.

The Mountain-Climbing Impulse

Rather than deciding that the opportunities of starting a school outweigh the costs, mountain climbers think that the challenge itself sounds like fun. A certain number of teachers engage in writing elaborate model curricula, in organizing exotic field trips, or in sponsoring time-consuming clubs because they enjoy the task. Some educators opt to start a program or a school simply because they enjoy creating or shaping something new. These individuals make use of the new opportunities produced by competition, but their activity is likely to produce only a limited expansion in capacity. The number of mountain climbers willing to make

---

communities.' . . . If they cared enough to do that, I would be glad to stay." Delgado's experience poses key questions: What summons the Delgados of the world to public service? How many Delgados are there? What keeps their fire burning? How can policymakers and administrators stoke that fire? And how do those efforts interact with efforts to unleash competitive markets? These questions are addressed in chapter 9.

14. See Sornson and Scott (1997).

an extraordinary commitment simply because it seems fun appears limited.[15]

The Missionary Impulse

The missionary's prime concern is doing good works. Just as a religious missionary seeks to save as many souls as possible, an education missionary tries to reach as many children as possible. The educators at El Sendero in Edgewood sought to bring Christ to students, those at Milwaukee's Highland Montessori sought to cultivate love of learning, while those in the Hope schools in Cleveland preached discipline and knowledge. Missionary educators may have varied understandings of what it means to "reach" or "save" children, but they share a desire to make a difference in children's lives. Missionary educators look beyond the walls of their schools, and they hire and train new faculty so as to reinforce and extend their own good works.

Missionaries are driven by a belief so strong that they willingly undertake costly activity in order to share that belief. Religious missionaries leave home, endure ridicule, and accept the rebuffs of nonbelievers because they believe that the souls they save are worth their suffering. Other than love of the job or love of the challenge, however, what motivates a public educator to undertake similar efforts? Desiring to teach children is rarely enough to spark a selfless crusade. Rather, public educators become missionaries when their devotion is not only to their students but also to the larger ethos and purpose of democratic schooling.

Some teachers are passionately committed to the democratic ethos of community, diversity, and shared citizenship. These educators see school choice as a threat not because they are worried about personal loss, but because it threatens a system they cherish. These entrepreneurs are certainly responding to the market, but they do not seek the rewards that the market offers. In fact, they are often opposed to the notions of incentives and consumerism central to market-based reform. Competition spurs those individuals to take proactive steps in order to forestall private alternatives, but their insensitivity to market incentives means that market incentives can do little to guide or shape the nature of their efforts.

---

15. This is particularly true when one considers how difficult, costly, and frustrating it is to launch a new school. For discussion, see Finn, Manno, and Vanourek (2000, pp. 100–17); Spencer (2000).

These educators are striving to advance a passionately held ethos. Consequently, they are unlikely to adopt strategies that violate their ethical precepts. Educators committed to the public school ethos resist targeting privileged children or offering programs focused on the high performers, even though such programs can convey substantial competitive advantages.[16] This self-imposed professional code limits the problems that choice-based reform might cause, keeps such educators committed to helping all children, and focuses educators on working with the students they have rather than on assembling a more ideal student population. Unfortunately, the ethically scrupulous educators and schools are at a disadvantage when confronting competitors more concerned with selective incentives than with professional codes of conduct. Over time, a system driven by extrinsic incentives is likely to reward those educators who focus on delivering consumer satisfaction at the expense of those who seek to advance abstract conceptions of the public interest.

Missionaries, Mercenaries, and Private Sector Capacity

Educational competition requires that a meaningful threat arise to challenge the public system. Such a threat requires both that nonpublic entrepreneurs have the opportunity to emerge and that individuals seize that opportunity. The size of the pool of private entrepreneurs limits program capacity, regardless of statutory or logistical limitations.

Currently, as in the public system, nonpublic educational entrepreneurs are also offered few extrinsic incentives. Voucher and charter school reimbursement rates are generally low, so those involved in running these schools claim neither enhanced compensation nor materially enhanced work environments. For-profit schooling offers a way to boost extrinsic incentives—by permitting investors to reap a financial windfall and by permitting entrepreneurs to tap the equity markets—but cultural biases against for-profit education, the uncertain road map to a financially successful enterprise, and the still-minuscule size of the for-profit K–12 sec-

---

16. For an excellent discussion of the hostility of conventional public school ideology to distinctive, or niche, schools, see Hill (1999, pp. 149–52). The principal of one of Milwaukee's innovative schools said, "Why don't I try to attract the high-SES [socioeconomic status] kids? Hell, that kind of defeats the whole purpose of what we're doing here. . . . You might as well ask why I don't kick out [the students] who are having trouble. The whole reason we're here is to help every kid. . . . And I like to think we're trying the hardest to help the kids who need the most help."

tor have so far limited its impact on education markets.[17] Of course, a significant expansion of for-profit schooling may radically alter this calculus.

Absent selective incentives to promote private sector education entrepreneurship, the expansion of private capacity rests on the same sources of intrinsic motivation that spur public educators. The result is that private capacity expansion is also constrained by the pool of intrinsically motivated individuals, the general preference for small schools, and the lack of interest in opening branch campuses or aggressive expansion.

Relying upon work embracers or mountain climbers to expand capacity is problematic. They intitiate extraordinary efforts only because they expect to enjoy either the effort or the fruits of the labor. Under the best of circumstances, entrepreneurship is exhausting and consuming. The more demanding or procedurally burdensome it is, the more likely it is that such entrepreneurs will decide that the rewards are not worth the cost. Especially given the razor-thin administrative staffs at most private schools and charter schools, even modest increases in paperwork or regulation are likely to reduce the extent of entrepreneurial activity.

Most of the interest in expansion is found among religious educators interested in proselytizing or doing "good works." Of course, much choice-based reform is constrained by concerns about maintaining the "wall" between church and state. Charter schooling prohibits religious activity, while voucher programs often exclude religious schools, limit permissible religious activities, or require that schools permit students to opt out of religious instruction. All of these measures will significantly constrain the expansion of capacity if they dissuade religiously minded entrepreneurs from opening new schools. If the costs and demands of starting a school are too daunting, even missionaries may decide they can best accomplish their works in ways other than running a school.[18] In the absence of reli-

17. In January 2000 there were only about 200 for-profit K–12 schools, with a combined enrollment of about 100,000 students. See William C. Symonds, "For-Profit Schools," *Business Week*, February 7, 2000, pp. 64–76.

18. As one Milwaukee private school administrator recalled, "When I came in . . . I was the seventh director in eight years. . . . The job just burned people out. We were providing what we felt was a quality education program . . . on grant dollars and volunteer time. People were volunteering, working for practically nothing, doing what amounts to missionary work in a sense." He continued, "If there was a group with some money out there for employability training, we were an employability training program. If there was money out there for pregnancy prevention, we became a pregnancy prevention program. We kept changing . . . to fit the needs of funding sources. . . . You can only do for a certain

gious involvement, it is difficult to cultivate competition beyond a certain point unless extrinsic motivation is utilized.

Many people enjoy teaching or working with children. That does not mean they enjoy managing a physical plant or coordinating field trips or keeping books. Typically, private sector entrepreneurs tackle these chores because they are materially or professionally compensated for their efforts. Currently, education does not provide such extrinsic compensations. In their absence, education entrepreneurs emerge and operate only as long as their intrinsic incentives outweigh the costs incurred.[19] When administrative activity makes running a charter or voucher school more difficult, time consuming, or frustrating, the development of competitive capacity will be retarded.

Conclusion

The response to choice-based competition in Milwaukee, Cleveland, and Edgewood proved to be generally mild, political in tone, focused on bolstering public support, driven by intrinsically motivated volunteers, and designed to avoid forcing unwilling employees to alter routines or procedures. Choice critics observe these outcomes and suggest that competition does not work in education, while advocates see these outcomes as evidence that competition has not yet had a fair trial or as proof that fundamental change is looming. In truth, the nature of education markets—as they currently exist—means that the primary effects of competition will be political. In the case of the MPS, the competitive shock was large enough and the political context was sufficiently receptive—due to the presence of a strong union, a responsive school board, and a provoucher community infrastructure—that the political response drove real changes.

When pushed to act, system leaders operate with few tools in a resistant and ambiguous environment. This creates an incentive to pursue reforms that do not require confronting entrenched constituencies. As a result,

---

period of time before you burn people out. They burned a lot of people out because not only were they the principal, the education leader, a teacher, and sometimes the janitor but they also had to do the book work, the fund-raising, and everything else. So good people came through the program but they couldn't stick with it. I could see early on that I was going to burn out as well."

19. For a systematic analysis of the schools that emerge under choice-based reform, see Mintrom (2000b). Mintrom examines the incidence of innovation among the 138 charter schools operating in Michigan in 1999, shedding light on who started charter schools, the programs they designed, and how they managed the schools.

the most common responses are increasing outreach and public relations or relaxing organizational constraints so that potential entrepreneurs can provide new programs and services. Ironically, these entrepreneurs are motivated by largely the same impulse as drives those who are expanding capacity outside the public system. The key distinction is that the most committed public entrepreneurs are missionaries for the public school ethos, while those outside the system are often pursuing a religious mission.

Given this reality, how might the forces of competition be strengthened? What would be the likely consequences of such an effort? And what might be the possible side effects? These questions are considered in chapter 9.

NINE

You Say You Want

a Revolution?

I do have a graduation thought to pass along to you. Whatever career you may choose for yourself . . . let me propose an avocation to be pursued along with it. . . . Make a career of humanity. Commit yourself to the noble struggle for equal rights.

MARTIN LUTHER KING JR., 1959 address to rally
prior to the Youth March for Integrated Schools

The point is, ladies and gentlemen, that greed, for lack of a better word, is good. Greed is right. Greed works. Greed clarifies, cuts through, and captures the essence of the evolutionary spirit. Greed, in all of its forms, greed for life, for money, for love, knowledge, has marked the upward surge of mankind. And greed, you mark my words, will not only save Teldar Paper but that other malfunctioning corporation called the USA.

GORDON GEKKO, fictional financier, address to
a shareholder meeting in the movie *Wall Street*

MIGHT COMPETITION SUCCEED where successive waves of well-intentioned school reform have failed? Can the market squeeze out inefficiency, unleash creative energy, and drive systemic improvement in the nation's public schools?

This study suggests that the initial competitive effects produced by the nation's first voucher programs were modest and subtle. Competition did not rapidly bulldoze away inefficiencies or drive systemic improvement in teaching and learning; nor did it lead school systems to revamp governance, management, or operations. In Milwaukee, however, it showed hints of loosening bureaucratic procedures and organizational routines,

219

driving incremental publicity-oriented change, fostering significant political developments, and producing new opportunities for entrepreneurs. These results are properly understood not as simple precursors of dramatic change, but as evidence that the political pressure unleashed by choice programs will yield complex outcomes. The lesson is not that markets cannot drive more profound change in education but that such effects will require changing the institutional and organizational context of urban schooling.

Though competition is billed as a way to reform bureaucratic, inefficient, unfocused urban public school systems, it is not clear that its introduction will be enough to exercise important procedural and professional constraints on these systems. The structure of the marketplace and the nature of the competing producers will prove pivotal. Policymakers can foster market competition by enhancing competitive capacity and by shifting education consumption from a collective to a divisible model. Similarly, they can help school systems compete more effectively by streamlining system governance, increasing the motivation of executives, empowering the system leadership, and taking steps to alter the nature and composition of the teacher work force. In short, making competition work as intended will require much more than the simple introduction of market mechanisms.

Policymakers will have to uproot the constraints they have imposed on the nascent educational marketplace and on school systems. Other constraints, those due more to circumstance than to policy, will have to be addressed more patiently and creatively. Ironically, many of the factors that have stymied earlier reform efforts, lending luster to the promise of choice-driven reform, may hinder market operations. Choice-driven competition is not a one-shot solution to addressing the ills of urban education but requires complementary efforts to reshape the targeted school systems. This observation should not come as a surprise to anyone who has witnessed the painful efforts to import markets into Russia or Eastern Europe after the collapse of the former Soviet Union, but its relevance is rarely acknowledged in the school choice debate.

Such a conclusion is fundamentally at odds with a tenet long held by many choice proponents, the powerful claim that choice-based reform will radically remake schooling, obviating the need for more conventional efforts to improve schooling.[1] If policymakers were willing to abolish public

---

1. Chubb and Moe (1990, p. 217) proposed that, "without being too literal about it, we think reformers would do well to entertain the notion that choice *is* a panacea . . .

school systems and create a free and open market in education, then there is a strong case to be made for the claim that markets alone would drive radical change. However, such measures are not under consideration.

In truth, the larger case advanced by sophisticated choice proponents is subtle and largely consistent with the analysis offered here. For instance, John Chubb and Terry Moe famously argued that the structure of private schooling clarifies school-level goals, makes it easier to monitor school performance, empowers administrators and teachers, and keeps educators attuned to the needs of their clientele.[2] In other words, the authors suggest that, *within the private sector,* markets *produce* the ancillary changes required to make competition effective. In the context of private schooling, the complementary changes required to make competition work are presumed to follow *automatically*. On the other hand, when school choice is introduced as a public policy intended to subject public schools to competition, the continued presence of state-imposed, political, and legal constraints ensures that such changes are anything but automatic.

Chapters 1 through 8 have examined how the introduction of competition affects urban school systems, asking what effects emerged, what factors shaped those effects, and what these portend for the future of education competition. Market advocates too often seize upon tentative results as a way to forestall critical consideration of how education competition works. Choice critics make the same mistake, too readily interpreting evidence of isolated problems as proof that markets will not or cannot work in education. The present study has not equipped me to judge whether policymakers should embrace competition or whether market forces will make urban schools "better." Such determinations ought to await the development of a fuller body of research and analysis. In short, I am sympathetic with those who suggest that it is too soon to evaluate the impact of these nascent voucher programs. However, I suggest that such complaints miss the larger lessons to be learned and that there are three fundamental choices to make regarding the promise of educational competition.

Effective policymaking requires understanding the nature and import of these three choices. First, we could abandon efforts to harness markets and concentrate on improving schools through other reform approaches.

---

choice is not like other reforms and should not be combined with them as part of a reformist strategy for improving America's public schools. Choice . . . has the capacity *all by itself* to bring about the kind of transformation that, for years, reformers have been seeking to engineer in myriad other ways."

2. Chubb and Moe (1990).

Second, we might embrace the uneven promise of constrained competition, as it now exists, and hope that effects will grow along with a developing competitive threat and evolutionary changes in the urban systems. Third, we might move aggressively to harness the potential of bulldozer-style competition, relying upon either a free market model or a model premised on a clear vision of accountability. This chapter seeks to develop a framework for assessing the merits of competition, the kinds of education markets we might construct, and the implications of each approach.

Four Challenges to Market-Driven Improvement

Imagine a private sector producer whose consumers disagree about what kind of product they want; who depends on the support of both consumers and nonconsumers; whose executives are largely unable to evaluate, hire, fire, reward, or sanction employees; and whose product is hard to judge. Any executive—whether Henry Ford, Jack Welch, or Bill Gates—would struggle in the face of such odds. Organizations, whether private or public, will compete only when they have the will and the ability to do so.

When proponents of market competition see intimations of things to come in the reactions of the Milwaukee and Edgewood school systems, they overlook the fact that markets do not necessarily infuse organizations with the will or the ability to compete. Conflicting goals will not melt away, leaders will not suddenly possess the tools they need, and employee motivations will not undergo a metamorphosis. Public school systems cannot unilaterally escape constraints rooted in legislative decisions, cultural norms, and the nature of schooling. These constraints can be loosened, but such change will come at a cost. If policymakers wish to increase the effects of competition, they can do so in four general ways.

Degree of threat. First, an effective marketplace requires the presence of a significant competitive threat. In the absence of meaningful competition, producers must fear the emergence of competitors. If producers' fear of the potential threat is small, or if they have the luxury of choosing not to respond, competition will have little effect. Unless there is the potential that competitors can steal large numbers of clients, unless clients are able and willing to switch providers, and unless lost clients result in real losses, public systems will have little to fear.

Executive motivation. Second, public school systems are guided by political, rather than economic, logic. Public officials are driven to win popular support, not to maximize profitability. The difference is crucial, as public officials will take steps that bolster the legitimacy and popular standing of their organization rather than those that necessarily yield a cheaper or "better" product. They will be loath to challenge organized, attentive, and influential constituencies, even when doing so may enhance organizational performance. Unless the inert majority becomes attentive and offers support for officials who challenge entrenched constituencies, public officials have little reason to do so.

Product ambiguity. Third, the market context of education is different from that in which the vast majority of producers operate. Disagreement about the definition of *quality* and ambiguity over how to assess outcomes make it difficult for large districts to forge agreement on what constitutes improved performance. This makes it difficult to benchmark and measure the performance of either the system or individual employees.

Leadership tools. Finally, urban school systems are highly constrained organizations. A lack of effective oversight and isolated classrooms leave teachers well equipped to resist administrative direction. Meanwhile, administrators have few tools with which to compel cooperation or coerce desired behaviors at the school level. The result is that teachers are largely free to act as they see fit, as long as they do not violate procedural or legal guidelines. This yields schools that rely heavily on professional dedication and intrinsic motivation to produce desired outcomes.

Sharpening the Pickax

Given these four constraints, what are policymakers to do? One option is to continue to promote competition without altering the broader status quo. Such a course is akin to embracing the pickax and forgoing efforts to unleash the ruthless, competitive bulldozer. This course will spur symbolic responses (and political counterattacks on system critics) and will chip away at the procedural impediments that stifle intrinsically motivated entrepreneurs.

To opt for the pickax approach is to place great faith in the desire of educators to "do well by doing good" and to accept the primacy of the public school ethos and intrinsic motivation, while rejecting the notion that educators should be motivated by self-interest or schools driven by market imperatives. The objective is to loosen the bureaucracy and to stir innovation, permitting entrepreneurial energy to flourish. If policymakers wish to continue to embrace the pickax, two kinds of changes are worth considering. The first addresses the need to turn up the competitive heat on school systems, which will heighten the political pressure on systems to take action. The second is to empower administrators while relaxing organizational constraints on entrepreneurial activity.

Creating a Marketplace

The scope and nature of school system response will depend in large part on the degree of competitive pressure. Executives will feel compelled to take action only if the immediate or potential threat is sufficiently fearsome.

The threat posed by choice plans has generally been mild. Voucher programs, due to limited private school capacity, program caps, statutory restrictions, and persistent legal challenges, have not threatened public school jobs or budgets. Meanwhile charter schools are generally small, are often subject to extensive regulation, and often target at-risk populations that public educators find onerous. Some choice programs, like those in Milwaukee and Cleveland, were crafted to limit the revenue lost by the impacted system. Policymakers can accelerate competition by increasing the number of choice schools, the size of these schools, or the financial loss that public systems suffer when they lose enrollment. Expanding the size of voucher and charter programs will involve more than just lifting the caps on these programs; it will also require private or public sector efforts to develop the capacity of choice schools.[3]

Early efforts to launch choice schools benefited from the ability to draw upon a large supply of frustrated educators and an array of funders eager to demonstrate the viability of school choice or to fund new models of schooling. However, although philanthropies are happy to seed models or promote new initiatives, they are generally much less willing to support ongoing operations. In addition, the opening of more than two thousand charter schools has siphoned many disgruntled teachers from the traditional public schools. The growth of competitive capacity may slow as shrinking foundation support, a smaller pool of dissatisfied educators, and the spread of supplemental resources over more schools make entrepreneurship less viable.

Currently, capacity limits the threat that choice schools pose to public school systems. For instance, while charter schooling has grown by leaps

---

3. For a thoughtful discussion on enhancing the supply of choice schools, see Hill (1999).

and bounds in recent years, with more than 400 schools opening in both 1999 and 2000, in 2001 voucher and charter programs of all stripes still enrolled only about 1 percent of the nation's students. Increasing competitive pressure demands a substantial increase in either the number of new schools or their size. The rate of charter school expansion has been impressive, especially in urban communities such as Philadelphia and Washington, D.C., where concern with public schooling is highest. However, even in those cities, if new charter schools are as small as existing charter schools (with an average enrollment of 150 to 200), meaningful competition will require a great number of new schools.[4]

Two groups of entrepreneurs will prove critical to expanding competitive capacity: religious educators compelled by a sense of mission and for-profit educators seeking high rates of return. Religious missionaries obliged to serve their faith will work diligently to attract additional students. Such educators have always opened and run schools; the difference under school choice is the increased potential student population. Of course, the missionary impulse is more common among members of evangelical sects, suggesting that the expansion of private schooling under vouchers may eventually alter the universe of religious schooling.[5]

It is the for-profit educators who have the most straightforward interest in adding capacity.[6] They are most likely to open big schools and establish chains of schools, because their bottom-line concern with profitability creates pressure to minimize costs and increase their customer base. For-profit educators have a major advantage in opening or expanding schools, because—if investors believe the firm is offering returns commensurate with the risks incurred—they can access capital markets for the necessary support. Nonprofit operators have a much more difficult time attracting such investment. The growth of for-profit operators will dramatically increase the capital available to open and expand schools, attract entrepreneurs into education provision, and lessen reliance upon philanthropic and government resources. Many conventional charter operators voice distaste for such a "chain" mentality, preferring small, one-

4. For a good descriptive overview of the state of charter schooling, see Rees (2001).

5. In recent decades, even as the number of Catholic schools has steadily declined, the number of evangelical schools has increased, from about 2,500 in 1972 to roughly 9,000 in 2000. See Sikkink (2001, p. 38).

6. McEwan and Carnoy (2000, p. 228) observe that these educators also emerged in Chile when it introduced a voucher system, noting that "the new players in education markets created by a large voucher plan are nonreligious, for-profit schools."

site schools. Regardless of the educational or intrinsic appeal of the "mom and pop" approach, the chain model is essential to fostering meaningful competitive pressure.

School choice legislation that restricts the participation of religious schools or for-profit schools substantially limits the potential impact of competition. More generally, rules or requirements that raise barriers to entry—by making entrepreneurship more costly or problematic—will serve to limit capacity expansion.[7] Of course, critics of choice have expressed concern that choice may expand the role of religious and for-profit schooling. Such critics are at least partially correct, if large-scale, sustainable competition is to emerge. A key task for those intent on cultivating a significant market will be to make the case for religious and for-profit schools and to convince the public and policymakers that these schools ought to be included in choice programs without being subjected to suffocating regulation.[8]

Equipping Leaders to Lead

Urban school systems are a managerial nightmare, ossified under the weight of rules, procedures, contractual language, and local politicking. Regardless of the competition they face, officials have few incentives to focus on outcomes, have little flexibility, and are vulnerable to conflicting political pressure. No matter the threat an organization faces, its leaders cannot respond unless they have the ability to do so. There are several ways in which policymakers might give school administrators the requisite tools; most are familiar from the reinventing government and effective management movements.[9]

Administrative energy can be focused more closely on productivity and performance by making available sophisticated and accessible informa-

7. For a brief overview of how and why barriers to market entry reduce entrepreneurial activity, see Schneider, Teske, and Mintrom (1995, pp. 75–78).

8. Legislators unwilling to formally allow religious participation in charter school programs or for-profit participation in some voucher programs have nonetheless left some cracks through which these providers have gotten involved in supporting expansion. For instance, for-profit operators have contracted to "manage" schools that are sponsored by nonprofit entities. Similarly, religiously motivated operators have opened many charter schools featuring curricula, pedagogy, and discipline that—even in the absence of formal religious instruction—are intended to advance particular moral precepts and beliefs.

9. For extensive discussions of the steps necessary to enhance the performance of public sector organizations, see Barzelay and Armajani (1992); Linden (1994); Osborne and Gaebler (1992).

tion systems. Performance and budget software, or accounting systems that make real costs clear and traceable, can help administrators track employee activity and performance. Absent such information, administrators are necessarily forced to focus on inputs and procedures. Particularly effective will be mechanisms that track student enrollment and school market performance, especially if linked to incentives that prompt administrators to treat the data seriously.

Once administrators have information on organizational performance and have incentives to care, they can act more effectively if empowered to fire, promote, reward, pay, and monitor teachers.[10] The more discretion administrators have, the larger the impact of such changes will be.[11] Of course, such reforms require changes in contracts, laws, and the norms of professional education administration. Absent such changes, administrators must rely upon personal charm and informal suasion to drive organizational improvement. Radically changing this state of affairs will inevitably raise legitimate concerns about managerial competence and fairness. Moreover, how such tools are designed and utilized is of great import and is a question that will require careful attention.[12]

The current culture of schooling leaves school systems ill equipped to respond to competition. The vast majority of teachers have not chosen the profession for any selective incentives that their employers can readily control, but out of a sense of mission, a love of the work, and because it allows them time to be with their families, provides job security, and allows them to work with children.[13] These are not the kinds of incentives that administrators can readily manipulate. Efforts to relax certification

10. If selective incentives are to be used, they must be of sufficient size. For instance, in the case of merit pay, it is important to "make the size of the performance pay increment substantial" and to recognize that the effects of material rewards will also vary with other factors, such as working conditions, personal tastes, and other opportunities. See Brandt (1990, p. 7). Most experiments with merit pay do not provide substantial bonuses for personal performance, instead opting for smaller awards or awards based on schoolwide performance (inviting collective action problems). Such reforms, while well intentioned and pleasing on their face, are unlikely to drive changes in individual behavior and have given rise to the claim "that we have tried merit pay many times before and it seldom works." Brandt (1990, p. 14).

11. For a general discussion regarding the use of incentives to influence teacher behavior, see Cohen (1996).

12. For concise, accessible discussions of how such selective incentives ought to be designed and implemented, see Kelley and others (2000); Kelley (1997). For a more extended treatment of these issues, see the relevant scholarship discussed in chapter 2.

13. Public Agenda (2000).

requirements, recruit nontraditional educators, and permit administrators to reward teachers for performance will help to attract more entrepreneurial personnel into the profession and will increase the number of potential teachers, giving teachers more reason to fear for their jobs.[14]

Finally, administrators are not trained in ways that prepare them to cope with market demands, nor are they selected for their ability to answer the challenge. One obvious step is to recruit administrators temperamentally suited and professionally equipped to manage in a competitive environment. Appropriate preparation would more closely resemble that of business executives, while recruitment should emphasize executive ability at least as much as educational experience. Both state certification processes and schools of education are responsible for the shape of the administrative work force and for the lack of managerial training administrators receive, and both will need to be revisited. Altering professional training and certification will affect the kinds of people who choose to enter education or to climb the administrative ranks, prompting additional changes in school culture.

Risks of the Pickax

The pickax route is alluring. It promises change without wrenching dislocations. However, even if policymakers address competitive capacity and administrative behavior, it is only a halfway measure. It does not compel change or alter the incentives that drive educational performance. Efforts to reform urban school systems have historically disappointed. Consequently, there are four particular risks inherent in the pickax model. First, this approach is akin to "pushing on a string." Resources and opportunities can be provided, but the effects will depend on whether entrepreneurs choose to cooperate. Market-driven reform is often hailed precisely because critics believe that good intentions and selfless devotion have failed to produce school improvement. To rely on the pickax is to bet that, given the opportunity, the nation's urban educators will deliver.

Second, public officials typically shy away from upsetting procedural routines or encouraging entrepreneurship out of deference to watchful constituencies and an autonomous organizational culture. While pickax

14. For an insightful discussion of the ways in which evaluation and compensation strategies might be used to alter educator behavior in productive ways, see Odden and Kelley (1997).

competition softens opposition among entrenched constituencies, galvanizes political support, makes administrators more willing to countenance freelancing by subordinates, and creates new opportunities for entrepreneurial personalities, the long-term promise of such changes is uncertain. More fundamentally, this approach is less a vision of conventional market-based reform than an expansive effort to promote traditional school reform by ratcheting up political pressure.

Third, it is not clear that changes produced by the pickax will necessarily be positive ones. Given the incoherence and autonomy that characterizes urban school systems, the accretion of new, semi-independent units may actually make it more different to allocate resources or provide services in an efficient or accountable manner.

Finally, as long as school systems are political entities with a well of public support, they will be tempted to answer competition, at least in part, by mobilizing public sentiment and appealing to lawmakers and the courts. This may come at the expense of more productive activity. Reducing the incidence of grievance politics requires minimizing the value of such appeals. Strong school choice laws, clear judicial declarations of legality, and broad political support for choice-based measures will render political and legal attacks less appealing. Political mobilization can also be made less effective by increasing the availability of concrete data on school system performance; such data can render sweeping moral claims less relevant. If school systems can supply data that convincingly show they are effective, moral appeals will be unnecessary; if they cannot, it will be more difficult to convince the community to overlook that fact.

Unchaining the Bulldozer

Proponents of education competition generally envision market impacts and systemic changes much more momentous than those produced by pickax competition. A more radical market approach, ambitious in scope and serious about answering the challenge, seeks to leverage the ruthless power of self-interest and extrinsic incentives. The result, often unacknowledged, is a transformative decision to fundamentally alter the culture, structure, and ordering of public schooling.

As in the case of pickax competition, bulldozer competition requires that a substantial market threat develop and that system officials be given the means to control their organizations. However, transformative competition requires two additional types of change. First, the self-interest of executives must be hitched to their competitive performance. Second, the basis on which school systems and their schools are competing must be made clear.[15]

The allure of the bulldozer is clear; the concern is that it will change school culture and practice in undesirable ways. The market presumption is that extrinsic incentives can be used to reinforce intrinsic motivation in the entrepreneurial and to substitute for it in others. This presumption works well where there is no fundamental conflict between intrinsic and extrinsic motivation. For instance, rewarding a coal miner for digging coal, an inventor for inventing, or a software designer for crafting software tends to create few difficulties. Problems can arise, however, in human service fields, where intrinsic and extrinsic motivation may clash.

In professions like the priesthood or social work or teaching, where the most committed workers are often motivated by a sense of personal mission, efforts to focus on demonstrated performance or material rewards can strike practitioners as misguided or offensive. Introducing selective incentives or monitoring performance more closely may alienate these individuals, as their conception of their role comes into conflict with organizational expectations. These educators desire autonomy and the ability to do what they deem proper, while the newly threatening sanctions and rewards demand that they operate in the prescribed manner and produce results others believe desirable. Many teachers are likely to find the profession less rewarding and may very well depart.

Meanwhile, introducing selective incentives will attract teachers comfortable with them and will gradually foster a culture that accepts those incentives. The result is that, while school culture becomes increasingly less hospitable to the intrinsically motivated teacher, it will become increasingly receptive to the teacher comfortable with managerial oversight and with rewards linked to demonstrated performance. Understanding how these effects will play out will require determining the extent of intrinsic motivation among current teachers, the rate at which selective incentives will attract new teachers, and the degree to which extrinsic motivation will compel teachers to perform.

Performance Incentives for Executives

Public school systems are governed by public officials whose position encourages them to juggle conflicting goals and focus on questions of eq-

---

15. For a discussion of these same issues in the context of efforts to improve policing, see Moore (1994).

uity. Simply placing such officials in a market or quasi market does not change the fact that they have reason to move cautiously and to adopt procedures that minimize controversy. As long as systems remain publicly governed, the need to assuage the larger community will vie with the incentive to focus on product quality. System officials will care about the customer to the extent that customers overlap with the voting public but will continue to be monitored, rewarded, and funded at the behest of the voters. How might executives be motivated to focus on enrollment or to pursue reforms that may alienate powerful constituencies?

Generally speaking, competition will not force publicly governed school systems to enhance organizational efficiency unless the personal or professional self-interest of officials or administrators is linked to their competitive performance. One way in which this can be done is through the emergence of a political constituency that has clear performance expectations and that provides a counterweight to entrenched constituencies. A political coalition with sufficient strength can push board members and administrators to challenge entrenched constituencies and can reward them for their actions.

It is not necessary, however, to rely on the serendipitous emergence of such a coalition. Policymakers can opt to reward and sanction executives and managers on the basis of competitive performance. If the job security, the salaries, and the prospects of central administrators and principals are linked more tightly to changes in enrollment, self-interest will induce them to compete for students.[16] One approach would be to compensate administrators based on enrollment or to make enrollment a prominent component of performance evaluation. Of course, such systems must be crafted with attention to unintended side effects. For instance, some students are more troublesome or more expensive than others and will therefore be pursued less avidly; appropriate adjustments will be necessary in these cases. Similarly, fluctuation in enrollment may be driven in part by factors other than performance. While such issues are significant and require careful attention in designing incentive structures, the larger point is that educators will compete for students if given reasons to do so. We sometimes see this at the school level, where administrative concern or public pressure can lead a principal at a given school to seek ways to recapture lost enrollment.

---

16. Osborne and Gaebler (1992, pp. 195–218) provide an extensive discussion of how selective incentives can be used to encourage enterprising behavior among public employees.

Clarifying the Product

There are two ways to encourage education competition to focus on outcomes rather than on more public activity. One is by permitting schools to target niche markets. Competition will inevitably emerge within each niche, as consumers compare the schools on the particular criteria of concern. Alternatively, school systems can more readily be pressed to compete if the standards by which the community is judging the system and its schools are made explicit.[17]

Within a given market niche, individual schools will compete to provide what consumers desire. Consumers value academic preparation, but they also value location, religious instruction, and other goods. While there is value in schools competing to offer more appealing religious instruction, more convenient transportation, or a particular reading program, the deeper hope is that schools will feel compelled to outperform one another in terms of more fundamental educational quality. We can clarify the dimensions on which schools are competing by freeing public schools to seek and cultivate their own market niche, while recognizing that such a model will not ensure that every school will adopt a primary focus on academics.

So long as school systems exist as collective political entities, prodding them to focus on improving performance will require altering the marketplace by increasing agreement on mission and by clarifying measures of output. More agreement on outcome goals—whatever those goals are determined to be—will enhance the likelihood that the market choices of consumers will compel systems to compete on those dimensions. Such agreement need not be formal. For instance, informal agreement about what schools should be doing and how to judge whether they are succeeding is relatively common in many private schools, small school systems, and high-performing suburban school systems. A useful parallel is higher education, where rating guides have pressed colleges to focus on the criteria used, even though most college and university officials believe the ranking scores are flawed measures of school quality. The fact that consumers rely upon certain criteria to make choices encourages organizations to

---

17. During the 1990s the notion of clarifying and standardizing educational objectives was most visibly embodied in the standards-based reform movement. Standards-based reforms were adopted widely by the states and enjoyed some success at the federal level. For discussion, see Schwartz and Robinson (2000).

improve their performance on the measured criteria, whatever the relationship of these criteria to "actual" organizational quality.

Clearer measures of product quality will focus attention on the measured dimensions of system performance. In practice, of course, every effort to rely upon such measures will encounter legitimate philosophical and practical concerns. These disputes are far too complex to address here. For the purposes of this discussion, it is necessary only to recognize that focusing attention on particular and measurable dimensions of schooling will induce educators to compete especially on those outcomes.

Two Visions of the Bulldozer

Tapping the raw power of market competition requires that consumers be able to readily assess substantive product quality. There are two general approaches that policymakers might adopt to help consumers make quality-conscious choices. Both shift the basis of competition away from symbolic appeals and toward substantive performance, doing so by simplifying and clarifying decisions about education consumption.

One approach uses a uniform outcome measure, such as a high-stakes testing regimen, to establish standards for judging school performance. By encouraging significant numbers of consumers to select schools on the basis of a particular outcome, such an approach compels educators to respond accordingly. The second approach does not establish a uniform measure of quality but instead poses a truly free marketplace in which schools are able to appeal to particular constituencies. Competition in such a market will take place among individual schools within a niche, as schools try to outperform one another on the criteria that their customers care about.[18]

Under either system, educators who refuse to acknowledge market directives will find themselves out of work, while those who respond effectively will be recognized and rewarded. Under such arrangements, the culture of schooling will become far less significant to reform efforts, because it will no longer be the driving force behind employee motivation

---

18. For instance, a market niche might consist of all constructivist schools in a community, in which case educators at those schools will compete to convince parents that theirs is the most effective constructivist school. Another niche might include college preparatory schools competing on the basis of college matriculation, the quality of the institutions that their graduates attend, or some other related metric. A third niche might cater to families concerned primarily about musical instruction. And so on.

and cooperation. In effect, then, the market bulldozer will repeal the rules that now govern school reform efforts. If policymakers wish to get serious about unleashing competition in education, they have a choice of two models: coercive accountability and the free market.

Coercive Accountability

Coercive accountability works by clarifying objectives and then driving producers to meet those objectives. The simplest, most straightforward way to force schools to improve performance is to clearly and succinctly define what constitutes a quality product, to make available simple proxies for quality, to enable consumers to easily respond to those proxies, and to give educators incentives to care about how consumers respond. Such an approach would presumably include assessments of student performance on a standardized instrument (typically, a test of content knowledge, though it could measure some radically different objective, such as how much students report enjoying learning or how developed their analytic prowess is). Schools could then be evaluated on the basis of student performance.

In such a system, families are likely to weight standardized assessment heavily when choosing schools. The extent to which families actually do this will depend in part on how widely publicized the scores are, on how relevant they are thought to be, and on personal preferences and values. So long as administrative incentives are linked to student enrollment and administrators have the ability to reward and sanction subordinates on the basis of their efforts, schools will have incentive and opportunity to boost their measured performance so as to attract students.

For this model to function, it is necessary to create differentiated incentives for education officials and administrators and to link these to student enrollment. Granting administrators new tools with which to compel cooperation will enable them to focus and control school-level efforts, as will initiatives that give them leeway to select their staffs and to create a work force sensitive to the selective incentives that principals can readily wield. This vision of an "accountable" market looks much more like that of an industrial concern than it does like the romantic notion of the public school, and with good reason. In fact, so long as school-level personnel are compensated on the basis of enrollment or outcome performance, and are therefore impelled to compete against one another for students, nonpublic competition is not even essential to this model. Those who embrace charter schooling or school choice as a way to let innovative schools flower are justified in fearing the implications of this narrow focus on specific, test-driven outcomes.

The appeal of this model is that it pressures all schools to focus on producing a quality education in a straightforward and systematic manner. Its downside is twofold. First, not all observers agree that the good being produced is in fact a quality good. Some critics suggest that assessments do not measure the meaningful learning that takes place in schools.[19] Such accountability also creates the risk that schools—unless carefully monitored and regulated or constrained by a sense of professionalism or mission—may enhance test performance by encouraging low performers to leave school, by squeezing out productive educational activities that do not contribute to test performance, by devoting substantial time to test preparation, or by trying to ensure that low-performing students are not tested. Advocates of accountability counter, with much merit, that such responses can be minimized and that the benefits outweigh such costs.[20]

Second, coercive accountability can undermine or marginalize the role of intrinsic motivation. On the one hand, the focus and clarity produced by accountability may foster more coherent school cultures, more cooperation among school faculty, and a higher degree of job satisfaction. On the other hand, defining the purpose of schooling so explicitly ensures that education approaches oriented to achieving other educational ends are likely to be perceived as ineffective. For instance, if a school program does a good job of developing creative writing or scientific reasoning but does not produce impressive outcomes on the performance measure, it will appear ineffective. To the degree that families view the outcome measure as reliable and valid, many will depart schools that fare poorly on the measure, regardless of the schools' "true" quality. This will limit the ability of schools to define their own mission and should prove deeply troubling to charter school proponents who wish to see a tremendous variety of schools take root and flourish. In the process, such change will likely dampen sources of the intrinsic motivation that inspires work-embracing and mountain-climbing entrepreneurs. In a system of coercive accountability, choice-based reform becomes intertwined with standards-driven reform.

19. See, for instance, Kohn (2000); McNeil (2000); Ohanian (1999).

20. For a discussion of how to limit the problems posed by efforts to boost test scores through cheating or undesirable practices, see Cizek (1999). For a discussion that asserts that the benefits of standards-driven accountability outweigh its costs, see Ravitch (2000).

Coercive accountability is in fact a peculiar kind of market-based reform. Classic markets collect and channel the self-interested preferences of discrete consumers without centralized direction. The resulting pressure steers the behavior of producers. Coercive accountability, on the other hand, is much more akin to a straightforward case of state coercion. If instead of relying upon consumer activity the state were to announce that it would sanction or fire employees at low-performing schools, it would be hard to discern any difference between the effects of market pressure and nonmarket coercion. From a policymaker's perspective, this point is, in some sense, academic. If the goal is to boost test scores, who really cares whether competition or standards improved performance? However, the distinction is theoretically important and has important practical consequences.

The Free Market

The free market model seeks to create a clear outcome and divisible good in a manner very different from that just discussed. Like coercive accountability, the free market model requires giving officials and administrators powerful personal and professional incentives to care about enrollment and then empowering them to control their organizations.

However, whereas coercive accountability drives improvement by forcing producers to compete on the basis of standardized outcomes, the free market permits producers to compete on the basis of whatever criteria they desire. If entry to the marketplace is simplified, profit seekers, missionaries, and work embracers will provide a variety of schools, emphasizing a variety of outcomes. Parents will be free to measure schools on the criteria they deem relevant, and the result will be competition among schools that appeal to parents with a given set of preferences. If, as chapter 2 suggests, some parents are concerned primarily with academics, others with school safety, and so on, different schools will cater to these different concerns.[21]

The resulting fragmentation will foster market niches. Within each niche consumers will choose schools based on the criteria they believe important. So long as school officials have incentives to pursue enrollment, they will respond by seeking to compete in an appropriate niche. In essence,

21. It is interesting to note that Cleveland and Milwaukee parents who said they were concerned primarily about the school program and curriculum then disagreed about what subject matter was most important. See Meissner, Browne, and Van Dunk (1997).

this model permits families to compare kinds of schools and then to measure each school against other, similar schools. Whereas coercive accountability forces every school to compete according to a common barometer, the free market permits each school to choose the standard by which it will be assessed. In this way, the free market is much more protective of traditional sources of intrinsic motivation than is coercive accountability, as it provides the opportunity for an array of schools with a variety of orientations and designs to flourish.

Finding such a system at odds with popular notions of public schooling, even market advocates rarely make the case for the free market option. The natural compromise is to embrace a free market system with "adequate" safeguards. The problem is that a market model with too many such safeguards yields an ambiguous environment, which rewards gestures rather than demonstrated performance.

The Problem with Trying to Have It Both Ways

Most market enthusiasts are uncomfortable with both of these strong visions of competition, while remaining unwilling to rely upon the gradualist pickax. They desire a hybrid system, one that marries the clear guidelines of coercive accountability with the opportunity for niche creation afforded by the free market. The problem with such an approach is that it inevitably results in blurred outcomes, forcing producers to compete on some other basis. Reducing the prominence of clear outcomes reduces the pressure for schools to improve measured performance. Meanwhile, standardizing required services curtails the emergence of niches and homogenizes school provision, making it more difficult for consumers to use niche-specific proxies to compare schools.

Coercive accountability and market accountability can be understood as the two ends of a continuum. It is possible, and probably appropriate, to temper an extreme version of either approach. However, a hybrid approach will make it more difficult to use either measured outcomes or niche-specific proxies to assess quality, encouraging consumers to shop— and educators to compete—on the basis of more symbolic proxies.

Public Education under a Competitive Regime

The question should not be, Will competition make schools "better"? Given the radically different visions of schooling implicit in our current system of education and in a market system of education, there is no simple way to weigh the promises and challenges of a competitive regime against the status quo. Instead, the less ambitious question should be, Will competition change schools in ways we want them to change? Competition will encourage schools to compete on the basis of outcomes that consumers reward. Such change will produce schools surprisingly different, for good or ill, from those that developed in the twentieth century. In the end, getting serious about education competition is a far more profound choice than we often acknowledge.

If we believe markets will improve schooling, then by all means let us proceed along that course. Let us do so, however, with a commitment to taking the steps required to construct productive markets. In and of themselves, markets are not an elixir and they will not magically improve schooling. What markets do is harness and channel self-interest. If they do so in ways that force schools to improve, then competition will prove beneficial. Whether they do so depends on structural, statutory, and cultural predicates.

Markets are shaped by context. It is often easy for us to overlook this point when contemplating private sector activity in the United States because, at least from a bird's-eye perspective, there is substantial homogeneity across the nation's private sector. Executives and investors generally seek to maximize their return on equity, employees are responsive to selective incentives, managers control an array of sanctions and rewards, and so on. These conditions are less common, or even absent, in public enterprises. I am not suggesting that private sector firms are interchangeable or that they are not also constrained in important ways. I am arguing only that lazy analogies between the public and private sectors obscure important differences. There is some evidence that competition may gradually gain momentum and that some constraints may loosen as educators and other local figures grow acclimated to a new institutional regime. However, if they are serious about reaping the potential benefits of competition, policymakers have the ability to significantly accelerate this process.

So long as school systems are governed by rickety bureaucracies, run by managers bereft of data or tools, staffed by employees who have little motivation beyond the intrinsic, charged with producing ill-defined and ambiguous outcomes, and faced with few penalties for poor performance, efforts at substantive improvement—whether market driven or not—will be stifled. This means that for critics of choice-based competition to be persuasive in their opposition to choice-based reform, they are obliged to offer a less radical vision of structural change that will equip systems to pursue meaningful improvement.

Unleashing competition requires harnessing individual self-interest, lashing it to clear outcome goals, creating a market characterized by substantial competition, and giving individuals the tools necessary to act in their own behalf. Schools in such a world will be characterized by far greater accountability, focus, and managerial influence than are today's public schools. Such a workplace, in which performance and ambition are recognized and rewarded, may well be attractive to many talented men and women who now see a decision to teach as a decision to forgo opportunity and ambition in the name of public service.

While they may attract this promising new breed of teacher, however, market-driven schools are also likely to alienate many educational entrepreneurs currently accorded iconic status.[22] An accountability-driven, incentive-driven approach is antithetical to the popular notion that schooling ought to be improved by infusing teaching with a greater sense of personal agency and calling.[23] The changes implicit in competition risk alienating many educators traditionally regarded as inspirational and selfless icons, fostering a school culture alien to our education heritage, or producing an incentive structure that distorts educational priorities. The entrepreneurs currently in the public schools should not be taken for granted. The intrinsically motivated educator is likely to feel uncomfortable and constrained as autonomy is reduced. It is possible that work-embracing and missionary educators may decide that other careers are more attractive than working in schools dominated by a bottom-line ethos. Under such a system, the democratic missionaries who currently lead the public school charge against the market assault may depart teaching for new causes.

22. Some critics, such as Molnar (1996) and Giroux (1999), argue that American education is already too commercial. These critics rightly view the reforms required to unchain the bulldozer as an assault on the values that they believe ought to be at the heart of schooling.

23. For a discussion of the need to enhance the sense of service and calling in teaching, see Hansen (1995). This belief—that effective school reform ought to foster intrinsic motivation and be rooted in enhanced professional autonomy—is central to the ideas of prominent school reformers such as Meier (1995) and Sizer (1996). In fact, in an extensive review of the research relating to urban teacher preparation, Weiner (2001, p. 369) protests that standardization is educationally destructive. She rejects the notion that such approaches might improve education, arguing that learning is enhanced by "contexts that are socioculturally, linguistically, and cognitively meaningful."

Betting on markets is a decision to trade an uneven system marked by the selfless and extraordinary performance of the few for the more predictable production of an incentive-sensitive work force managed by performance-conscious executives. The selfless zeal that characterizes the best classrooms, and the rudderless autonomy that characterizes many others, would be slowly displaced by a steadier, less whimsical motivation. This is not simply a matter of "improving" schools; it is a decision to alter the nature and culture of K–12 education. While perhaps desirable, such a change is not a casual one.

The Choice Ahead

Decades of attention to the problems of urban school systems have failed to improve matters. Against this backdrop, the impersonal mechanism of education competition is appealing because of the very real possibility that it might drive improvement through resistant systems. However, two caveats are in order. First, competition is likely to deliver the promised systemic change only if it is complemented by broader changes to the structure and organization of school systems. Even then, its effects will depend in part upon contextual factors over which policymakers enjoy limited control. Second, the promised benefits of competition will not come without significant costs.

Unleashing transformative competition will require significantly altering public education. Without such changes, the effects of competition are likely to be sporadic and largely political. Many market proponents finesse the inevitable trade-offs, disavowing any interest in the harsher aspects of competition while lauding the gentle benefits of innovation. However, they simultaneously suggest that school choice will deliver systemic improvement. Proponents cannot have it both ways; they must forgo systemic improvement and accept whatever succor the pickax may bring, or they must embrace the market bulldozer in all its terrible majesty.

I am not suggesting that the costs of competition render it undesirable or that choice advocates ought to settle for the pickax. Public policy always involves trade-offs; rejecting the promise of markets leaves urban systems to struggle with existing constraints. The challenge for voters and policymakers is to assess costs and benefits with their eyes wide open.

A particular risk is that many assumptions regarding the promise of competition depend, to a degree that is not fully appreciated, on the goodwill of educators. Among the most effective ways for schools to compete is by skimming off the best students, by purging students who are not cost-effective, or by skimping on unobserved services in order to focus on those services that customers do observe (whether this be a school's test scores or its physical plant). The same challenge emerges in for-profit health care, where price competition pressures health professionals to cut corners. In both health care and education, professional ethics and culture provide the bulwark that restrains the temptations of self-interest. In changing the culture of schooling, in attracting to the profession educators less motivated by a commitment to the democratic ethos, the protections provided by ethics and culture are likely to weaken. If this proves to be the case, it will require new efforts to restrict undesirable competitive practices.

School choice has long been viewed as the answer to numerous problems: it is a way to foster the flowering of new schools and to promote standards, to support religious education and to harness the power of the market. As much as we might wish it otherwise, school choice cannot fulfill all of these hopes. Given their conflicting goals, it is unclear whether market advocates really wish to embrace choice-driven competition. For instance, many advocates of charter schooling trumpet the promised freedom of choice while evincing hostility to unbridled markets and for-profit operators. This is not an untenable position, as one can support school choice and not education markets, but it suggests a need to avoid broad claims regarding the promise of competition.

The inability of markets to readily transform urban school systems highlights the structural and organizational problems that these systems face. The manner in which systems respond to choice-induced competition makes clear just how difficult it is to reshape urban systems through good faith and a reliance on intrinsic motivation. However, when pressed to offer systemic approaches to improving urban education, many critics of education markets respond with little more than lofty ideals, faith in the goodwill of teachers, and the conviction that schools will get the job done if they are simply given "enough" money and if teachers would just do the "right" things. While intuitively appealing, this is a bankrupt approach, one that has disappointed for three decades and has left millions of children to pay the price. If choice opponents can do no better, then their lack of useful alternatives provides a compelling argument that market competition may be necessary to bring meaningful improvement to urban schooling. To be taken seriously, critics must offer more than high hopes, good intentions, and a steady supply of new pedagogical and curricular innovations.

The statutes, bureaucracy, and procedural routines that hamper school officials are designed into the very structure of urban public school systems. Competition provides one way to chip away at these barriers, though its success will depend on complementary changes. Too often the education debate proceeds as if those discussing education markets were in one room and those discussing the political constraints on school reform were in another. In fact, education competition cannot be divorced from discussions about testing, teacher certification, school governance, education administration, or the other frustrating conversations that many school choice proponents have long wished to avoid. In the end, the fate of education markets, for good or ill, is intertwined with broader issues of education politics and policy.

References

Acemoglu, Daron, and Robert Shimer. 1999. "Efficient Unemployment Insurance." *Journal of Political Economy* 107: 893–928.

Allison, Graham T. 1971. *Essence of Decision: Explaining the Cuban Missile Crisis.* Boston: Little, Brown.

Angus, David L. 2001. *Professionalism and the Public Good: A Brief History of Teacher Certification.* Washington: Fordham Foundation.

Anyon, Jean. 1997. *Ghetto Schooling: A Political Economy of Urban Educational Reform.* Teachers College Press.

Armor, David J., and Brett M. Peiser. 1997. "Competition in Education: A Case Study of Interdistrict Choice." Pioneer Paper 12. Boston: Pioneer Institute for Public Policy.

———. 1998. "Interdistrict Choice in Massachusetts." In *Learning from School Choice,* edited by Paul E. Peterson and Bryan C. Hassel. Brookings.

Arnold, R. Douglas. 1990. *The Logic of Congressional Action.* Yale University Press.

Aud, Susan. 1999. "Competition in Education: A 1999 Update of School Choice in Massachusetts." Boston: Pioneer Institute for Public Policy.

Baldwin, Beatrice. 1995. "Lessons Learned from Louisiana's Teacher Evaluation Experience." In *Teacher Evaluation Policy: From Accountability to Professional Development,* edited by Daniel L. Duke. SUNY Press.

Ballou, Dale, and Michael Podgursky. 1997. *Teacher Pay and Teacher Quality.* Kalamazoo, Mich.: Upjohn Institute.

———. 2000. "Gaining Control of Professional Licensing and Advancement." In *Conflicting Missions? Teachers Unions and Educational Reform,* edited by Tom Loveless. Brookings.

———. 2001. "Let the Market Decide." *Education Matters* 1(1): 16–25.

Barber, Benjamin R. 1992. *An Aristocracy of Everyone: The Politics of Education and the Future of America.* Ballantine.

243

Barth, Roland S. 1980. *Run School Run.* Harvard University Press.

Barzelay, Michael, with Babak J. Armajani. 1992. *Breaking through Bureaucracy: A New Vision for Managing in Government.* University of California Press.

Beales, Janet R., and Maureen Wahl. 1995. *Given the Choice: A Study of the PAVE Program and School Choice in Milwaukee.* Los Angeles: Reason Foundation.

Besanko, David, David Dranove, and Mark Shanley. 2000. *Economics of Strategy.* 2d ed. Wiley and Sons.

Bierlein, Louann A. 1993. *Controversial Issues in Educational Policy.* Newbury Park, Calif.: Sage.

Bishop, John H. 2000. "Privatizing Education: Lessons from Canada, Europe, and Asia." In *Vouchers and the Provision of Public Services,* edited by C. Eugene Steuerle and others. Brookings, Committee for Economic Development, and Urban Institute.

Bjorgan, Roger, Chen-Ching Liu, and Jacques Lawarree. 1999. "Financial Risk Management in a Competitive Electricity Market." *IEEE Transactions on Power Systems* 14:1285–307.

Black, Gordon S. 1989. *The Lack of Confidence in Public Education in Wisconsin.* Milwaukee: Wisconsin Policy Research Institute.

Blum Center. 1998. *Educational Freedom Report* 60. Milwaukee (June 19).

Borland, Melvin V., and Roy M. Howsen. 1992. "Student Academic Achievement and the Degree of Market Concentration in Education." *Economics of Education Review* 11: 31–39.

Bradford, David F., and Daniel N. Shaviro. 2000. "The Economics of Vouchers." In *Vouchers and the Provision of Public Services,* edited by C. Eugene Steuerle and others. Brookings, Committee for Economic Development, and Urban Institute.

Brandt, Richard M. 1990. *Incentive Pay and Career Ladders for Today's Teachers: A Study of Current Programs and Practices.* SUNY Press.

Bridges, Edwin M. 1986. *The Incompetent Teacher.* Philadelphia: Falmer.

Brouillette, Liane. 1996. *A Geology of School Reform: The Successive Restructurings of a School District.* SUNY Press.

Bryk, Anthony S., David Kerbow, and Sharon Rollow. 1997. "Chicago School Reform." In *New Schools for a New Century: The Redesign of Urban Education,* edited by Diane Ravitch and Joseph P. Viteritti. Yale University Press.

Bryk, Anthony, and others. 1997. *Charting Chicago School Reform: Democratic Localism as a Lever for Change.* Boulder, Colo.: Westview.

Buchanan, James M. 1968. *The Demand and Supply of Public Goods.* Chicago: Rand McNally.

Buckeye Institute. 1998a. *Giving Choice a Chance: Cleveland and the Future of School Reform.* Dayton, Ohio.

———. 1998b. *Public Choices, Private Costs: An Analysis of Spending and Achievement in Ohio Public Schools.* Dayton, Ohio.

Butler, Esther. 1997. "The Changing Role of the Cleveland Public School Board, 1965–1995." Ph.D. dissertation, Cleveland State University.

Campbell, David E. 2001. "Making Democratic Education Work." In *Charter Schools, Vouchers, and Public Education,* edited by Paul E. Peterson and David Campbell. Brookings.

Cannell, John. 1987. *Nationally Normed Elementary Achievement Testing in America's Public Schools.* Princeton, N.J.: Eye on Education.

Carl, James C. 1995. "The Politics of Education in a New Key: The 1988 Chicago School Reform Act and the 1990 Milwaukee Parental Choice Program." Ph.D. dissertation, University of Wisconsin–Madison.

Carlson, John A. 1998. "Risk Aversion, Foreign Exchange Speculation, and Gambler's Ruin." *Economica* 65:441–54.

Carnegie Foundation for the Advancement of Teaching. 1992. *School Choice: A Special Report.* Princeton, N.J.

CEO Foundation. 1999. *A Report on the First Semester of the Horizon Voucher Program.* San Antonio, Texas.

———. 2000. *Horizon Scholarship Program, Second Annual Report.* San Antonio, Texas.

Charter School Resource Center of Texas. 2000. *Directory of Operational Texas Open Enrollment Charter Schools.* San Antonio.

Chubb, John, and Terry Moe. 1990. *Politics, Markets, and America's Schools.* Brookings.

Chung, Chung-Cheng, and Michael Szenberg. 1996. "The Effects of Deregulation on the U.S. Airline Industry." *Journal of Applied Business Research* 12(3): 133–40.

Cibulka, James G., and Frederick I. Olson. 1993. "The Organization and Politics of the Milwaukee Public School System, 1920–1986." In *Seeds of Crisis: Public Schooling in Milwaukee since 1920,* edited by John L. Rury and Frank A. Cassell. University of Wisconsin Press.

Citizens League of Greater Cleveland. 1995. *Using the Power of Collaboration to Help Cleveland's Children.*

Cizek, Gregory J. 1999. *Cheating on Tests: How to Do It, Detect It, and Prevent It.* Mahwah, N.J.: Erlbaum.

"Cleveland Looks at Desegregation Case, *Reed* v. *Rhodes.*" 1992. *Cleveland Public Schools Spectrum* 5(4): 1–3.

Cleveland City School District. 1998. *Comprehensive Annual Financial Report for Fiscal Year Ended June 30, 1998.* Cleveland, Ohio: CPS Treasurer's Department.

Cleveland Public Schools. 1998. *District Annual Report.*

Cleveland Teachers Union. 1995. *Critique: The Official Publication of the Cleveland Teachers Union.* September.

———. 1996. *Critique: The Official Publication of the Cleveland Teachers Union.* December.

Clotfelter, Charles T., and Helen F. Ladd. 1996. "Recognizing and Rewarding Success in Public Schools." In *Holding Schools Accountable: Performance-Based Reform in Education,* edited by Helen F. Ladd. Brookings.

Clowes, George A. 2001. "Court Rejects Cleveland Vouchers." *School Reform News* 5(February): 1.

Cohen, David K. 1996. "Rewarding Teachers for Student Performance." In *Rewards and Reform: Creating Educational Incentives That Work,* edited by Susan H. Fuhrman and Jennifer A. O'Day. San Francisco: Jossey-Bass.

Cohen, David K., and Eleanor Farrar. 1977. "Power to the Parents? The Story of Education Vouchers." *Public Interest* 48: 72–97.

Collins, Catherine, and Douglas Frantz. 1993. *Teachers: Talking Out of School.* Boston: Little, Brown.

Conlan, Timothy J., and David R. Beam. 2000. "Symbolic Coalitions and the New Politics of Ideas." Paper prepared for annual meeting of the American Political Science Association. Washington, August 31–September 3.

Consortium on Productivity in the Schools. 1995. *Using What We Have to Get the Schools We Need: A Productivity Focus for American Education.* New York.

Cortez, Albert, and others. 1999. *Students for Sale: The Use of Public Money for Private Schooling.* San Antonio: Intercultural Development Research Association.

Coulson, Andrew. 1999. *Market Education, the Unknown History.* New Brunswick, N.J.: Transaction.

Crandall, Robert W., and Harold Furchtgott-Roth. 1996. *Cable TV: Regulation or Competition.* Brookings.

Crenson, Matthew A. 1971. *The Un-Politics of Air Pollution.* Johns Hopkins University Press.

Darling-Hammond, Linda. 1996. "Restructuring Schools for High Performance." In *Rewards and Reform: Creating Educational Incentives That Work,* edited by Susan H. Fuhrman and Jennifer A. O'Day. San Francisco: Jossey-Bass.

Dee, Thomas S. 1998. "Competition and the Quality of Public Schools." *Economics of Education Review* 17(4): 419–27.

Derthick, Martha. 1990. *Agency under Stress: The Social Security Administration in the American Government.* Brookings.

DiIulio, John J., Jr. 1994. "What Is Deregulating the Public Service?" In *Deregulating the Public Service: Can Government Be Improved?* edited by John J. DiIulio Jr. Brookings.

Dougherty, J. Chrys, and Stephen L. Becker. 1995. *An Analysis of Public-Private School Choice in Texas.* San Antonio: Texas Public Policy Foundation.

Dougherty, John A. 1997. "More than One Struggle: African-American School Reform Movements in Milwaukee, 1930–1980." Ph.D. dissertation, University of Wisconsin–Madison.

Douglas, James. 1987. "Political Theories of Nonprofit Organization." In *The Nonprofit Sector: A Research Handbook,* edited by Walter W. Powell. Yale University Press.

Duesterberg, Thomas, and Kenneth Gordon. 1997. *Competition and Deregulation in Telecommunications: The Case for a New Paradigm.* Indianapolis: Hudson Institute.

Duke, Daniel L. 1995. "Conflict and Consensus in the Reform of Teacher Evaluation." In *Teacher Evaluation Policy: From Accountability to Professional Development,* edited by Daniel L. Duke. SUNY Press.

Dworkin, Anthony G. 1987. *Teacher Burnout in the Public Schools: Structural Causes and Consequences for Children.* SUNY Press.

Edelman, Murray. 1972. *The Symbolic Uses of Politics.* University of Illinois Press.

Elmore, Richard F. 1986. *Choice in Public Education.* Philadelphia: Center for Policy Research in Education.

————. 1990. "Choice as an Instrument of Public Policy: Evidence from Education and Health Care." In *Choice and Control in American Education,* edited by William Clune and John Witte. Vol. 1, *The Theory of Choice and Control in Education.* New York: Falmer.

————. 1996. "Getting to Scale with Good Educational Practice." *Harvard Educational Review* 66: 1–26.

Epple, Dennis, and Richard Romano. 1998. "Competition between Private and Public Schools, Vouchers, and Peer-Group Effects." *American Economic Review* 88:33–62.

Etzioni, Amitai, ed. 1969. *The Semiprofessions and Their Organization: Teachers, Nurses, Social Workers.* Free Press.

Fass, Paula S. 1991. *Outside In: Minorities and the Transformation of American Education.* Oxford University Press.

Finn, Chester E. 1991. *We Must Take Charge: Our Schools and Our Future.* Free Press.

Finn, Chester E., Bruno V. Manno, and Gregg Vanourek. 2000. *Charter Schools in Action: Renewing Public Education.* Princeton University Press.

Fisher, Franklin M. 1991. *International Organization, Economics, and the Law.* MIT Press.

Fiske, Edward B., and Helen F. Ladd. 2000. *When Schools Compete: A Cautionary Tale.* Brookings.

Flipse, Marry S. 1992. "Asia's Littlest Dragon: An Analysis of the Laos Foreign Investment Code and Decree." *Law and Policy in International Business* 23:199–237.

Fried, Robert L. 1995. *The Passionate Teacher: A Practical Guide.* Boston: Beacon.

Friedman, Milton. 1982. *Capitalism and Freedom.* University of Chicago Press.

Fuchs, Ester R. 1992. *Mayors and Money: Fiscal Policy in New York and Chicago.* University of Chicago Press.

Fullan, Michael. 1991. *The New Meaning of Educational Change.* Teachers College Press.

Fuller, Howard L. 1985. "The Impact of the Milwaukee Public School System's Desegregation Plan on Black Students and the Black Community, 1976–1982." Ed.D. dissertation, Marquette University.

Fuller, Howard L., and George A. Mitchell. 1999. *The Fiscal Impact of School Choice on the Milwaukee Public Schools.* Institute for the Transformation of Learning, Marquette University.

Fuller, Howard L., George A. Mitchell, and Michael E. Hartmann. 1997. *The Milwaukee Public Schools' Teacher Union Contract: Its History, Content, and Impact on Education.* Institute for the Transformation of Learning, Marquette University.

———. 2000. "Collective Bargaining in Milwaukee Public Schools." In *Conflicting Missions? Teachers Unions and Educational Reform,* edited by Tom Loveless. Brookings.

Fusarelli, Lance D. 1999. "Reinventing Urban Education in Texas: Charter Schools, Smaller Schools, and the New Institutionalism." *Education and Urban Society* 31: 214–24.

———. 2002. "Texas: Charter Schools and the Struggle for Equity." In *The Charter School Landscape: Politics, Policies, and Prospects,* edited by Sandra Vergari. University of Pittsburgh Press.

Gilles, Stephen G. 1998. "Why Parents Should Choose." In *Learning from School Choice,* edited by Paul E. Peterson and Bryan C. Hassel. Brookings.

Giroux, Henry A. 1999. "Schools for Sale: Public Education, Corporate Culture, and the Citizen-Consumer." *Educational Forum* 63:140–49.

Goeree, Jacob K., and Charles A. Holt. 1999. "Rent-Seeking and the Inefficiency of Nonmarket Allocations." *Journal of Economic Perspectives* 13: 217–40.

Gorard, Stephen. 1997. *School Choice in an Established Market.* Aldershot, England: Ashgate.

Greene, Jay P. 1998. "Civic Values in Public and Private Schools." In *Learning from School Choice,* edited by Paul E. Peterson and Bryan C. Hassel. Brookings.

———. 2001. *An Evaluation of the Florida A-Plus Accountability and School Choice Program.* New York: Manhattan Institute.

Greene, Jay P., William G. Howell, and Paul E. Peterson. 1997. "An Evaluation of the Cleveland Scholarship Program." Occasional Paper. Program on Education Policy and Governance, Harvard University.

———. 1998. "Lessons from the Cleveland Scholarship Program." In *Learning from School Choice,* edited by Paul E. Peterson and Bryan C. Hassel. Brookings.

Greene, Jay P., and Nicole Mellow. 1998. "Integration Where It Counts: A Study of Racial Integration in Public and Private School Lunchrooms." Working Paper. Austin, Tex.: Public Policy Clinic.

Greene, Jay P., Paul E. Peterson, and Jiangtao Du. 1998. "School Choice in Milwaukee: A Randomized Experiment." In *Learning from School Choice,* edited by Paul E. Peterson and Bryan C. Hassel. Brookings.

———. 1999. "Effectiveness of School Choice: The Milwaukee Experiment." *Education and Urban Society* 31(2): 190–213.

Grover, Herbert J. 1990–91. "Private School Choice Is Wrong." *Educational Leadership* 48 (December–January): 51.

Gustafson, Thane. 1999. *Capitalism Russian Style.* Cambridge University Press.

Gutmann, Amy. 1987. *Democratic Education.* Princeton University Press.

Hansen, David T. 1995. *The Call to Teach.* Teachers College Press.

Hansmann, Henry. 1980. "The Role of Nonprofit Enterprise." *Yale Law Journal* 89: 835–901.

————. 1987. "Economic Theories of Nonprofit Organization." In *The Nonprofit Sector: A Research Handbook,* edited by Walter W. Powell. Yale University Press.

Hanushek, Eric A. 1997. "Outcomes, Incentives, and Beliefs: Reflections on Analysis of the Economics of Schools." *Educational Evaluation and Policy Analysis* 19: 310–18.

Hassel, Bryan C. 1998. "Charter Schools: Politics and Practice in Four States." In *Learning from School Choice,* edited by Paul E. Peterson and Bryan C. Hassel. Brookings.

————. 1999. *The Charter School Challenge.* Brookings.

Hazlett, Thomas W., and Matthew L. Spitzer. 1997. *Public Policy toward Cable Television: The Economics of Rate Controls.* MIT Press.

Heclo, Hugh. 1977. *A Government of Strangers: Executive Politics in Washington.* Brookings.

Henig, Jeffrey R. 1994. *Rethinking School Choice: Limits of the Market Metaphor.* Princeton University Press.

Henig, Jeffrey R., and others. 1999. *The Color of School Reform: Race, Politics, and the Challenge of Urban Education.* Princeton University Press.

Hess, Frederick M. 1999. *Spinning Wheels: The Politics of Urban School Reform.* Brookings.

————. 2000. "Setting the Caged Bird Free: The Struggle to Decentralize an Urban School System." Paper prepared for a conference on Making the Grade: Assessing the Reform of Houston's Public Schools. Houston, Tex., October 23–24.

Hess, Frederick M., Robert Maranto, and Scott Milliman. 2001. "Responding to Competition: School Leaders and School Culture." In *Charter Schools, Vouchers, and Public Education,* edited by Paul E. Peterson and David Campbell. Brookings.

————. Forthcoming a. "Coping with Competition: How Charter Schooling Affected Public School Outreach in Arizona." *Policy Studies Journal.*

————. Forthcoming b. "Little Districts in Big Trouble: How Four Arizona School Systems Responded to Charter Competition." *Teachers College Record.*

Hill, Paul T. 1999. "The Supply Side of School Choice." In *School Choice and Social Controversy: Politics, Policy, and Law,* edited by Stephen D. Sugarman and Frank R. Kemerer. Brookings.

Hill, Paul T., Christine Campbell, and James Harvey. 2000. *It Takes A City: Getting Serious about Urban School Reform.* Brookings.

Hill, Paul T., and Mary Beth Celio. 1998. *Fixing Urban Schools.* Brookings.

Hirsch, E. D. 1987. *Cultural Literacy: What Every American Needs to Know.* Boston: Houghton Mifflin.

Hirschman, Albert O. 1970. *Exit, Voice, and Loyalty.* Harvard University Press.

Holt, Bert L. 1999. "Cleveland Scholarship and Tutoring Program, Overview of Distribution and Outcome, 1995–1999 and 1999–2000." Scholarship Application Distribution Report. Cleveland.

Horowitz, Donald L. 1977. *The Courts and Social Policy.* Brookings.

Howell, William G., and others. 2001. "Raising Black Achievement." *Education Matters* 1(2): 46–54.

Hoxby, Caroline M. 1994. "Do Private Schools Provide Competition for Public Schools?" Working Paper 4978. Cambridge, Mass.: National Bureau of Economic Research.

———. 1998. "Analyzing School Choice Reforms That Use America's Traditional Forms of Parental Choice." In *Learning from School Choice*, edited by Paul E. Peterson and Bryan C. Hassel. Brookings.

———. 2000. "Does Competition among Public Schools Benefit Students and Taxpayers?" *American Economic Review* 90: 1209–38.

———. 2001. "School Choice and School Productivity (Or, Could School Choice Be a Tide That Lifts All Boats?)." Paper prepared for National Bureau of Economic Research Conference on the Economics of School Choice. Islamorada, Fla., February 22–24.

Hussar, William J. 1998. "Predicting the Need for Newly Hired Teachers in the United States to 2008–09." Washington: National Center for Education Statistics.

Jefferson, Carolyn. 1991. "An Historical Analysis of the Relation between the Great Migration and the Administrative Policies and Practices of Racial Isolation in the Cleveland Public Schools." Ph.D. dissertation, Cleveland State University.

Jepsen, Christopher. 1999. "The Effects of Private School Competition on Student Achievement." Northwestern University.

Johnson, Susan M. 1996. *Leading to Change: The Challenge of the New Superintendency.* San Francisco: Jossey-Bass.

Johnson, Susan M., and Susan M. Kardos. 2000. "Reform Bargaining and Its Promise for School Improvement." In *Conflicting Missions? Teachers Unions and Educational Reform*, edited by Tom Loveless. Brookings.

Kahneman, Daniel, and Amos Tversky. 1982. "The Psychology of Preferences." *Scientific American* 286(January): 160–73.

Kane, Thomas J., and Douglas O. Staiger. 2001. "Volatility in School Test Scores: Implications for Test-Based Accountability Systems." Paper prepared for Brookings Conference on Accountability and Its Consequences for Students. Washington, May 15–16.

Kanter, Rosabeth M. 2001. "The Ten Deadly Mistakes of Wanna-Dots." *Harvard Business Review* (January): 91–100.

Katznelson, Ira, and Margaret Weir. 1985. *Schooling for All: Class, Race, and the Decline of the Democratic Ideal.* Basic Books.

Kelley, Carolyn. 1997. "Teacher Compensation and Organization." *Educational Evaluation and Policy Analysis* 19(1): 15–28.

Kelley, Carolyn, and others. 2000. "The Motivational Effects of School-Based Performance Awards." Policy Brief. Philadelphia: Consortium for Policy Research in Education.

Kennedy, Mary M. 1999. "Approximations to Indicators of Student Outcomes." *Educational Evaluation and Policy Analysis* 21: 345–63.

Kerchner, Charles T., and Julia E. Koppich. 2000. "Organizing around Quality: The Frontiers of Teacher Unionism." In *Conflicting Missions? Teachers Unions and Educational Reform*, edited by Tom Loveless. Brookings.

Key, V. O. 1949. *Southern Politics in State and Nation*. Vintage.

King, Byron. 1993. "Cincinnati: Betting on an Unfinished Season." In *A Union of Professionals: Labor Relations and Educational Reform*, edited by Charles T. Kerchner and Julia E. Koppich. Teachers College Press.

Kingdon, John. 1995. *Agendas, Alternatives, and Public Policies*. 2d ed. HarperCollins.

Kohn, Alfie. 2000. *The Case against Standardized Testing: Raising the Scores, Ruining the Schools*. Portsmouth, N.H.: Heineman.

Kolderie, Ted. 1995. *A Major Education Reform—The Charter Idea: Update and Prospects*. Minneapolis: City Prospects.

Kreps, David. 1990. "Corporate Culture and Economic Theory." In *Perspectives on Positive Political Economy*, edited by James E. Alt and Kenneth A. Shepsle. Cambridge University Press.

Kritek, William J., and Delbert K. Clear. 1993. "Teachers and Principals in the Milwaukee Public Schools." In *Seeds of Crisis: Public Schooling in Milwaukee since 1920*, edited by John L. Rury and Frank A. Cassell. University of Wisconsin Press.

Ladd, Helen F., and Edward B. Fiske. 2001. "The Uneven Playing Field of School Choice: Evidence from New Zealand." *Journal of Policy Analysis and Management* 20(1): 43–63.

Ladner, Matthew, and Matthew J. Brouillette. 2000. *The Impact of Limited School Choice on Public School Districts*. Midland, Mich.: Mackinac Center for Public Policy.

Landsberger, Michael, and Isaac Meilijson. 1996. "Extraction of Surplus under Adverse Selection: The Case of Insurance Markets." *Journal of Economic Theory* 69: 234–40.

Lee, Valerie E., Robert G. Croninger, and Julia B. Smith. 1996. "Equity and Choice in Detroit." In *Who Chooses? Who Loses? Culture, Institutions, and the Unequal Effects of School Choice*, edited by Bruce Fuller and Richard F. Elmore. Teachers College Press.

Levin, Henry M. 1987. "Education as a Public and Private Good." *Journal of Policy Analysis and Management* 6: 628–41.

———. 1993. "The Economics of Educational Choice." *Economics of Education Review* 10: 137–58.

———. 1998. "Educational Vouchers: Effectiveness, Choice, and Costs." *Journal of Policy Analysis and Management* 17: 373–92.

Levine, Michael. 1987. "Airline Competition in Deregulated Markets: Theory, Firm Strategy, and Public Policy." *Yale Journal on Regulation* 4: 393–494.

Levine, Marc V., and John F. Zipp. 1993. "A City at Risk: The Changing Social and Economic Context of Public Schooling in Milwaukee." In *Seeds of Crisis: Public Schooling in Milwaukee since 1920*, edited by John L. Rury and Frank A. Cassell. University of Wisconsin Press.

Lezotte, Lawrence. 1992. "Learn from Effective Schools." *Social Policy* 22: 34–36.

Lieberman, Myron. 1993. *Public Education: An Autopsy*. Harvard University Press.

———. 1997. *The Teacher Unions*. Free Press.

Linden, Russell M. 1994. *Seamless Government: A Practical Guide to Reengineering in the Public Sector*. San Francisco: Jossey-Bass.

Linn, Robert L. 2000. "Assessments and Accountability." *Educational Researcher* 29: 2, 4–16.

Lipsky, Michael. 1980. *Street-Level Bureaucracy: Dilemmas of the Individual in Public Services*. Russell Sage Foundation.

Long, Mary J. 1996. "*San Antonio v. Rodriguez* and the Next Twenty Years of State Court Cases." Ph.D. dissertation, Loyola University.

Lortie, Dan C. 1975. *Schoolteacher: A Sociological Study*. University of Chicago Press.

Loveless, Tom, and Claudia Jasin. 1998. "Starting from Scratch: Political and Organizational Challenges Facing Charter Schools." *Educational Administration Quarterly* 34(1): 9–30.

Lupia, Arthur. 1992. "Busy Voters, Agenda Control, and the Power of Information." *American Political Science Review* 86: 390–404.

———. 1994. "Short Cuts versus Encyclopedias: Information and Voting Behavior in California Insurance Reform Election." *American Political Science Review* 88: 63–76.

Macedo, Stephen. 2000. *Democracy and Distrust: Civic Education in a Multicultural Democracy*. Harvard University Press.

Maguire, Sheila. 2000. *Surviving, and Maybe Thriving, on Vouchers*. New York: Public/Private Ventures.

March, James G., and Johan Olsen. 1987. *Ambiguity and Choice in Organizations*. Oslo, Norway: Universitetsforlaget.

Martinez, Valerie, Kenneth Godwin, and Frank R. Kemerer. 1995. "Private Vouchers in San Antonio: The CEO Program." In *Private Vouchers*, edited by Terry Moe. Stanford, Calif.: Hoover Institution Press.

———. 1996. "Public School Choice in San Antonio: Who Chooses and with What Effects?" In *Who Chooses? Who Loses? Culture, Institutions, and the Unequal Effects of School Choice*, edited by Bruce Fuller and Richard F. Elmore. Teachers College Press.

McAvoy, Paul W. 1996. *The Failure of Antitrust and Regulation to Establish Competition in Long-Distance Telephone Services*. MIT Press.

McDermott, Kathryn A. 2000. "Barriers to Large-Scale Success of Models for Urban School Reform." *Educational Evaluation and Policy Analysis* 22: 83–89.

McEwan, Patrick J. 2001. "The Potential Impact of Large-Scale Voucher Programs." *Review of Educational Research* 70: 103–50.

McEwan, Patrick J., and Martin Carnoy. 2000. "Effectiveness and Efficiency of Private Schools in Chile's Voucher System." *Educational Evaluation and Policy Analysis* 22: 213–40.

McGroaty, Daniel. 1996. *Break These Chains: The Battle for School Choice*. Rocklin, Calif.: Prima.

———. 2000. *Trinnietta Gets a Chance: Six Families and Their School Choice Experience*. Washington: Heritage Foundation.

McLaughlin, Milbrey W. 1987. "Learning from Experience: Lessons from Policy Implementation." *Educational Evaluation and Policy Analysis* 9: 171–78.

———. 1991. "The Rand Change Agent Study: Ten Years Later." In *Education Policy Implementation,* edited by Allan Odden. SUNY Press.

McLellan, Jeffrey A. 2000. "Rise, Fall, and Reasons Why: U.S. Catholic Elementary Education, 1940–1995." In *Catholic Schools at the Crossroads: Survival and Transformation,* edited by James Youniss and John L. Convey. Teachers College Press.

McNeil, Linda M. 2000. *Contradictions of School Reform: Educational Costs of Standardized Testing.* Routledge.

Mead, Julie F. 2000. "City Charter Schools: The Legal and Political Issues That Surfaced When the City of Milwaukee Gained the Authority to Charter." Paper prepared for Annual Meeting of the American Educational Research Association. New Orleans, April 24–29.

Meier, Deborah. 1995. *The Power of Their Ideas: Lessons for America from a Small School in Harlem.* Boston: Beacon.

Meissner, David G., Jeffrey C. Browne, and Emily Van Dunk. 1997. *School Choice in Cleveland and Milwaukee: What Parents Look For.* Milwaukee: Public Policy Forum.

Melnick, R. Shep. 1994. *Between the Lines: Interpreting Welfare Rights.* Brookings.

Metcalf, Kim. 1999. "Evaluation of the Cleveland Scholarship and Tutoring Program, 1996–99." Indiana Center for Evaluation, Indiana University.

Metcalf, Kim K., and others. 1998a. *A Comparative Evaluation of the Cleveland Scholarship and Tutoring Grant Program: Year One (1996–97).* Indiana Center for Evaluation, Indiana University.

———. 1998b. *Evaluation of the Cleveland Scholarship Program: Second-Year Report (1997–98).* Indiana Center for Evaluation, Indiana University.

Meyer, John, and Brian Rowan. 1983. "The Structure of Educational Organizations." In *The Dynamics of Organizational Change in Education,* edited by J. Victor Baldridge and Terrence Deal. Berkeley, Calif.: McCutchan.

———. 1991. "Institutionalized Organizations: Formal Structure as Myth and Ceremony." In *The New Institutionalism in Organizational Analysis,* edited by Walter W. Powell and Paul J. DiMaggio. University of Chicago Press.

Meyer, John, W. Richard Scott, and Terrence Deal. 1983. "Research on School and District Organization." In *The Dynamics of Organizational Change in Education,* edited by J. Victor Baldridge and Terrence Deal. Berkeley, Calif.: McCutchan.

Miller, Gary. 1992. *Managerial Dilemmas: The Political Economy of Hierarchy.* Cambridge University Press.

Millman, Jason, ed. 1997. *Grading Teachers, Grading Schools.* Thousand Oaks, Calif.: Corwin.

Millott, Marc Dean, and Robin Lake. 1996. "So You Want to Start a Charter School?" Institute for Public Policy Management, University of Washington.

Milwaukee Public Schools. 1997. *Innovative Schools Program Final Report.*

———. 1998a. *Special Report: School Board Elections and Election Districts.*

———. 1998b. *District Demographic and Enrollment Analysis 1992–2002*. Division of Facilities and Maintenance Services.

Miner, Barbara. 1994. "The Power and the Money: Bradley Foundation Bankrolls Conservative Agenda." *Rethinking Schools* 8(3): 1–16.

Mintrom, Michael. 2000a. *Policy Entrepreneurs and School Choice*. Georgetown University Press.

———. 2000b. "Leveraging Local Innovation: The Case of Michigan's Charter Schools." Michigan State University.

Mitchell, George. 1989. *An Evaluation of State-Financed School Integration in Metropolitan Milwaukee*. Milwaukee: Wisconsin Policy Research Institute.

———. 1992. *The Milwaukee Parental Choice Program*. Milwaukee: Wisconsin Policy Research Institute.

Mitchell, Susan. 1994. *Why MPS Doesn't Work: Barriers to Reform in the Milwaukee Public Schools*. Milwaukee: Wisconsin Policy Research Institute.

———. 1999. *How School Choice Almost Died in Wisconsin*. Milwaukee: Wisconsin Policy Research Institute.

Moe, Terry. 1989. "The Politics of Bureaucratic Structure." In *Can the Government Govern?* edited by John E. Chubb and Paul E. Peterson. Brookings.

———. 2001. *Schools, Vouchers, and the American Public*. Brookings.

Molnar, Alex. 1996. *Giving Kids the Business: The Commercialization of America's Schools*. Boulder, Colo.: Westview.

Monk, David. 1992. "Educational Productivity Research: An Update and Assessment of Its Role in Education Finance Reform." *Educational Evaluation and Policy Analysis* 14(4): 307–32.

Moore, Mark H. 1994. "Policing: Deregulating or Redefining Accountability?" In *Deregulating the Public Service: Can Government Be Improved?* edited by John J. DiIulio Jr. Brookings.

———. 1995. *Creating Public Value: Strategic Management in Government*. Harvard University Press.

Moore, Thomas. 1998. *Tax Funding for Private School Alternatives*. Milwaukee: Institute for Wisconsin's Future.

Morken, Hubert, and Jo Renee Formicola. 1999. *The Politics of School Choice*. Lanham, Md.: Rowman and Littlefield.

Morrison, Steven, and Clifford Winston. 1990. "The Dynamics of Airline Pricing and Competition." *American Economic Review* 80: 389–93.

———. 1995. *The Evolution of the Airline Industry*. Brookings.

Mueller, John. 1999. *Capitalism, Democracy, and Ralph's Pretty Good Grocery*. Princeton University Press.

Murnane, Richard J., and Frank S. Levy. 1995. "What General Motors Can Teach U.S. Schools about the Proper Role of Markets in Education Reform." *Phi Delta Kappan* 78(October): 108–14.

National Center for Education Statistics. 1999. *Snapshots of Private Schools in the United States: Results from the Schools and Staffing Survey*. Washington: Office of Educational Research and Improvement.

Nelson, Richard. 1977. *The Moon and the Ghetto: An Essay on Public Policy Analysis*. Norton.

Nelson, Richard, and Michael Krashinsky. 1973. "Two Major Issues of Public Policy: Public Policy and Organization of Supply." In *Public Subsidy for Day Care of Young Children,* edited by Richard Nelson and Dennis Young. Lexington, Mass.: Heath.

Niskanen, William A. 1971. *Bureaucracy and Representative Government.* Chicago: Aldine.

Norquist, John O. 1998. *The Wealth of Cities: Revitalizing the Centers of American Life.* Reading, Mass.: Addison-Wesley.

North, Douglass C. 1990. *Institutions, Institutional Change, and Economic Performance.* Cambridge University Press.

O'Day, Jennifer A. 1996. "Introduction: Incentives and School Improvement." In *Rewards and Reform: Creating Educational Incentives That Work,* edited by Susan H. Fuhrman and Jennifer A. O'Day. San Francisco: Jossey-Bass.

Odden, Allan R. 1996. "Incentives, School Organization, and Teacher Compensation." In *Rewards and Reform: Creating Educational Incentives That Work,* edited by Susan H. Fuhrman and Jennifer A. O'Day. San Francisco: Jossey-Bass.

Odden, Allan, and William H. Clune. 1998. "School Finance Systems: Aging Structures in Need of Renovation." *Educational Evaluation and Policy Analysis* 20: 157–78.

Odden, Allan R., and Carolyn Kelley. 1997. *Paying Teachers for What They Know and Do: New and Smarter Compensation Strategies to Improve Schools.* Thousand Oaks, Calif.: Corwin.

Odden, Allan R., and Lawrence O. Picus. 2000. *School Finance: A Policy Perspective.* 2d ed. Boston: McGraw-Hill.

Ohanian, Susan. 1999. *One Size Fits Few: The Folly of Educational Standards.* Portsmouth, N.H.: Heinemann.

Ohio Department of Education. 1997. *What Really Matters in American Education.* Columbus.

Olson, Lynn. 2000. "Finding and Keeping Competent Teachers." *Education Week: Quality Counts 2000* 19(18): 12–18.

Olson, Mancur. 1971. *The Logic of Collective Action.* Harvard University Press.

Orfield, Gary, and Carole Ashkinaze. 1991. *The Closing Door: Conservative Policy and Black Opportunity.* University of Chicago Press.

Orr, Marion. 1999. *Black Social Capital: The Politics of School Reform in Baltimore, 1986–1998.* University of Kansas Press.

Osborne, David, and Ted Gaebler. 1992. *Reinventing Government.* Reading, Mass.: Addison-Wesley.

O'Shea, James, and Charles Madigan. 1997. *Dangerous Company: The Consulting Powerhouses and the Businesses They Save and Ruin.* Random House.

Ouchi, William. 1980. "Markets, Bureaucracies, and Clans." *Administrative Sciences Quarterly* 25: 129–41.

Parker, Allan E., and Michael David Weiss. 1991. "Litigating *Edgewood*: Constitutional Standards and Application to Educational Choice." *Review of Litigation* 10(3): 599–624.

Peltzman, Sam. 1993. "The Political Economy of the Decline of American Public Education." *Journal of Law and Economics* 36: 331–70.

Petersburs, John J. 1998. "Analysis of the Milwaukee Parental Choice Program in Light of the First Amendment Establishment Clause Federal Supreme Court Cases." Ph.D. dissertation, Marquette University.

Peterson, Paul E. 1976. *School Politics, Chicago Style.* University of Chicago Press.

———. 1999. "Vouchers and Test Scores: What the Numbers Show." *Policy Review* (January–February): 10–15.

Peterson, Paul E., David Myers, and William G. Howell. 1999. "An Evaluation of the Horizon Scholarship Program in the Edgewood Independent School District, San Antonio, Texas: The First Year." Program on Education Policy and Governance, Harvard University.

Peterson, Paul E., and Chad Noyes. 1997. "School Choice in Milwaukee." In *New Schools for a New Century: The Redesign of Urban Education,* edited by Diane Ravitch and Joseph P. Viteritti. Yale University Press.

Petro, Jim. 1998. "Cleveland Scholarship and Tutoring Program: Special Audit Report." Columbus: State of Ohio.

Pindyck, Robert S., and Daniel L. Rubinfeld. 1998. *Microeconomics,* 4th ed. Upper Saddle River, N.J.: Prentice Hall.

Plank, Stephen, and others. 1993. "Effects of Choice in Education." In *School Choice: Examining the Evidence,* edited by Edith Rasell and Richard Rothstein. Washington: Economic Policy Institute.

Popov, Vladimir. 1999. "The Financial System in Russia Compared to Other Transition Economies: The Anglo-American versus the German-Japanese Model." *Comparative Economic Studies* 41: 1–4.

Portz, John, Lana Stein, and Robin R. Jones. 1999. *City Schools and City Politics: Institutions and Leadership in Pittsburgh, Boston, and St. Louis.* University of Kansas Press.

Powell, Arthur G., Eleanor Farrar, and David K. Cohen. 1985. *The Shopping Mall High School: Winners and Losers in the Educational Marketplace.* Boston: Houghton Mifflin.

Powell, Brian, and Lala Carr Steelman. 1996. "Bewitched, Bothered, and Bewildering: The Use and Misuse of State SAT and ACT Scores." *Harvard Educational Review* 66: 27–59.

Provenzo, Eugene F., and Gary N. McCloskey. 1996. *Schoolteachers and Schooling: Ethoses in Conflict.* Norwood, N.J.: Ablex.

Public Agenda. 1994. "What Americans Expect from the Public Schools." New York.

———. 1999. *On Thin Ice: How Advocates and Opponents Could Misread the Public's Views on Vouchers and Charter Schools.* New York.

———. 2000. *A Sense of Calling: Who Teaches and Why.* New York.

Public Policy Forum. 2000. *School Finance Laws Mute Competition.* Milwaukee.

———. 2001. *9,200 Choose Voucher Schools.* Milwaukee.

Raadschelders, Jos. C. N., and Mark R. Rutgers. 1996. "The Evolution of Civil Service Systems." In *Civil Service Systems in Comparative Perspective,* edited by A. G. Hans and others. Indiana University Press.

Ravitch, Diane. 2000. *Left Back: A Century of Failed School Reforms.* Simon and Schuster.

Ravitch, Diane, and Joseph P. Viteritti. 1997. "New York: The Obsolete Factory." In *New Schools for a New Century: The Redesign of Urban Education,* edited by Diane Ravitch and Joseph P. Viteritti. Yale University Press.

Rees, Nina Shokraii. 1999. "Public School Benefits of Private School Vouchers." *Policy Review* (January–February): 16–19.

———. 2001. *School Choice: What's Happening in the States, 2001.* Washington: Heritage Foundation.

Rich, Wilbur. 1996. *Black Mayors and School Politics: The Failure of Reform in Detroit, Gary, and Newark.* Garland.

Robyn, Dorothy. 1987. *Breaking the Special Interests: Trucking Deregulation and the Politics of Policy Reform.* University of Chicago Press.

Roch, Christine H. 2000. "Policy, Networks, and Information: The Role of Opinion Leaders in the Flow of Information about Education." Paper prepared for Annual Meeting of the American Political Science Association. Washington, August 31–September 3.

Rofes, Eric. 1998. "How Are School Districts Responding to Charter Laws and Charter Schools?" Policy Analysis for California Education, University of California–Berkeley.

Rose, Lowell C., and Alec M. Gallup. 1998. "The Thirtieth Annual Phi Delta Kappa/Gallup Poll of the Public's Attitudes toward the Public Schools." *Phi Delta Kappan* 79 (September): 41–56.

Rosen, Harvey S. 1999. *Public Finance.* 5th ed. Irwin–McGraw-Hill.

Rouse, Cecelia-Elena. 1998. "Private School Vouchers and Student Achievement: An Evaluation of the Milwaukee Parental Choice Program." *Quarterly Journal of Economics* 113(2): 553–602.

Sander, William L. 1999. "Private Schools and Public School Achievement." *Journal of Human Resources* 34: 697–709.

Sanders, Eugene T. 1999. *Urban School Leadership: Issues and Strategies.* Larchmont, N.Y.: Eye on Education.

Sawhill, Isabel V., and Shannon L. Smith. 2000. "Vouchers for Elementary and Secondary Education." In *Vouchers and the Provision of Public Services,* edited by C. Eugene Steuerle and others. Brookings, Committee for Economic Development, and Urban Institute.

Scheingold, Stuart A. 1974. *The Politics of Rights: Lawyers, Public Policy, and Political Change.* Yale University Press.

Schlesinger, Leonard A., and others. 1987. *Chronicles of Corporate Change: Management Lessons from AT&T and Its Offspring.* Lexington, Mass.: Heath.

Schneider, Mark. 1999. "Information and Choice in Educational Privatization." Paper prepared for Conference on Setting the Agenda for the Study of Privatization in Education. Teachers College, Columbia University, April 8–10.

Schneider, Mark, Paul Teske, and Melissa Marschall. 2000. *Choosing Schools: Consumer Choice and the Quality of American Schools.* Princeton University Press.

Schneider, Mark, and Paul Teske, with Michael Mintrom. 1995. *Public Entrepreneurs: Agents for Change in American Government.* Princeton University Press.

Schneider, Mark, and others. 1998. "Shopping for Schools: In the Land of the Blind, the One-Eyed Parent May Be Enough." *American Journal of Political Science* 42(3): 769–93.

Schumpeter, Joseph A. 1942. *Capitalism, Socialism, and Democracy.* 5th ed. Harper and Row.

Schwartz, Robert B., and Marian A. Robinson. 2000. "Goals 2000 and the Standards Movement." *Brookings Papers on Education Policy, 2000:* 173–214.

Scott, Andrew, and Harald Uhlig. 1999. "Fickle Investors: An Impediment to Growth?" *European Economic Review* 43: 1345–47.

Shanker, Albert. 1993. *Restoring the Academic Mission of the School.* Washington: American Federation of Teachers.

Shubik, Martin. 1982. *Game Theory in the Social Sciences: Concepts and Solutions.* MIT Press.

———. 1984. *A Game Theoretic Approach to Political Economy.* MIT Press.

Sikkink, David. 2001. "Speaking in Many Tongues." *Education Matters* 1(2): 36–44.

Simon, Herbert A. 1979. *Models of Thought.* Yale University Press.

———. 1997. *Administrative Behavior: A Study of Decision-Making Processes in Administrative Organizations.* Free Press.

Sizer, Theodore R. 1996. *Horace's Hope: What Works for the American High School.* Boston: Houghton Mifflin.

Smith, Kevin B., and Kenneth J. Meier. 1995. *The Case against School Choice: Politics, Markets, and Fools.* Armonk, N.Y.: Sharpe.

Sornson, Robert, and James Scott. 1997. *Teaching and Joy.* Alexandria, Va.: Association for Supervision and Curriculum Development.

Spencer, Jim. 2000. "Whose Idea Was This Anyway? The Challenging Metamorphosis from Private to Charter." In *School Choice in the Real World: Lessons from Arizona Charter Schools,* edited by Robert Maranto and others. Boulder, Colo.: Westview.

Steuerle, C. Eugene. 2000. "Common Issues for Voucher Programs." In *Vouchers and the Provision of Public Services,* edited by C. Eugene Steuerle and others. Brookings, Committee for Economic Development, and Urban Institute.

Stiglitz, Joseph E. 2000. *Economics of the Public Sector.* 3d ed. Norton.

Stolee, Michael. 1993. "The Milwaukee Desegregation Case." In *Seeds of Crisis: Public Schooling in Milwaukee since 1920,* edited by John L. Rury and Frank A. Cassell. University of Wisconsin Press.

Stolp, Stephen, and Stuart C. Smith. 1997. "Cultural Leadership." In *School Leadership: Handbook for Excellence,* edited by Stuart C. Smith and Philip K. Piele. University of Oregon Press.

Stone, Clarence N. 1998. "Civic Capacity and Urban School Reform." In *Changing Urban Education,* edited by Clarence N. Stone. University of Kansas Press.

Stone, Deborah. 1997. *Policy Paradox: The Arts of Political Decision Making.* Norton.

Stone, Joe A. 2000. "Collective Bargaining and Public Schools." In *Conflicting Missions? Teachers Unions and Educational Reform,* edited by Tom Loveless. Brookings.

Stout, Robert T., Marilyn Tallerico, and Kent P. Scribner. 1995. "Values: The 'What' of the Politics of Education." In *The Study of Educational Politics*, edited by J. Scribner and D. Layton. Washington: Falmer.

Supik, Josie Danini, and Roy L. Johnson. 1999. *Missing: Texas's Youth Dropout and Attrition in Texas Public High Schools*. San Antonio: Intercultural Development Research Association.

Teske, Paul, Samuel Best, and Michael Mintrom. 1995. *Deregulating Freight Transportation*. Washington: American Enterprise Institute.

Teske, Paul, and others. 2001. "Can Charter Schools Change Traditional Public Schools?" In *Charter Schools, Vouchers, and Public Education*, edited by Paul E. Peterson and David Campbell. Brookings.

Thompson, James. 1967. *Organizations in Action: Social Science Bases of Administrative Theory*. McGraw-Hill.

Tiebout, Charles M. 1956. "A Pure Theory of Local Expenditures." *Journal of Political Economy* 64: 416–24.

Tyack, David. 1974. *The One Best System*. Harvard University Press.

Tyack, David, Michael Kirst, and Elisabeth Hansot. 1983. "Educational Reform: Retrospect and Prospect." In *The Dynamics of Organizational Change in Education*, edited by J. Victor Baldridge and Terrence Deal. Berkeley, Calif.: McCutchan.

Underwood, Julie. 1991. "Choice in Education: The Wisconsin Experience." *West's Education Law Reporter* 68: 229–47.

Vanourek, Gregg, and others. 1997. "Final Report." Hudson Institute Charter Schools in Action Project (October) (www.edexcellence.net/chart/chart1htm).

Viteritti, Joseph P. 1999. *Choosing Equality: School Choice, the Constitution, and Civil Society*. Brookings.

Vogelsang, Ingo, and Bridget M. Mitchell. 1997. *Telecommunications Competition: The Last Ten Miles*. MIT Press.

Wagner, Tony. 1994. *How Schools Change: Lessons from Three Communities*. Boston: Beacon.

Walford, Geoffrey. 1994. *Choice and Equity in Education*. Great Britain: Cassell.

Walker, Decker. 1992. "Curriculum Policymaking." In *Encyclopedia of Educational Research*, edited by Marvin Alkin and others. 6th ed. Macmillan.

Wasley, Patricia A. 1991. *Teachers Who Lead: The Rhetoric of Reform and the Realities of Practice*. Teachers College Press.

Weaver, R. Kent. 1986. "The Politics of Blame Avoidance." *Journal of Public Policy* 6: 371–98.

Weick, Karl. 1976. "Educational Organizations as Loosely Coupled Systems." *Administrative Science Quarterly* 21: 1–19.

Weiner, Lois. 2001. "Research in the 90s: Implications for Urban Teacher Preparation." *Review of Educational Research* 70: 369–406.

Weinschrott, David J., and Sally B. Kilgore. 1998. "Evidence from the Indianapolis Voucher Program." In *Learning from School Choice*, edited by Paul E. Peterson and Bryan C. Hassel. Brookings.

Wells, Amy Stuart. 1998. *Beyond the Rhetoric of Charter School Reform: A Study of Ten California School Districts*. UCLA Charter School Study.

Wells, Amy Stuart, and Janelle Scott. 1999. "Evaluation and Privatization of Charter Schools." Paper prepared for Conference on Setting the Agenda for the Study of Privatization in Education. Teachers College, New York, April 8–10.

WestEd. 2000. *Analysis and Implications of California Proposition 38: Will Vouchers Improve Student Access to Private Schools?* San Francisco.

Westheimer, Joel. 1998. *Among School Teachers: Community Autonomy and Ideology in Teachers' Work*. Teachers College Press.

Whitty, Geoff, Sally Power, and David Halpin. 1998. *Devolution and Choice in Education: The School, the State, and the Market*. Great Britain: Acer.

Wiley, Richard E. 1984. "The End of Monopoly: Regulatory Change and the Promotion of Competition." In *Disconnecting Bell: The Impact of the AT&T Divestiture*, edited by Harry M. Shooshan III. Pergamon.

Williams, Michael R. 1997. *The Parent-Centered Early School: Highland Community School of Milwaukee*. Garland.

Willms, J. Douglas, and Frank H. Echols. 1993. "The Scottish Experience of Parental School Choice." In *School Choice: Examining the Evidence*, edited by Edith Rasell and Richard Rothstein. Washington: Economic Policy Institute.

Wilson, James Q. 1989. *Bureaucracy: What Government Agencies Do and Why They Do It*. Basic Books.

———. 1994. "Can the Bureaucracy Be Deregulated? Lesson from Government Agencies." In *Deregulating the Public Service: Can Government Be Improved?* edited by John J.DiIulio Jr. Brookings.

Wirt, Frederick M., and Michael W. Kirst. 1989. *Schools in Conflict*. Berkeley, Calif.: McCutchan.

Wisconsin Department of Public Instruction. 1999. *Wisconsin Charter Schools*. Madison.

———. 1998. "The Milwaukee Voucher Experiment." *Educational Evaluation and Policy Analysis* 20(4): 229–52.

———. 2000. *The Market Approach to Education: An Analysis of America's First Voucher Program*. Harvard University Press.

Wohlstetter, Priscilla, and others. 1997. *Organizing for Successful School-Based Management*. Alexandria, Va.: Association for Supervision and Curriculum Development.

Wolf, Patrick J., and others. 2001. "Private Schooling and Political Tolerance." In *Charter Schools, Vouchers, and Public Education*, edited by Paul E. Peterson and David Campbell. Brookings.

Woods, Philip A., Carl Bagley, and Ron Glatter. 1998. *School Choice and Competition: Markets in the Public Interest?* London: Routledge.

Wrinkle, Robert D., Joseph Stewart Jr., and J. L. Polinard. 1999. "Public School Quality, Private Schools, and Race." *American Journal of Political Science* 43(4): 1248–53.

Zaller, John. 1992. *The Nature and Origins of Mass Opinion*. Cambridge University Press.

Index